Make Believe

Make Believe

THE BROADWAY MUSICAL IN THE 1920S

ETHAN MORDDEN

New York   Oxford

Oxford University Press

1997

Oxford University Press

Oxford   New York
Athens   Auckland   Bangkok   Bogotá   Bombay
Buenos Aires   Calcutta   Cape Town   Dar es Salaam
Delhi   Florence   Hong Kong   Istanbul   Karachi
Kuala Lumpur   Madras   Madrid   Melbourne
Mexico City   Nairobi   Paris   Singapore
Taipei   Tokyo   Toronto

and associated companies in
Berlin   Ibadan

Library of Congress Cataloging-in-Publication Data
Mordden, Ethan
Make believe : the Broadway musical in the 1920s
/ Ethan Mordden.
p.   cm.
Includes index.
ISBN 978-0-19-510594-0
1. Musicals—United States—History and criticism.
2. Broadway (New York, N.Y.)—History.   3. Popular music—United
States—1921–1930—History and criticism. I. Title.
ML1711.M75   1997
782.1'4'09747109042—dc20   96-40962

To the late Bill Tynes

because Eddie Cantor,
Marilyn Miller, and Florenz Ziegfeld
were his favorite things

Acknowledgments

Thank you to Mary Ann Chack of the Shubert Archives; to Mark Trent Goldberg of Roxbury Recordings; to Mark D. Kaufmann; to Bob Gottlieb; to Ken Mandelbaum, for his always generous sharing of expertise and research material; to my ingenious agent, Joe Spieler; and especially to my editor, Sheldon Meyer, whose encompassing knowledge and intelligence enrich every manuscript he touches. This is our seventh book together; many thanks.

Contents

Make Believe

1

Little Angel Cake

THE STATE OF MUSICAL COMEDY

Reminiscing with her father about her show-biz past, a young woman recalls her greatest triumph, singing "Tee-Oodle-Um-Bum-Bo" in red satin pants. She favors us with a nostalgic chorus of the song, whereupon her father chimes in with the second chorus. Then the orchestra cranks up the tempo, the two exit, and a line of chorus girls dances on to pursue the number, all dressed in red satin pants. We have no idea who these woman are, how they all got hold of replicas of the heroine's old costume, and why they have suddenly erupted into her apartment.

Or: the curtain rises upon an operetta's third act to reveal "a room of state at the Royal Palace" in Karlsberg as "ladies and gentlemen of the Court are dancing a quadrille." Uniforms and fancy dress emphasize the high tone of the affair, the violins saw regally away, and a lackey announces, "The Grand Duchess Anastasia"—to whom a handy countess addresses perhaps the most extraneous line of the decade: "Dear Duchess, isn't it an *enchanting* ball?"

Meanwhile, in a musical comedy with a Palm Beach country-club setting, a downstage curtain decorated in a palm-tree motif covers a set change while the plot's Hispanic Temptress slinks on to sing "In the Swim at Miami (where the smart set love to play)." In her honor, the verse reeks of tango, though the chorus suddenly veers into a go-everywhere fox trot and though the number in any case has nothing to

3

do with her character or her role in the story. At least the stage is now
ready for the action to continue; but first we get a "Bubble Dance" performed by Beth Beri—simply because the producer caught Beri's act in
vaudeville and liked it.

Now for a snippet of humorous dialogue. Star comic applies for a job
as bus boy. Tavern proprietress has seen him already. "Didn't I tell you
then," she asks, going into traditional business of sizing him up, flirting,
and posing, "that I wanted an *older boy*?" Winking at the audience, star
comic replies, "Yes, ma'am. That's why I came back today."

Finally, consider the Eleven O'Clock Number, the star shot just before the folding up of the plot and the everybody-onstage-for-the-last-
reprise finale. This one has two stars, dancing siblings who now appear
in eccentric costume, she in Alpine togs with an outlandishly feathered
hat. The book writers gamely try (and fail) to rationalize the outfit; it's
really there to provision a song called "Swiss Miss," which will allow the
pair to dilate comically upon the rituals of mountain courtship, then to
go into a mock-Tyrolean dance capped by their trademark "run-around"
exit, in which they lope along in ever-widening circles to the orchestra's
Germanic oompah and the pealing of bells till they disappear from sight
and the audience goes crazy.

This is the Broadway musical of the 1920s as we recall it: recklessly
built upon the despotism of performing talent, dotty with corny humor
of a bygone era, riddled with cliché and convention, its storylines cease-
lessly humiliated by irrelevant songs and specialty acts. The shows I've
just invoked—respectively, *La, La Lucille, The Student Prince, Kid
Boots, The Stepping Stones,* and *Lady, Be Good!*—typify the musical in
the five years that followed the end of World War I. Yet the 1920s as a
whole saw the form so refine and transform itself that, by the decade's
finish, the "Tee-Oodle-Um-Bum-Bo" chorus line, the Bubble Dances,
the nineteenth-century comedy, and the unmotivated star shot would be
virtually extinct, unknown to the better writers and unpopular even with
second-raters.

The 1920s, in fact, marked an end to the American musical as it been
established at the start of the twentieth century by its two more or less
founding practitioners, Victor Herbert and George M. Cohan.* The
one's surpassing musicianship and the other's sparky theatricality

---

* There were, of course, creators of note before Herbert and Cohan, such as Edward E. Rice, Charles Hoyt, and Edward Harrigan and Tony Hart. But theirs was
generally an epoch of eclectic primitivism, gently educated by such foreign masters
as Gilbert and Sullivan and Jacques Offenbach.

shaped models for others to try, especially in Herbert's versatility—for, while he is popularly remembered for his operettas, like *Naughty Marietta* (1910), he wrote in all the forms available, from revue and extravaganza (fairy-tale spectacle centered on a star comic) to saucy shows with a trendy flavor like *Miss Dolly Dollars* (1905) and *The Princess "Pat"* (1915). Indeed, while recruiting solid singers for virtually all his shows, Herbert identified the difference between musical comedy and "comic opera" (as they called operetta in his day) by the way he weighted his scores toward the majestic big tune (as in *Naughty Marietta*'s "Ah! Sweet Mystery of Life" and "'Neath the Southern Moon") or toward livelier and more intimate numbers, such as Dolly's entrance spot, "Just Get Out and Walk," endearing piffle about Dolly's automobile in which she speaks of filling hospitals with pedestrians and imitates the buzz of the motor.

Symphonist, cellist, bandmaster, unofficial president of the pop composers' community, and god of the parlor pianist, Herbert was extraordinarily influential. But, as the 1920s neared, his well of melody began to dry out. After *Naughty Marietta*, only *Sweethearts* (1913) and *Eileen* (1917) found him in top form. His shows were the most integrated of the time, his incidental music the most ingenious, his (own) orchestrations the very sound of Big Broadway. But Herbert's insistent use of the waltzes, marches, and comic ditties in finicky $\frac{6}{8}$ time that European operetta favored marked him as a not entirely naturalized immigrant. When Cohan marched, as in his war anthem "Over There," one heard the vigor of the smart-alec, big-shouldered Yankee dandy. When Herbert marched, it was right into a beer garden with a madcap duchess and a magic knight or two.

Consider the last musical of Herbert's lifetime, *Orange Blossoms* (1922).* Like Herbert's preceding four shows, *The Velvet Lady* (1919), *Angel Face* (1919), *My Golden Girl* (1920), and *The Girl in the Spotlight* (1920), *Orange Blossoms* meant to seem contemporary, "in the know," as they put it then. Adultery, nightclubs, and racy backstage life had kept the preceding quartet salty, and *Orange Blossoms* was based on a "naughty" French comedy, *La Passerelle,* staged in New York in 1903 (and again in 1914) as *The Marriage of Kitty, Orange Blossoms*'s original title. We get a "legacy with a catch" plot, very common in musicals at this time: roué hero, his eye on a Brazilian divorcée, marries innocent heroine as a ruse to outwit the terms of a will but falls in love with hero-

---

* *The Dream Girl* (1924), the last title in Herbert's catalogue, was produced posthumously.

ine instead. Fred de Gresac (the pseudonym of the wife of the opera baritone Victor Maurel, Verdi's first Iago and Falstaff), *La Passerelle's* coauthor, gave Herbert a verbose script that was cut in rehearsals and tryouts to a fine tautness, and the cast was excellent. Herbert had lately been leaning toward musical comedy specialists such as Donald Brian, Eddie Dowling, Georgia O'Ramey, and Jack Donahue—"personalities" rather than voices—and *Orange Blossoms* continued this trend with Queenie Smith and Nancy Welford in supporting roles, Hal Skelly as a comic detective (on the beach, eying the girls in their bathing suits, he cries, "Gee! I wish I was the ocean!"), and, especially, Edith Day in the lead.

The 1920s comprised, on a certain level, an age of heroines, and Day was one of the great ones, a dark beauty who fielded a shockingly good voice for a musical-comedy all-arounder, agile in comedy and a seasoned dancer. Maybe better than good—the recordings that Day left behind reveal a strong supple soprano of great expressive purpose. One can see why, quitting New York in mid-decade to settle in England, she reigned as "Queen of Drury Lane" in three consecutive smash hits (*Rose-Marie, The Desert Song,* and *Show Boat*), filling that vast auditorium in a time when theatre speaker systems were unheard of. The voice had a bright, even glaring edge and the interpretations an air of wicked command. Day was too good for musical comedy, born for operetta.

But Herbert wasn't really in the operetta business any more. Struggling to maintain his position as First Composer of Broadway, he had seen the rise of Rudolf Friml, Sigmund Romberg, Irving Berlin, and Jerome Kern (and Cole Porter, George Gershwin, Vincent Youmans, and Richard Rodgers had all put in at least token appearances by September 1922, when *Orange Blossoms* opened). It was Kern whom Herbert designated as his heir: and Kern, then, wrote musical comedy, not operetta. So Herbert and his lyricist, B. G. De Sylva, gave Day little to bite into musically beyond the show's waltzy hit, "A Kiss in the Dark," a trick song in that, out of context, it sounds like a hymn to flirtation but, in the show, recalls the heroine's fearful encounter with an amorous stranger—the very man she will marry. The rest of *Orange Blossoms's* score, despite a sly French flavor in hommages to Messager and an Offenbachian galop in a dance number, found Herbert either fecklessly recycling his old style or fecklessly trying to sound fresh—the oh-so-delicate woodwind syncopations capping the vocal line in "Legend of the Glowworm" over here and the irritatingly zippy march "A Dream of Orange Blossoms" over there.

At 95 performances, *Orange Blossoms* was hardly a flop; *The Dream*

Girl did even better. As with nearly all Herbert shows, piano-vocal scores were published, palm court orchestras proudly sawed out medleys of the principal tunes, and the casts went touring. But, after *Eileen,* not one of Herbert's musicals had any real impact, because his music had lost its grip on the national ear.

George M. Cohan, however, was on a roll, or so it seemed. At the turn of the century, when he and the rest of the Four Cohans (father Jerry, mother Nellie, and sister Josie) burst out of vaudeville onto Broadway, the critics were offended and the public often baffled. Whether as playwright, songwriter (both words and music), director, or star, Cohan was thought vulgar, with his know-it-all persona and arrogant jingoism, his incessant slang and jokes about the "rubens" and "kiwanies" in the sticks. In the world according to Cohan, once you left New York it was all Bridgeport. Yet it was the audiences outside New York that first took to him. "Back to the woods where you belong!" was how Cohan characterized his first critical reception.

Over time, however, even Broadway came to enjoy this New Yorker's New Yorker. Now the slang seemed hip, the flagwaving droll, a running gag. Cohan's fans especially enjoyed the way he spoofed the theatre's growing obsession with fourth-wall naturalism, appealing to the audience for patience whenever a player threatened to get Serious, or allowing characters to comment on the action *during* it. Here's a taste of *The American Idea* (1908), in which a pair of Brooklyn wisenheimers in Paris charm a pair of American girls away from French royalty. Watch how the actor tells the public what he's doing *while he's doing it*:

> (*A man enters, stage right.*)
> MAN: He was a man of medium height, say forty years of age.
> He arrived in Paris Thursday morning and was driven direct-
> ly to the Elysée Palace Hotel. As he stepped from the cab and
> approached the Court Portal, a bell-boy appeared and said:
> BOY: Baggage, monsieur?

Cohan also won respect as a producer-cum-play doctor, the master of what he openly called "Cohanization." This often involved a wholesale rewrite of someone else's work, as when he refashioned a feeble Ruritanian operetta called *Cherry Blossoms* into a campy burlesque, *The Royal Vagabond* (1919). It was a success, but the most impressive Cohanization made one of the major hits of the 1920s out of an unpretentious little piece called *The House That Jack Built,* with book and lyrics by Frank Mandel and Otto Harbach and music by Louis Hirsch. Its eponymous hero (Jack McGowan) is a young idealist who wants to construct bungalows for low-income families—ten dollars down and ten dollars a month. Little happens, all told. Jack's mother (Georgia Caine) loses the fortune Jack has been counting on as a grubstake, and Jack's head is turned by an aggressive flapper (Florrie Millership). But then Jack discovers oil, not to mention the ingenue who has loved him all along, Mary (Janet Velie).

Mary was Cohan's favorite name, and he took charge of the work lovingly, not by rewriting but by giving it energy while stressing its sentiment. Cohan filled the show with dance—at that, goofy, slambang, crazy dance. Cohan expanded the chorus boys' salute to the heroine, "Mary," with an encore of his own "Mary's a Grand Old Name" and "So Long, Mary" from Forty-Five Minutes From Broadway (1906). Cohan plugged the main love song, "The Love Nest," throughout the evening.* Cohan even used the tune as the show's opening, in a daring subversion of convention: after the overture, the audience heard a lone male voice singing a capella about this wonderful everyman's home with its "dream room for two." Then the curtain rose, disclosing Jack alone in his mother's living room, beaming down on a giant model home. And, last of all, Cohan changed the show's title, during the Boston tryout, to Mary (1920).

As we shall see, the 1920s appreciated mainly performing talent. Eventually, with the arrival of what appeared to be a first generation of all-American Broadway songwriters, the creative talent, too, came into prominence. But the men who staged musicals were all but unknown—except Cohan. Critics even spoke of a Cohan "style," a tribute later given to George Abbott and Hassard Short and still later to the director-choreographers who rose up in the late 1940s and 1950s. Yet Julian Mitchell, Mary's codirector (with Cohan), had an astonishing curriculum vitae, taking in such landmarks as A Trip To Chinatown (1891); The Fortune Teller (1898); several of Joe Weber and Lew Fields's burlesques; The Wizard of Oz (1903) and its imitation, Babes in Toyland (1903); the first seven editions of Ziegfeld's Follies; from revue through musical

---

* Because out-of-town audiences remained Cohan's most loyal supporters, Cohan held the show over for unprecedented runs in Philadelphia and Boston before coming to New York, by which time "The Love Nest" had become the nation's number-one tune. One critic called it the "Every Little Movement" of the age, referring to the almost intolerably ubiquitous hit from Karl Hoschna's Madame Sherry (1910). Wags declared that "The Love Nest" was best performed by simply repeating the first line, "Just a love nest, cozy and warm" over and over, whether it fit the notes or not. Longtime television viewers will know it as the theme of The George Burns and Gracie Allen Show.

comedy to operetta, from Hoyt and Herbert to Kern and Hammerstein, from the 1880s to the mid-1920s, when he died virtually in harness. To top it all, the man was deaf.

Edward Royce, like Mitchell both a director and a choreographer, claims even greater history, from the trend-setting Gaiety musicals and Viennese operettas in London in the early 1900s, on to all of the key Princess shows* in the late 1910s, thence to such influential works—each of a different kind—as *Apple Blossoms, Irene,* and *Sally,* at the turn of the decade into the 1920s. Clearly, these two men were essential collaborators in the development of the musical's performing style.

But the conjuring names were those of the stars—Marilyn Miller, Fred Stone, Al Jolson, even Lillian Russell, retired in 1912 but retaining immense cachet as the shapely Queen of Comic Opera in the days before *The Merry Widow* changed all the rules. (In *very* brief: before *The Merry Widow,* the romantic musical was elegant. After *The Merry Widow,* the romantic musical was sensual.) Russell was the First Love of a generation of American boys. Miller replaced her; Stone tickled them; and Jolson stirred them. Or there were the producers: Ziegfeld, Charles Dillingham, Arthur Hammerstein (son of Oscar the Great and uncle of Oscar the Next). Directors? There was only Cohan. He left so strong an impression that *Mary*'s reviews mentioned the King of Broadway more than *Mary*'s authors.

As author himself, however, Cohan was almost in trouble. Everyone knew that he was repeating himself—as he had been almost from the beginning. Same old *kinds* of songs, same old flag, the Irish, the class-war stuff. Both *Little Nellie Kelly* (1922) and *The Rise of Rosie O'Reilly* (1923) were Cinderella shows, and, though Cohan did not appear in them, his presence was deeply felt: in the billing of Nellie's heroine, Elizabeth Hines, as "Our Own Little American Girl"; in the hoptoad tempo of the stagings; or in the unapologetic simplicity of the scores, as in *Rosie*'s "I Never Met a Girl Like You," "Love Dreams," "When June Comes Along with a Song," and, of course, the inevitable Cohan "a pretty girl should have a plain name" number, "A Ring To the Name of Rosie."

What saved the shows was, as always, Cohan's vigor and charm and the fact that he was preaching to the converted. He didn't have a public: he had fans, especially of what had become his trademark, near nonstop dancing. "A Terpsichorean convulsion," Alan Dale (of the *Telegraph*) called *Little Nellie Kelly.* "An explosion of all the joints, the

* See page 15.

tendons, and the cartilages. . . Everything and everybody jigged, and contorted, and twisted, and cavorted, and pirouetted, and tripped it, and trotted, and raced, and rushed, and rampaged, and rioted, and footed it, and embonpointed it, and made a general dancing rough-house."

Cohan filled *Little Nellie Kelly* with vaudeville dancing acts—the Lorraine Sisters, Cunningham and Clements, Joseph Niemeyer and Aileen Hamilton, Carl Hemmer, James and Mercer Templeton. But, in truth, *everyone* in the show danced (with the exception of that Cohan standby, the pretentious dowager). In the first number, "Over the 'Phone," the butler picks up and the young millionaire hero dances in, answering the butler in rhyme and breaking into song when he takes the receiver, and presently the stage simply fills with hoofing people.

A Cohan musical was a fantasy—*that* was his charm. He made no attempt to normalize his stories, sophisticate his characters, pretend that he wasn't putting on a lot of fun for you. Nellie, a department store clerk, has been invited to the millionaire's mansion on some lovably implausible pretext, and her entrance is a Big One, announced by three butlers and leading into a number "All in the Wearing." Says Nellie, "My goodness, I've never had such a fuss made over me before in all my life," and someone replies, "Wait till the second act."

It's the same old Cohan. The millionaire falls for Nellie, but the dowager, his aunt, opposes the match. Comes now the Cohan twist: so do the snobbish maid and butler! Then the Cohan romantic complication: Nellie's old boy friend, Jerry Conroy. ("From the Bronx," the script informs us, as if that explained everything.) There's the Cohan proletarian sympathy: Nellie is not only Irish but the daughter of a cop. And, of course, the Cohan mystery subplot requiring the appearance of a comic detective: the dowager's pearls are stolen, and Jerry is suspected. At length, Jerry gets Nellie, the company reprises the show's hit, a Bowery waltz called "Nellie Kelly I Love You," and, during the curtain calls, all cry out, "Come again! Tell the folks at home about us!" A George M. Cohan show.

The Cinderella musical was not peculiar to Cohan. It was the rage of the era: *Poor Little Ritz Girl* (1920); *The Right Girl* (1921); *Two Little Girls in Blue* (1921); *The O'Brien Girl* (1921), also with Elizabeth Hines in the Cinderella role; Jerome Kern's *Good Morning, Dearie* (1921); *Suzette* (1921); *Sue, Dear* (1922); *Daffy Dill* (1922), which even included a song entitled "Prince Charming"; Victor Herbert's *Orange Blossoms,* of course; the W. C. Fields vehicle *Poppy* (1923); *The Magic Ring* (1923); *Mary Jane McKane* (1923), with the young Oscar Hammerstein's goof on the tale in that *his* Cinderella dresses down, not up, to win her prince; *Lollipop* (1924), for which Vincent Youmans wrote his first score without a co-composer; *Plain Jane* (1924), which was *Mary Jane McKane*'s original title; *Marjorie* (1924), yet again with Elizabeth Hines; *The Magnolia Lady* (1924); *Princess April* (1924) . . . and that's but a partial listing.

The initiating title in this series is *Irene* (1919), another clerk-has-adventure-in-millionaire's-mansion show, though Irene gets her millionaire. Here was a small-scale piece that became a shockingly big hit, running over a year and a half at a time when musicals could pay off inside of a month and 200 performances (about half a year) marked a smash hit. *Irene* popularized not only the Cinderella tale but the New York City setting. In the early 1900s, comic operas took place in Europe, the Orient, and other exotic places, and musical comedy took place in small-town America. Only gradually did the musical's endemic hustle and smarts seem to require Manhattan as its natural background, and it occurred just as George Gershwin and Cole Porter and Rodgers and Hart were seen as the certain replacements of Victor Herbert and even George M. Cohan, whose city had come to seem naive, almost folksy.

Irene also popularized Edith Day. Her international stardom began here, especially when she played the show in both New York and London. The show held another ace, for, from a routinely tuneful Harry Tierney–Joseph McCarthy score came the deathless "Alice Blue Gown." But perhaps *Irene*'s main contribution was as set-up for the Show of the Decade, the one to be insistently invoked by veterans as embodying the ideals of beauty, spectacle, and "heart interest," the one that confirmed the hegemony of Broadway's greatest showman and Broadway's greatest musical star, the one that invented the idea that a merely pleasing show, wedded to gigantic publicity, would yield a colossal hit: Jerome Kern's . . . or should we say Marilyn Miller's . . . no, better, Florenz Ziegfeld's *Sally* (1920).

The most bewitched heterosexual in the history of the theatre, Ziegfeld had discovered, ravished, and presented many a beauty in his *Follies* revues. Now he had something special to produce, a *talented* beauty, blonde and leggy with a smile-in-a-million, a distinctive dancer of both tap and ballet, who sang and projected character. Musical comedy women stars were pretty; Miller was spectacular. Like her coevals Geraldine Farrar and Greta Garbo, Miller could change face from one photograph to the next, a rich look playing games with your eyes. *Sally*

was Ziegfeld's presentation of but also *to* Marilynn* Miller, the Hope
Diamond as musical. In the program, Miller was billed three times, as

> Sally of the Alley, a Foundling
> Mme. Nockerova, a Wild Rose
> Premiere Star of the Follies

There you read the plot in little. Sally, an orphan, is assigned a dish-
washing job in a restaurant where the most noticeable waiter is a more
or less Russian duke in exile. (The specified country is Czeckogovinia.)
He's the star comic, Leon Errol, a specialist in rubber-legs shtick and
sympathetic to Miller. Her love interest is Blair Farquhar (Irving Fish-
er), a society prince and novelist—right, another Cinderella story. Sally
attends a ball posing as a Slavic femme fatale, quarrels with Blair (on
the scantiest motivation since Leontes' denunciation of his wife in the
first scene of *The Winter's Tale*), and becomes a *Follies* star in a "Butterfly Ballet" composed by Victor Herbert.

Getting Herbert to step in for the ballet alone was Ziegfeld's idea of
piling Ossa upon Pelion, for *Sally*'s authors were already top men: book
writer Guy Bolton, lyricists P. G. Wodehouse and Clifford Grey, and
composer Jerome Kern, not to mention the sets of Joseph Urban, by far
Broadway's outstanding designer. Miller's above-the-title costar, Errol,
was a longtime *Follies* favorite, and there was a second lead comic, Walter Catlett. Ziegfeld even found a place for Dolores, as a society matron.
(When Ziegfeld's faithful assistant, talent scout, and *Follies* lyricist,
Gene Buck, pointed out that the role calls not for a showgirl but for an
old woman, Ziegfeld replied, "Nobody wants to look at an old woman.")
Sally was a sum of parties of the First Part, almost recklessly over-
talented.

What of the quality of the show itself? Given Miller's charm, Errol's
weird brilliance, three all-time-hit Kern songs, and the general air of
spectacle (five eminent couturiers shared billing for costumes), how
could anyone know what *was* the quality of the show itself? The Ziegfeld

---

* Rising from vaudeville into Broadway revue, from the Shuberts to Ziegfeld,
Miller (originally Mary Ellen Reynolds) retained the odd spelling of her first name
despite Ziegfeld's discouragement. "Glorifying the American Girl" was his slogan, and
American girls had American names. Lillian Lorraine. Vera Maxwell. Imogene Wilson. Virginia Biddle. Merle Finley. Hazel Forbes. Mary Hay. Drucilla Strain was as
far as Ziegfeld would go, though he did allow one mannequin to go on with one
name in the European manner, the tall and terminally haughty Dolores. It was during *Sally*'s post-Broadway tour that Miller finally dropped the double "n," to Ziegfeld's
intense relief.

touch lay in *Ziegfeld*'s quality as ringmaster of talent. What he started with was just another New York City Cinderella musical, like *Irene*. What he finished with was the Show of the Decade.

Bolton's book is serviceable in a literal sense: at the service of the performers. It framed the elements of sexy innocence and unimposing self-esteem that so ingratiated Miller to her audience, unleashed Errol and Catlett, and kept the story moving. True, there's that inept creation of a second-act tiff between the heroine and her social scion, to provision suspense before the happy third-act curtain, in a tableau of three matrimonial couples (Miller and her beau, Catlett and the soubrette, Mary Hay, and, straining credibility, Errol and Dolores) at Downtown's famous Church Around the Corner. The humor is constant, if variable. When the society boy hands Errol the menu for a special dinner, Errol reads out, "'Two Young Children,' 'A Touch of Arsenic.'" Our hero says, "Oh, excuse me. Those are all chapter headings in my novel. The menu is on the other side." Ugh. But then Catlett's girl friend recalls "the night my poor grandpa had his ribs broken in two places." Says Catlett, "Well, your grandpa shouldn't go into such places."

What disappoints about *Sally* is the score. Besides the three standards ("Look for the Silver Lining," "Whip-Poor-Will," and "Wild Rose"), this is astonishingly tuneless music from Jerome Kern in his early-middle prime. The title song is unconventionally structured in the form ABCCD, but each part bears no relation to any other part, as if the song had been composed by those five costume designers. Sally's first character number, "You Can't Keep a Good Girl Down," should suggest her indomitable spirit, but it comes off as a dead march, and "The Lorelei," "(On the banks of) the Schnitza-Komisski," and "Little Church Around the Corner" are three of the lamest comedy songs of all time.

Still, Ziegfeld was not only a master showman but a master publicist, and by the time *Sally* had closed its seventeen-month New York run, in April 1922, Ziegfeld had the story of the year to work with: Miller's engagement to Jack Pickford, the younger brother of movie star Mary Pickford, at that time the world's most famous woman. Jack, too, acted in movies, but what he mostly did was create scandals, especially the one that resulted in the extremely mysterious death, at the age of twenty-one, of his first wife, Olive Thomas, a Ziegfeld showgirl—in fact, one of the master's personal favorites. It was believed—by Ziegfeld, anyway—that Jack had hooked Olive on drugs *and* given her syphilis *and*, maybe, murdered her or at least facilitated her suicide.

So, after firing off a few PR salvos about Miller's appendicitis attack—in fact, she suffered from lifelong erratic health and was to die at age thirty-seven from, it appears, a botched medical procedure—Ziegfeld went on to the Miller-Pickford wedding, in July, at Pickfair, the White House of Hollywood, home of Little Mary and Douglas Fairbanks. The nation gaped as the stories poured out: Ziegfeld accuses Jack Pickford, Miller's mother is not happy, Little Mary's mother is not happy, Jack was dishonorably discharged from the Navy, Jack will sue Ziegfeld . . . all this as *Sally* ended its summer hiatus and launched its national tour. In 1923, rumors of a Miller-Pickford divorce capped the fun. By the time *Sally* closed, in mid-1924, it had played three-and-a-half years* and grossed well over five million dollars—almost certainly the most that any musical had earned within its first few years of life.

The Show of the Decade should surely have become a classic—not just famous but insistently revived. It was filmed, for starters, by First National in 1925—a silent, obviously—with Colleen Moore and Errol. Then sound came in, and Warner Brothers, which had bought control of First National in late 1928, found itself with an ideal property in an era raving over movie musicals: Marilyn Miller in her movie debut remaking *Sally* as an all-talking, all-singing, all-dancing Technicolor special, with Joe E. Brown taking over for Errol. The film was a hit; then *Sally* vanished.

Surely it should have been restaged. London, which had enjoyed *Sally* in 1921 with Dorothy Dickson, enjoyed it all over again in 1942 with Jessie Matthews, the piece retitled *Wild Rose*. Back on Broadway, however, who could duplicate Miller, Errol, Ziegfeld? The show passed into legend, a polite way of saying that it had been disqualified from further consideration. Suddenly, in 1948, one of the most forgotten of all Broadway revivals presented Bambi Linn and Willie Howard in a terribly underpowered production with a new script and heavy substitutions in the score, all from other Kern shows. Truth to tell, these infusions from *Leave It to Jane, The Cabaret Girl, The Riviera Girl,* and *Sitting Pretty* made *Sally* sing more tunefully. But the money and power and self-belief—the Ziegfeld—were lacking. So was Miller. Although her *Sally* film does not survive in the original color, the black-and-white reading available on laser disc includes three minutes of color recently retrieved in England. Luckily, this falls at the very center of Sally, in "Wild Rose," as Miller accepts the adoration of the male chorus while going through an amazing series of high kicks, turns, and prances, at one point giving

---

* For the 1924–25 season, Ziegfeld licensed *Sally* to a firm specializing in cut-down versions of Broadway hits for split weeks and one-night stands in the smaller towns, and the show ran for yet another year.

a stagey wink at someone in the "audience," just as she must have, night after night, when *Sally* played the New Amsterdam to not just sellout but turnaway business. In black and white, barred by the decades from knowing exactly how Miller filled a theatre with radiance, we are dubious. But in color she returns and is extraordinary. We see, for these few awesome minutes, why the 1920s so believed in the Absolute Power of the Performer.

When *Sally* was new, its fallout was heavy. It reestablished Ziegfeld as a master of musical comedy after he renounced the form to concentrate on revue. It proclaimed Miller, just twenty-two, as the queen of musical comedy. It gave Errol a shot at high stardom, one he missed in a poor choice of vehicles. It affirmed New York as the setting for the musical's rags-to-riches sagas, whether in *Irene*'s famous "tenement scene" of Irish girls chatting on fire escapes or *Sally*'s Greenwich Village cabaret, bon-ton mansion, and *Follies* debut. It presented the first major instance of the Broadway-Hollywood connection that, at least in terms of sales of rights for film adaptation, kept the stage musical solvent during hard times. And it left an astonishing resonance for a show that simply wasn't there any more. At the mid-century mark, the twenties-spoofing *Gentlemen Prefer Blondes,* showing New Yorkers, in Europe, singing the "Homesick Blues," characterizes their longing for American culture by rhyming "Rudy Vallee" with "a show like *Sally.*"

Yet *Sally* made no real history. Its celebration of the ingenue and the comic as the musical's essential stars honored a tradition that dated back well into the nineteenth century, to the days of George L. Fox and Lillian Russell. The spectacular aspect of *Sally,* too, belonged to the musical's remote past. Musical spectacles in the 1920s were usually revues or operettas—musical *comedies* were getting tauter, slimmer, faster. No question, *Sally* had a vogue. It was surely big *Sally* rather than dainty *Irene* or dancey *Mary* that prompted the Shuberts to produce *Sally, Irene and Mary* (1922), an old-fashioned Cohan imitation using tintypes of the three heroines and references to their shows, with a staggeringly talky book and a lifeless score. Yet, with that magic name pushing it forth, it was a hit. *Sally* was the Show of the Decade, all right: the preceding one. It's interesting to learn that, when Guy Bolton, P. G. Wodehouse, and Jerome Kern conceived it, it was an intimate piece. They even called it *The Little Thing.* And it was, as a few of you may have guessed, a Princess Theatre show.

We need to backtrack a bit here, for the Princess musical of the second half of the 1910s is universally regarded as the most influential form between Gilbert and Sullivan and Rodgers and Hammerstein. Conceived for a jeweled *boîte* of a house on Thirty-Ninth Street in the shadow of the Sixth Avenue El, the series actually modeled itself on the format of a Victor Herbert title, *The Only Girl* (1914): contemporary New York City locale, "natural" rather than hokey comedy, songs fitted to the play rather than vice versa, and earnest central couple enmeshed in farcical action run by eccentric supporting characters.

The Only Girl was a tremendous but only momentary hit, and Herbert was fading, anyway. The Princess shows had what *The Only Girl* lacked—Jerome Kern, young and hungry and on the rise. Besides, as a *series* the Princess shows could enjoy an annual *réclâme*. Then, too, the 299-seat Princess Theatre itself was something of a magnet, not only for its cozy beauty but the elitism of its audience. The Princess had no second balcony filled with rowdy Cohan fans, no family packages such as thronged to Fred Stone's shows. The cognoscenti found it chic to know about Princess musicals; even Dorothy Parker checked in with a rave.

With such prominence, the Princess shows get credit as the first fully integrated musicals. This is nonsense. What, two generations after Gilbert and Sullivan and Offenbach? Oh, maybe the first fully integrated *American* musicals? No. Herbert and Cohan in their very distinct ways were the instigators there. But the Princess shows did have an air of a certain kind that was at once American, contemporary, and very charming. That, all together, in show after show by more or less the same writers did seem to portend something. It was a unified series, perhaps too much so. Half-baked historians celebrate their lack of convention; on the contrary, they were extremely conventional *in their own way.*

There was, for instance, the use of the show's title as a curtain line. "Oh, boy!" wails the hero of that show to cue in the intermission, as the soubrette drags him off into delicious mischief; again, just before the second-act finale, the entire cast exclaims, "Oh, boy!" in delight at the denouement. Or take the emphasis on choreography as a structural component—not, usually, as self-contained numbers but as hoofing by the singers immediately after their vocals. *Oh, Lady! Lady!!* is typical; of its fourteen numbers (not counting the two act finales), ten were topped off by a dance. There were the punning names by which the small choruses were billed—Miss May Anne Ayes, Miss B. Ava Little, Mr. Con Kearny, a throwback to the days of Charles Hoyt.* There was,

---

* Hoyt's *A Trip to Chinatown*'s principals include Rashleigh Gay, Welland Strong, Willie Grow, and Wilder Daly, a typical trifle of the 1880s and '90s but rare after about 1910.

for the latter half of the cycle, the second (or third) act trio for two men and one woman on some topic of at most glancing relevance to the plot, as in *Oh, Boy!*'s "Flubby-Dub the Caveman" or *Leave It to Jane*'s "Sir Galahad"—or, for that matter, *Sally*'s "The Lorelei," though Sally was no Princess show.* There was Kern's musical wit, in the droll punctuational beeps and buzzes that stipple his music between the actual vocal lines, or in, say, the blithe quotation of Borodin's Polovyetski Dances from *Prince Igor* at the mention of "Russian dancers" in *Oh, Boy!*'s opening chorus.

There was Wodehouse's wit as well—and here the Princess manner turned up something new. The early 1900s enjoyed a very few good lyricists, mainly Victor Herbert's partners Henry Blossom and Harry B. Smith. Blossom was a wag; and the absurdly prolific Smith, who worked on as many as five or six shows a year (in a career that lasted forty-five years!), was a proficient and at times imaginative talent. And Schuyler Greene helped style the first two Princess titles, *Nobody Home* and *Very Good Eddie*, with lyrics of charm and point.

But none before Wodehouse brought to the writing of song lyrics naturalism and whimsey, tenderness and savvy. Like Blossom and Smith, Wodehouse wrote both book and lyrics, but his books are ordinary. His lyrics are poetry. He was unpredictable, slipping jests into love songs and fey bits of wisdom into comic numbers. He seasoned his verses with an aficionado's zest for trendy American folkways, though he was not only English but a stay-at-home. ("I get it all from the newspapers," he explained.) He introduced enjambment into musical comedy lyrics, as in this snippet from *Oh, Boy!*:

> What bad luck! It's
> Coming down in buckets.

Wodehouse also introduced a salient feature of the modern musical, the song that treats a historical figure through a modern worldview and contemporary slang, the kind of thing Cole Porter popularized ("As Columbus announced when he knew he was bounced . . ."). One finds no instance of this before Wodehouse joined Kern and Guy Bolton on their third Princess collaboration, *Have a Heart.*

This show's main comedy song is "Napoleon," an ode as much to the despotic producer-realtor Abe Erlanger (known, among other things, as

---

* "The Lorelei" was originally written for *The Night Boat* (1920), when Kern, albeit with non-Princess collaborators Anne Caldwell (book and lyrics) and Charles Dillingham (producer), was still very much in the Princess mood.

"the little Napoleon") as to the Corsican general. Erlanger was the most powerful manager on The Street and the most hated. "It is as though Nature had said to itself, 'I'll make a toad,'" Bolton later remarked, "and then halfway through had changed its mind and said, 'No, by golly, I won't, I'll make a czar of the American theater.'" Shrimpy comic Billy B. Van put the number over:

> Napoleon was the ladies' pet
> He liked to have them handy.
> He used to blow in half his pay
> On violets and candy.

Wodehouse had a way of getting right into his characters as they sang, not just connecting the dots as Broadway's many hacks did but conceiving an original picture. Listen as *Oh, Lady! Lady!!*'s heroine hymns a waltz in honor of her fiancé:

> When his pretty eyes gazed into mine,
> Suddenly the sun began to shine
> And the birds began to trill.
> Nature shouted, "Here comes Bill!"*

Perhaps it was precisely because Wodehouse was not a born lyricist but a novelist and playwright that he viewed musical comedy so freshly: not knowing the clichés, he couldn't use them. Or did he in fact know and love them but, say, from afar, ever skewing or recoining them? *Oh, Boy!*'s "Nesting Time in Flatbush" rescues cliché from itself, when the verse begins

> I've always liked the sort of song you hear so much today
> Called "When It's Something-Or-Other Time in Someplace Far
>   Away."

and Kern signs in on the fun by launching the couplet with a quotation of the big D Major theme from the first movement of Tchaikofsky's Sixth Symphony, as if reminding pop music that it has not only its quirks but its superiors as well.

It was this paradoxical combination of the satiric and the wistful that most elementally identified the Princess spirit, which is why Wodehouse

---

* This is the number that replaced the so famously dropped "Bill," probably because the latter song's loving catalogue of its subject's faults ("I know that Apollo would beat him all hollow") misled the audience about a character who is in fact thoroughly appealing. Good thing it *was* dropped, for that freed Kern to try it out again in *Show Boat*—and imagine *Show Boat* without "Bill"!

appears to be the key person in this little revolution that supposedly influenced all that followed it—i.e., the twenties musical. Some historians emphasize agent Elizabeth Marbury or even the Princess's managers, F. Ray Comstock and William Elliott, as the conceivers of the
Princess format, Marbury especially. I see these three as, mainly, audience members at four or five viewings of Herbert's *The Only Girl,* which
was in effect the first Princess show. As for Kern's role in the revolution, by 1915, when the series began, he had just come into notice for
a superb clutch of songs interpolated into *The Girl From Utah* (1914)
and had enjoyed his first runaway national hit, "You're Here and I'm
Here."* Kern was the glory of the Princess shows but not the novelty,
not the revolutionary. And Guy Bolton, who wrote the scripts (sometimes with Wodehouse), was a chameleon, giving each era what it needed in any form it wanted. His credits include idiotic Ziegfeld spectacles,
revamped European musicals, homegrown American and very different-
ly flavored English operettas, revues, crazy musical comedies like *The
Ramblers* (1926), crass, war-weary musical comedies like *Follow The
Girls* (1944), clueless musical comedies like *Ankles Aweigh* (1955), and
even the last of the floperettas, *Anya* (1965), starring among others that
queen of song, Lillian Gish.

So, in all the world of the Princess show, the genius of the place was
. . . no, the genius was Kern. But the place itself was Wodehouse. His
strangely formal informality, his love of madcaps erupting into and
wrecking your dearest plans, his use of the jewel thief and detective and
Quaker aunt and pint-size yet solve-it-all elevator operator (the one who
sings "Napoleon") gave the series its variety but also its unity—its ability, really, to do the same magical thing over and over in different ways.

Oddly, every critic cites a different list of Princess shows. Some think
of them as exclusively a Kern-Bolton-Wodehouse preserve, all other
titles to be ignored. The Princess management itself counted all musicals produced at the Princess, no matter who wrote them, though *Oh,
Boy!* was such a hit that it had to be moved to and played most of its
run at the much larger Casino Theatre. Nobody seems to count the
Princess show that folded out of town, as if nothing exists unless it plays
New York. My own Princess list expands to every title that has some
bearing on the development of this unique style, after *The Only Girl:*

---

* The impact that this irresistible two-step enjoyed in 1914 is incalculable. We
can, somewhat, gauge it in RKO's *The Story of Vernon and Irene Castle.* To demon-
strate the vogue these two dancers enjoyed, the film presents miniatures of Fred Astaire and Ginger Rogers dancing across a map of the United States, capturing the
nation. The music they dance to? "You're Here and I'm Here," *the* hit of the day.

Nobody Home (1915), the first try; *Very Good Eddie* (1915), the first hit; *Go To It* (1916), by John Golden, Anne Caldwell, and John E. Hazzard, and despite the absence of Kern and Bolton more or less in their fashion; *Have a Heart* (1917), when Wodehouse signed on, but produced by Henry Savage, not Comstock and Elliott—and not at the Princess itself; *Oh, Boy!* (1917), by far the biggest success of the series; *Leave It To Jane* (1917), which Comstock and Elliott produced at another house; *Oh, Lady! Lady!!* (1918), the summit of the series, with Kern, Bolton, and Wodehouse in top form; *Oh, My Dear!* (1918), the other Princess show not composed by Kern, Louis Hirsch brought in to work with Bolton and Wodehouse; and *Zip! Goes a Million,* about which more shortly. Some might also include *Sitting Pretty* (1924), a Kern-Bolton-Wodehouse Broadway comeback (though the trio had meanwhile produced two London shows) after six years, very much in the Princess style.

We cannot proceed without asking to what extent the Princess shows actually influenced the twenties musical. Vastly, on one hand; on another, hardly at all. Certainly, the shows' love of up-to-date American settings led others to seek more naturalistic plot premises (except in operetta, of course), and the Princess insistence on character comedy hastened the end of the stock gags and puns that had been overwhelming scripts for decades. Then, too, the new composers who rose up in the 1920s owed much to the way Kern helped originate a grammar for the *music* in musical comedy—much as Victor Herbert had done, yes, but this time with a distinctly American tang. Richard Rodgers, George Gershwin, and Vincent Youmans all mentioned revisiting Princess shows in their youth just to hear the scores again. And surely Wodehouse comparably freed the lyricists who followed him, for there was little brilliance in the verses before him, and after him there were Lorenz Hart, Ira Gershwin, Cole Porter, and Oscar Hammerstein. All of a sudden.

There is one problem in all this. The timelessly sweet, wishful, and ineffable charm that was the very essence of Princess art was of no use to the twenties musical. We think of *Rose-Marie, The Desert Song, The "Cocoanuts", A Connecticut Yankee, Oh, Kay!, Good News!, George White's Scandals,* and *Earl Carroll's Vanities.* Big stuff, brash and crazy, or, like *Rose-Marie* and *The Desert Song,* passionate. Not charming. Sure, there were plenty of charming twenties shows, but they were also sexy, while the Princess shows were almost virginal. Moreover, a good half of the series was concerned with small-town America, while twenties musical comedy had relocated to Manhattan. The 1920 census was the first to find more Americans living in urban than in rural areas (admittedly with a very generous definition of "urban" as virtually any gathering of houses with a working post office). When historian Richard Hofstadter wrote, "The United States was born in the country and has moved to the city," he might have been discussing the twenties musical. What the show had *been* was "Mary's a Grand Old Name," "Ah! Sweet Mystery of Life," and "Sir Galahad." What the show would *be* was "Manhattan," "Black Bottom," and "Little Jazz Bird": city music.

We can get a fix on precisely when the eras turn over in the last Princess show, *Zip! Goes a Million,* which was planned to be the first musical of the new decade, due in town on January 5, 1920. Because of a mysterious rift between Wodehouse and his partners, B. G. De Sylva came in as lyricist. Otherwise, the corps was as of old. As so often previously, Bolton was adapting an old comedy hit, Winchell Smith and Byron Ongley's *Brewster's Millions* (1906), from George Barr McCutcheon's novel of 1902 about a young man who must spend, to the last penny and without recklessness, a million dollars in a year in order to inherit seven millions. The fun begins when he hires his best friends as his assistants, for the terms of the contract forbid him to tell anyone what he's up to—so the more he spends the more they try to block him.

The play, very closely based upon the dialogue-heavy novel, had not only retained McCutcheon's romance for the hero and his childhood sweetheart but also included a secondary comic love couple, indispensable for Princess-show structure. Thus, all Bolton had to do was update a bit (Brewster was now a war veteran) and to drop one of the original four acts, an unnecessary episode set aboard a steamship; Kern and De Sylva would run up the old Princess magic in the score. Oddly, considering De Sylva's future as one of the voices of the Jazz Age (in two years he would collaborate with the two Gershwins on "I'll Build a Stairway to Paradise"), here he really struggled to duplicate the gentler art of Wodehouse. Helpful also was the hiring, as Monty Brewster, of Harry Fox, a personable juvenile who had won renown singing "I'm Always Chasing Rainbows" in *Oh, Look!* (1918), a flop that became a hit on the post-Broadway tour, when the exotic Dolly Sisters joined the cast. Fox redoubled the excitement by marrying one of them and looked like becoming one thing the ensemble-oriented Princess series never had: a star. The casts had always offered sharp talent, and such *eventual* headliners as Vivienne Segal, Constance Binney, and Oscar Shaw had played leads (not to mention Marion Davies in a supporting role in *Oh, Boy!*). But Fox was almost famous already. Kern even nudged the young man's fame along by quoting Fox's "Rainbows" theme song in the introduction to his entrance solo—easy to do, as the tune had been lifted from the *Più lento* section of Chopin's "Fantaisie-Impromptu."

Zip! Goes a Million began its tryout with a Name, a presold story, and a fine score. Kern was clearly trying to cut his way out of the strait patterns of show music, at least in certain small ways: the haunting "wrong" note that begins the primary couple's first duet, "Forget Me Not"; the broad lines of the second couple's "Give a Little Thought To Me" (a new lyric for the verse and chorus of "I Believed All They Said," from *Rock-A-Bye-Baby* the year before), the first instance I know of in which a single melodic germ, varied by pitch and harmony, is repeated through an entire refrain; the energetic yet sorrowful strains of "The Little Backyard Band," a nostalgic ode to the vagabond play-for-pennies groups of suburban America, scored for Sousa march time (in the verse) and then dummkopf oompah waltz (in the chorus), capturing exactly the air of defiance-in-dejection that characterizes Monty and his buddies, trying to rally around a lifelong friendship despite *their* fervent belief that *he* has lost his mind; the direly pianissimo ending of Act Two; even De Sylva's anticipation of E. Y. Harburg in the silly word games on "mandolin" in "The Mandolin and the Man." *Zip!* also boasted three numbers that became all-time standards—"Whip-Poor-Will," "Look for the Silver Lining" (both of which ended up in *Sally* a year later), and, reclaimed from *Oh, Lady! Lady!!* with a new lyric devoted to the charm of the greenback, "Bill."

Yet the production closed in Washington, D. C., in late 1919, two stops ahead of New York; to this day, no one knows why, for both reviews and business were good. One can speculate. The picture of a man frittering away a million dollars is a bit distasteful, though he has sound motivation—revenge upon the grandfather who more or less disinherited the hero's mother to death. Besides, the story consistently succeeded in later film versions and as an English stage musical in 1951 starring George Formby and called, coincidentally, *Zip Goes a Million.*

Maybe the score was a problem. For all their inventiveness, the songs too often don't connect with the story, as in "Telephone Girls," a tribute to switchboard operators that refers to Manhattan telephone exchanges: cute but irrelevant. Maybe the notion of lifelong friends holding fast in adversity didn't suit the Princess style, in which not level-headed but *crackpot* characters prevail: screwball comedy.

Maybe Bolton's book ran to the verbose. The last known copy of the script, Bolton's own, was lost in London during the Blitz. However, the orchestra parts, from overture to bows, were uncovered in the famous archeological dig in the Warner Brothers Music warehouse in Secaucus, New Jersey, in 1982. A number of Hollywood studios had bought music publishing firms in the very late 1920s, when sound, especially music, became essential in film production; Warners bought T. B. Harms, publisher of all the major Broadway writers save the *samizdat* Irving Berlin. Because it was customary, upon the closing of a show's final post-Broadway tour, to store orchestra parts and any attendant ephemera (such as unused songs and lyric sketches) with the music publisher, the former Harms and now Warners music warehouse contained a library of the Broadway musical in its golden age. As we will see again and again in these pages, the authenticity of modern revivals depends almost entirely upon the Secaucus trove.

Zip! Goes a Million offers an instance of this. For a season of concert stagings of Princess shows in 1985, John McGlinn elected to bring back the two best of the line, *Oh, Boy!* and *Oh, Lady! Lady!!*, along with the least known of the Kerns, *Zip! Goes a Million*. McGlinn commissioned a new book from Mark D. Kaufmann, who worked from the novel and play and around the extant score. This, to modern sensibilities, is writing backward—but it is precisely how shows were written when *Zip!* was new. Songs were not created for a finished book but rather preceded the book or were written "alongside" it at the same time, which explains why so many songs of the 1910s and '20s don't fit smoothly into the script.

In the end, Kaufmann's stylish resuscitation confounded history with a wonderful evening, a lost show found and a flop coming off as a hit, not least because of the cast, the superb Jeanne Lehmann as the ever so serious heroine and an unusually high-powered Cris Gronendaal as Monty. Kaufmann's best innovation was the building of an extremely minor character in the play, Trixie, into a major comic figure, a musical-comedy nontalent whom Monty stars in a show guaranteed (he hopes) to lose a fortune, *Helga the Bratwurst Girl*. In a sustained set piece, the reading of an especially derisive Philadelphia review, Kaufmann created something the world had never actually seen—a musical worse than *Legs Diamond*. "We open at the Princess in two weeks!" the elated Monty booms. Another rewarding addition was the interpolation of a number dropped from Kern and Anne Caldwell's *She's a Good Fellow* (1919), "Semiramis," another of those antiquity-in-modern-terms capers, which gave a main chance to Judy Blazer's merrily Assyrian Trixie.

So what went wrong with the original *Zip! Goes a Million*? Could it simply be that the Princess era was over? *Zip!*'s middle act takes place in New York City, but it's basically about villagers adhering to a villager code of honor in business and loyalty to friends. This is suitable for a play of 1906, whose first-act finish would be followed by the curtain's flying up again upon a stylized "tableau": Monty, with pad, figuring out how much he'll have to spend per week to dissipate the fortune.

And isn't there a sense of the all-too-bygone days in a score with so many *gentle* titles? It's all so bully and sentimental—"You Tell 'Em," "The Language of Love," "Forget Me Not," "Whip-Poor-Will," "The Little Backyard Band," "Look for the Silver Lining." Had the Princess manner lost its vigor? One of the numbers offers a mockup of an old-time ballad performed in the styles of George M. Cohan, the Princess itself, and Al Jolson. This pastiche genre had been stock material since Victor Herbert's youth, a cliché by 1910. And what are we to make of a spoof of Princess style *in a Princess show*?* Had the series gone decadent? More pertinently, wasn't the Princess style now wholly old hat? Within five years, the series had fallen out of fashion.

Ironically, De Sylva had worked on a far more trendy piece just before *Zip! Goes a Million*—*La, La, Lucille* (1919), announced as "A New, Up-to-the-Minute Musical Comedy of Class and Distinction." New is right: it was not only De Sylva's first show but the first show to be entirely composed by the twenty-year-old George Gershwin, who had thus far been represented by the odd interpolation and a "mostly by" score for a terrible revue that closed out of town.

True, *La, La, Lucille*'s producer was an old-timer, Alfred E. Aarons,† and the French farce that supplied the plot stood in a long line of French farces that had fed Broadway musical story lines, especially in comic opera—Ivan Caryll's *The Pink Lady* (1911) and *Oh! Oh! Delphine* (1912), for instance, and we've just met Victor Herbert's *Orange Blossoms*. Like Herbert's show (and *Zip! Goes a Million*), *La, La, Lucille* offered a legacy-with-a-catch premise: husband (John E. Hazzard) must divorce his ex-showgirl wife (Janet Velie) or renounce his bluenose aunt's fortune. The show's structure, as in so many musicals from about 1910 to 1925, is pure three-act Georges Feydeau. Act One: problem stated, alleged solution agreed upon. Act Two: "solution" leads to endless complications. Act Three: true solution found. This sort of layout tends to deposit most of the fun in Act Two. Here, husband fakes assignation with bribed, unattractive co-respondent, to be discovered by wife, with divorce (and inheritance, and then remarriage) to follow. But the

---

* The score also contains a reference to *Leave It to Jane* in "Telephone Girls." The pastiche number, by the way, is excellent satire. Cohan and Jolson are easy—flag; mammy. But the Princess takeoff moves from a version of *Oh, Lady! Lady!!*'s "You Found Me and I Found You," complete with Frank Saddler's original tick-tock xylophone scoring, to end with the words "Till the clouds roll by."

† Not, as sometimes reported, Alex A. Aarons, Alfred's son and, in partnership with Vinton Freedley, the producer of most of Gershwin's famous musicals, from *Lady, Be Good!* to *Girl Crazy*.

hotel chosen for the occasion is overrun with grotesques—the co-respondent's jealous, knife-throwing husband, an Irish house detective, an eloping couple with a gift for getting into the wrong room . . . and Lucille, who finds husband not with co-respondent but with eloping bride. Oh, she'll divorce him, all right! For *good!*

Of course, it all ends well. The aunt turns out to be very much alive; she was only testing her nephew's devotion. And *Lucille's* book writer, Fred Jackson, spread his fun around in some outrageous, even Co-hanesque ways. The third act began exactly where the second had ended, without an opening number. Or take this moment with the central couple:

LUCILLE: Oh, dear! I don't know what to do.
JOHN: Well, let's sing.

And the orchestra strikes up "It's Hard to Tell"—and that music tells us why *Zip!* and its charm were Before and *Lucille* and its energy are Now. This is the show with "Tee-Oodle-Um-Bum-Bo"—remember the chorus girls in red satin pants?—but also with "There's More to the Kiss Than the X-X-X" (risqué), "Somehow It Seldom Comes True" (a wistful ballad with *swing*), and, most of all, "Nobody But You," one of Gershwin's very earliest songs in the jazzy style that all Broadway was to employ but that Gershwin in particular embodied, upstart, Jewish, unapologetic.

Not that *Lucille* marked a complete break with everything that *Zip! Goes a Million* represented. "From Now On," another of Gershwin's jazzy *Lucille* numbers, employs a slinky chromatic hook that is just like the one that Kern used to distinguish *Zip!'s* "Whip-Poor-Will"—a coincidence that reminds us how much revolution can share with the ancien régime. Still, there is a hustle to *La, La, Lucille* that the Princess style missed. Kern, Bolton, and Wodehouse might have replied that there's a beguiling innocence in the Princess style that *Lucille* misses. But this was the 1920s: innocence was over. World War I, the revival of the Ku Klux Klan, the "Red Scare" and the labor unrest of 1919, the popular scorning of Prohibition, the Sacco and Vanzetti case, and many great and small signs of social upheaval were bound to change the nation's view of itself, and the theatre could no longer play to the public it had known.

Even Jerome Kern, who was never attracted to the cynical or at least satiric kind of book that attracted the Gershwins, Rodgers and Hart, and Cole Porter, did put the old style behind him in one of his early-twenties musicals. *The Night Boat* (1920) and *Sitting Pretty* (1924) were pure Princess; *Sally* (1920), we know, was monumentally old-fashioned;

and *The Stepping Stones* (1923) was a Fred Stone extravaganza, its format about as contemporary as a back number of the *Police Gazette*.

But *Good Morning, Dearie* (1921) brought Kern to a somewhat modern-day New York, complete with an Irish gangster, a fight scene brought off so realistically that a large number of critics remarked upon it, and a generally saucy attitude. It's another Cinderella show: Rose-Marie (Louise Groody), assistant in a dress shop, is the gangster's old girl friend. He's about to get out of prison, but she wants no part of him, especially after she meets a society boy (Oscar Shaw). It's he and the gangster (Harland Dixon) who have the fight, and we should mention the comic detective (William Kent) who also turns shtick as a pseudo-Chinese waiter and a drunk servant. That's the show, all of it; and *Good Morning, Dearie* got universal raves, no easy pickings in a time when New York was stuffed with dailies. Even President Harding liked it. But then, *Good Morning, Dearie* was a piece that ran more on its performing talents than on its creative talents.

Louise Groody, for example. She was never a star in the Miss America Marilyn Miller sense of the term. But she was pretty, adroit, a "good enough" singer, and a darling. Oscar Shaw is that tiresome guy doing matinee idol profiles and Jack Buchanan chortles in the Marx Brothers film *The Cocoanuts*, but by the taste of the 1920s he would have been what Italian opera critics call "correct" as the society guy. Better yet was Harland Dixon's "Chesty" Costello, not only a singing but a dancing gangster. A vaudeville knockout in the team of Doyle and Dixon, this versatile performer was on call throughout the decade as a kind of indispensable party guest—looks great in a suit, fascinates by dancing with his legs going wild though his torso stays rigid, and breaks them up on every line. Ada Lewis, an old, old favorite as Rose-Marie's boss—she dated back not only to the age of those proto-musical creators Harrigan and Hart but to the Harrigan and Hart troupe itself—was first choice in those plump, tough, yet sensual grande dame parts that were America's version of the Gilbert and Sullivan Katisha-Buttercup-Dame Carruthers *Fach*. As for William Kent, he was yet another singing comic, adept at that stream-of-consciousness nonsense patter so popular in this age, very useful in self-contained sketch scenes involving pseudo-Chinese waiters.

But what of *Good Morning, Dearie* as written? It's a despair of Jerome Kern's admirers that between his Princess shows and his later identity as the king of the Broadway Art Score (think of "Smoke Gets in Your Eyes," "The Song Is You," or "All the Things You Are"), he seems temporarily to have lost power. One way of looking at it is: first Kern had

P. G. Wodehouse. Later he had Otto Harbach and Oscar Hammerstein. In between he had Anne Caldwell.

That's not a jibe. Caldwell is a forgotten but—judging by historians' comments—misunderstood figure who was, in fact, one, the first major woman writer of Broadway musicals,* two, not an ingenious librettist but a sometimes ingenious lyricist, and three, the closest thing to P. G. Wodehouse that Kern could have found in his Caldwell period (1919–25). Kern wanted nothing but charm from the musical, and I mean *Florodora* charm, the old stuff. Caldwell understood the old stuff but wanted to get into the new stuff: a transitional talent.

Consider *Good Morning, Dearie*'s love scene. Groody and Shaw are alone in the dress shop, and a clumsy book scene leads into "Rose-Marie," the heroine's wistfully autobiographical ballad. As the music continues, the hero tries out the song's first line—"Rose-Marie, little blossom grown on a love tree"—thereby turning the number into courtship. Blushing, Rose-Marie tries to steer the conversation away from this erotic precipice. As the orchestra hums away, she nervously babbles out the cue lines for "Didn't You Believe (that the bears would catch the naughty children?)," a bouncy salute to the innocence of childhood and evidence that these two are growing close. The playbill announced this eight-minute scene as a "Musical scena," and so it is: a mixture of underscored dialogue and two songs that advances the plot without our noticing how it was done.

Most of *Good Morning, Dearie* was on a lower level. Each of the two acts had two scenes, the set changes covered by irrelevant chorus girl parades. The score in toto lay well below the Princess level. There was a ton of specialty numbers and songs for the heck of it. For example, the lovers consider their honeymoon options, and "Niagara Falls" begins, Rose-Marie jump-starting the music by producing a railroad timetable; the song's trio section is a rhyming recitation of the various American cities the two will *not* be going to. It's not great Caldwell. It's even minor Kern. But the couple's third duet, "Blue Danube Blues," finds Caldwell and Kern inspired, he to adapt Johann Strauss's familiar waltz into a fox trot, this to be sung against a ragtime strain; and she to

---

* Fans of Rida Johnson Young and Dorothy Donnelly may question this statement. Young precedes Caldwell chronologically and, as lyricist of *Naughty Marietta,* can be called deathless on "Ah! Sweet Mystery of Life" alone. But her other work, save *Maytime,* is truly obscure. Donnelly's only important credits are *Blossom Time* and *The Student Prince,* and she began writing *after* Caldwell did. One odd fact: all three women started as performers; Donnelly was Broadway's first Candida, in 1903, at the Princess.

hone in on the shyness of a youth wanting to dance with a "girlie sweet." "At her stare," Caldwell continues, "he's well aware that he has lots of hands and feet." Be fair; was Wodehouse better? As the two coalesce, Caldwell writes, "Now my man I've found, Mister Stickaround." That's lovely.

So *Good Morning, Dearie* was spotty as a composition but filled with performing talent; no wonder all the critics went for it. They went for a lot worse. It was generally believed that critics went easy on musicals—critics themselves admitted it—because a feeble thriller or a funereal comedy was a dead loss but an idiotic musical might at least field a toothsome chorus line, a droll comic, or a nifty tune or two.

Certainly, the critics went easy on *The Gingham Girl* (1922), at 422 performances a smash hit. (By comparison, *Good Morning, Dearie*, the outstanding musical comedy hit of the previous season, ran 347 performances, outdistanced only by the operetta *Blossom Time*.) Yet *The Gingham Girl* is a terrible show. The tale of a country boy who lights out for The City to be joined at length by his hometown sweetheart, the piece does get some mileage out of rube humor. In Act One, in Crossville Corners, New Hampshire, the hero, John, is asked if he's got a sleeper for the train. "Been in this town twenty years," he replies, "don't need any more sleep."

Even city folk subscribe to the me-versus-the-world attitude of the comedy. In a Manhattan café, goodtime gal Mazie inquires of a waiter if he's seen her date.

> WAITER: A gentleman?
> MAZIE: I don't know yet. It's just a short acquaintance.

In Act Three, in the office of the heroine's burgeoning new business, Bluebird Cookies, Mazie turns up looking for work.

> MARY: Haven't we met before?
> MAZIE: Wouldn't be a bit surprised. Everyone in New York knows
>   me. I've been thrown out of some of our very best cafés.

Note that this is another Cinderella show. Note also the Cohanesque flavor of the John and Mary coupling, the loud-checked-suited-hick-takes-on-the-slicks gags, and especially the first-act finale, at the Crossville Corners railroad station, when the hero sings of how he'll take the town to the chorus's punctuation of a repeated "Atta boy, John!" We even get a quotation of "Give My Regards to Broadway."

Clearly, Cohan cast a long shadow. But then *The Gingham Girl*'s producers, Laurence Schwab and Daniel Kusell, had been packaging acts for vaudeville, among whose folk Cohan was regarded as a cross between George Washington and Saint Patrick. Kusell himself wrote *The Gingham Girl*'s book, and the composer and the lyricist, Albert Von Tilzer and Neville Fleeson, were derivative talents, as likely to use Cohan for a model as to strike out on their own. Take *Honey Girl* (1920), a musical with a horse-racing background. The good news about its score is that it's perfectly acceptable second-rate Kern. The bad news is that Kern didn't write it: Von Tilzer and Fleeson did. It's also got a bit of Victor Herbert in it: "I'm Losing My Heart to Someone" not only traces over the concept, waltz time, and general contours of *Naughty Marietta*'s "I'm Falling in Love with Someone" but even jumps up to a high note on the word "girl" as Herbert's original does. *The Gingham Girl*, too, has its dash of Herbert. "Tell Her While the Waltz Is Playing" is embarrassingly like unto "Ask Her While the Band Is Playing," from *Algeria* (1908).

The worst thing about *The Gingham Girl*'s score is its generic nature, a problem with many early twenties musicals. Back in 1915, the genially acerbic critic George Jean Nathan made a list of the standard musical comedy song cues, which included: "Yes, but there's only one girl in the world for me!" and "Yes, but there's only one town in the world for me!" and "Yes, but there's only one street in the world for me!" *The Gingham Girl*'s songs respond to these tired ideas—"The Twinkle in Your Eye," "You Must Learn the Latest Dances," "As Long As I Have You," "That Wonderful Thing We Call Love," "Love and Kisses" (the show's out-of-town title). Naturally, there would be a Greenwich Village number, a cliché in musicals set in New York. But how much more P. G. Wodehouse got out of the subject in *Oh, Lady! Lady!!* four years earlier, citing someone's eighty-three-year-old Aunt Matilda:

> She learned the ukelele, she breakfasted at Polly's,
> And, what is worse, she wrote free verse,
> And now she's in the *Follies!*

The Gingham Girl's Village scene does include a few bohemians—She Who Wears Batik, She Who Throws Bombs, even She Who Wears a Derby. But, when these girls start singing, we learn no more than that Village life is so merry "we simply laugh our worries away." That could be Kokomo, Brigadoon, anywhere.

No question, *The Gingham Girl* makes space for the New Dance Sensation, a fixture of the decade from first to last. In this number, a soloist or two, backed by the chorus, purports to introduce "the latest step," gets one all ready to learn it, then provides at most minimal instruction. This ritual seems to date back to the very early 1910s, as in Rudolf Friml's first two shows: *The Firefly* (1912) offered "The Latest Thing from Paris," *High Jinks* (1913) "The Dixiana Rise." Real popularity came with "The Syncopated Walk" in Irving Berlin's *Watch Your Step* (1914).

Instantly, a craze erupted. A Princess show succumbed, in *Nobody Home*'s "The Chaplin Walk," though Kern usually disdained the genre, preferring songs about dance in general. *Going Up* (1917) had "The Tickle Toe," one of the least communicative in this series ("sort of cute and so exciting" is the bulk of the tutorial). *The Scandals of 1920* offered "The Scandal Walk." But by then the dam had burst: *Mary* had "The Tom Tom Toddle," *Good Morning, Dearie* "The Teddy Toddle," *Little Nellie Kelly* "The Hinky Dee," *Sally, Irene and Mary* "The Flippety Flop" ("Glide a little, slide a little, then you hop"), *The Rise of Rosie O'Reilly* "The Marathon Step," *Sweet Little Devil* "The Jijibo," *The "Cocoanuts"* "The Monkey Doodle-Doo." The New Dance Sensation was almost exclusive to musical comedy, though the operetta *Rose-Marie* (1924) included two *old* dance sensations in "Totem Tom-Tom" and "The Minuet of the Minute." *The Gingham Girl*'s entry was "The Forty-Second Street and Broadway Strut," hard-driving, with plenty of "blue" notes and, like the rest of the score, utterly forgettable.

What, then, saved *The Gingham Girl*? It was at least neatly produced. It also had a Thing: eight dancing beauties who appeared throughout the show in various guises and also in many a publicity handout. It had a strong cast of tender talents, especially Eddie Buzzell, a chip of the Cohan block (later chosen to play Cohan's role in Warner Brothers' early talkie of *Little Johnny Jones*) as John and, as Mary, the delightful Helen Ford, soon to help launch Rodgers and Hart with key appearances in *Dearest Enemy* and *Peggy-Ann*. It had the dependable Sammy Lee for choreography. But, mainly, it had tradition supporting it, for it was made of echoes of Ziegfeld and Miller's *Sally*, Edith Day's *Irene*, and George M. Cohan's *Mary*. Like so many other titles of the early 1920s, *The Gingham Girl* is a musical of the past. Seeking the musical that says *now*, we should talk about *Lady, Be Good!* (1924).

One might think of this show as the one in which Ira Gershwin finally joined his already established brother, George, to give Broadway a distinctive new style in musical comedy, jazzy and witty and so up to the minute that there's not a waltz in the entire score. Or one could call this the show that decisively proclaimed the stardom of Fred and Adele Astaire. One could view it as Guy Bolton's definitive break with his Princess manner, for his book, written with incipiently longtime partner

Fred Thompson, is full of the nutty moxie we associate with the twenties musical—the eagerness to run to the next stupid joke, the next turbulent number.

I see *Lady, Be Good!* as none of the above so much as the first collaboration of Alex A. Aarons and Vinton Freedley, the only prominent producing office that was founded when the decade got into gear and which gave up more or less after the big financial blowout in 1929. Aarons and Freedley produced seven Gershwin shows, but they also worked with Rodgers and Hart and De Sylva, Brown, and Henderson: discovered Ethel Merman and glorified Gertrude Lawrence and Bert Lahr; built the Alvin* Theatre; and enriched the musical-comedy scene with Florida millionaires, boxing, bootleggers, and Havana gambling, the matter of the day. The Aarons and Freedley musical *was* the 1920s, and *Lady, Be Good!* can be seen as the ground zero of the explosion.

Let me emphasize that this was not a progressive show, not "good" history. Like most musical comedies of the early 1920s, *Lady, Be Good!* isn't about anything. It begins with a premise—homeless brother and sister, scrabbling for cash, get into romantic and legal entanglements that, like a lie, get more entangled the longer they get told. However, the premise is an excuse, and the entanglements are absurd: that's the fun. *Sally,* for all its chancy realism, is about something—an orphan wants to be somebody. *Irene* is about something—the slum poor can teach Society about honesty and fairness. *Mary* is about something—a young man with a dream. *Lady, Be Good!* is about the treat of seeing the Astaires in an Aarons-Freedley musical with a Gershwin score.

Ponder this: *Lady, Be Good!* has nine principals. One of them, Jeff White, is not truly a character, just a name that the authors pasted on Cliff Edwards, the pleasantly androgynous-voiced singer who was known as "Ukelele Ike." Edwards had little more than three spots in the show: a few lines leading into "Fascinating Rhythm" in Act One; then, in Act Two, a few other lines in a comic scene; and, finally, a specialty spot that had nothing to do with the story, in which Edwards sang whatever he chose and, like a good sport, a number that the Gershwins wrote for him, "Little Jazz Bird."

The other eight principals maintain a close relationship to the action. The Astaires, as the evicted siblings, and Walter Catlett, as their lawyer, held the center of the piece, with a romantic vis-à-vis for each. There is another couple, of the kind Bolton doted on, the incorrigibly dizzy

* Named for *Al*ex and *Vint*on, who lost it in 1932. Now it's called the Neil Simon. Zip goes a million.

Englishman (Gerald Oliver Smith) and the young woman (Patricia Clarke) trying to "reform" him.

It *sounds* reasonable, and it does all interlock. For instance, lawyer gets sister to impersonate a Mexican widow (but the supposedly dead husband is in fact sister's beau, who turns up right in the middle of the charade). Or, for instance, dizzy Brit gets job as house detective, becomes suspicious of lawyer, and handcuffs himself to the lawyer (then can't find the key, so the two can play frantic chain-gang comedy for the last fifteen minutes of the evening). Yet these eight people relate to each other farcically rather than characterologically. In the modern musical, character dictates action—*Oklahoma!, Guys and Dolls, Gypsy, Into the Woods, Kiss of the Spider Woman.* In the twenties musical, action dictates action—so much so that, when the finale finds all eight leads pairing off for a four-way wedding, it is less through desire than through simple symmetry.

Of course, it was Catlett's comic style, that of the fast-talking yet perennially bumbling conniver, that audiences counted on, not his psychological motivation. And it was the Astaires who were expected to flesh out their characters, not the authors. A script like *Lady, Be Good!*'s didn't give its characters personality: its performers did. We of today know how easy this must have been for Astaire, but when working with his sister he tended, protectively, to play to her, and it was she who was thought the mainstay of the act. Stark Young spent the first half of his *Times* review entirely on her—"ADELE ASTAIRE FASCINATES" ran the headline—and could say no better of Fred than that he "participates enthusiastically and successfully in most of Miss Astaire's dance offerings."

This was typical. Out of town, the show was called *Black-Eyed Susan,* the name of Adele's character (with an allusion, one presumes, to her masquerade as the Mexican widow). Backstage, however, Fred was the act's muscle. Sammy Lee designed the chorus dancing for "A Wonderful Party," "End of a String" (in which the girls claimed the boys by unwinding great pastel-colored ribbons), "Fascinating Rhythm," "Linger in the Lobby," and so on. (After the sprightly two- and three-person dances of the Princess era, twenties shows preferred Big Numbers.) But Fred laid out his and Adele's choreography himself, and a lot of the *Lady, Be Good!* flavor must have been tasted in "The Half of It, Dearie, Blues," "Swiss Miss," "I'd Rather Charleston" (written for the 1926 London production, with the Astaires and with William Kent in Catlett's part), and especially "Hang On To Me."

This last title was the show's first number, at the close of the first scene. (Here is another musical, years before *Oklahoma!,* that raises its curtain on a bit of orchestral sketching but no bustly chorus or even any singing at all.) We actually view the Astaires' eviction—Adele makes her entrance being carried out in bed—and then see them getting tearfully gallant about it:

DICK: It will be all right, Susie. I'll take care of you.
SUSIE: After all, there's two of us. It doesn't seem so bad when you've got someone to hang on to.

That leads into the song, whose dance finds the pair merrily moving into their new abode, the street: straightening the rug, hanging up the "God Bless Our Home" sampler, and, when a rainstorm hits, continuing the dance under an umbrella till all stage lights darkened to a single spotlight that irised out for the close.

Now, in terms of the story, that's a fine establishing sequence. But what audiences of 1924 were really learning was that those wonderful Astaire kids had finally made it. Needless to say, they were especially winning when playing siblings. Tradition has it that they more or less had to play brother and sister, or Just Good Friends. No. They were the love plot in both *For Goodness Sake* (1922) and the Kern-Caldwell backstager *The Bunch and Judy* (1922), which suggests the innocent nature of love plots in this epoch.

The Astaires and Catlett and the overall nutty atmosphere of the show, fine as all this was, does not mark *Lady, Be Good!* as uniquely as does the work of the Gershwins. After *La, La, Lucille,* George became George White's house composer for his annual *Scandals* revues in five successive editions, working mostly with *Lucille*'s lyricists, B. G. De Sylva and Arthur Jackson. Little of the rhapsodic, blue Gershwin we admire came through in this series, save "I'll Build a Stairway to Paradise," "Throw Her in High!," "Mah-Jongg," and "Somebody Loves Me."* Nevertheless, an occasional tune in various other shows gives us a Gershwin almost bursting with the new sound, a still very young but confident and self-directed Gershwin—"Innocent Ingenue Baby," a rippling melody punctuated with jagged riffs; the ghetto raveup "Nashville Nightingale"; or the frantic New Dance Sensation "The Jijibo."

Working with brother Ira must have finally liberated George, because not only was it the fondest collaboration in the musical's history but

---

* We should also mention *Blue Monday Blues,* a mini-opera presented in the *Scandals of 1922.* With its all-black dramatis personae, tragic narrative, and wailing vocal line, it is often regarded as a forerunner of *Porgy and Bess.* In truth, the piece is rather terrible; White removed it from the show after a chorus of scorn from the critics.

from the start it found George totally in form, a well of melody in a par-adise-garden of jazz. The two must have known they were destined to combine talents, but the unknown Ira feared appearing to have cashed in on his precocious brother's fame. Under the pseudonym "Arthur Francis," Ira tried and failed to establish himself—his one Broadway show, *Two Little Girls in Blue* (1921), was not the kind that makes rep-utations. "Francis" worked for Gershwin on a few songs here and there till Ira, under his own name, collaborated with Desmond Carter on the lyrics to George's *Primrose* (1924), a London show.

This production seems an odd occasion for the ultra-American George to produce his first really wonderful score—and it's a big one, seventeen songs plus three finales and a ballet—but he did so with dis-arming imitations of the English style in musical comedy even while try-ing out the Jazz Thing. "Berkely Square and Kew" (a honeymoon-cottage number with a twist: the couple will maintain separate resi-dences) and the wistful "Isn't It Wonderful" could have been composed by an Englishman; Heather Thatcher's big third-act solo, "I Make Hay When the Moon Shines," was clearly meant to stir memories of Gertie Millar's rendition of "Moonstruck" in *Our Miss Gibbs* fifteen years ear-lier. Yet "Naughty Baby" is one of the snazziest studies in syncopation and chromatically altered harmony to that date, pure Gershwin and pure Broadway.

And that must be why the *Lady, Be Good!* score, immediately after, seems so . . . well, it's a tired word, but: fresh. Something new-minted after that ponderous *Sally* and that crypto-operetta *Irene,* and that elec-trically humdrum *Mary* with its dirgelike love song. *Lady, Be Good!* has, on the contrary, "Fascinating Rhythm." Those shows move; this one *springs.* Think of the stamping "break," between the vocal lines of "The Half of It, Dearie, Blues," George's anticipation in music of what Fred Astaire will do when he dances it. Think of Vic Arden and Phil Ohman, the duo-pianist team in *Lady, Be Good!*'s pit, helping George define his sound as something apart, a giant jazz keyboard with too many blue notes. Think of the bouncing orchestral ritornello that binds the choral numbers "A Wonderful Party" and "End of a String"; or, in the first-act finale, the heroine's mournful reprise of a snatch of her love song, "So Am I," against the chorus's merry salute to marriage, reminding us that, amid the foolery, real feelings are being hurt.

Historians sometimes cite the hit titles of a score as if such were proof of quality: the more hits, the better the score. Nonsense. *Sally* spun off three hits, yet the rest of the music clunks. *Lady, Be Good!* added only "Fascinating Rhythm" and "Oh, Lady Be Good" to the catalogue of standards, yet it bubbles with surprise and delight. George had rhythm and George had harmony and George had energy; but what George (and Ira) mainly had was imagination. From now on, the very notion of a musical comedy score as a set of ten or twelve infinitely repeatable genre items—"There's only one song in the world for me!"—begins to go out of style.

The Second Violin

THE STATE OF OPERETTA

On one level, the history of the American musical can be seen in the development of the tension between lean-and-hungry musical comedy and fat-and-besotted operetta. For fifty years, from the late 1800s to the mid-1920s, operetta continually outperformed musical comedy in artistry, as when Gilbert and Sullivan and Offenbach played side by side with homegrown farces and revue-like contraptions. For the next fifty years, into the 1970s, musical comedy increasingly adopted operetta's musical strength while retaining its own smarts and humor. Since then, musical comedy and operetta have virtually vanished as distinct forms. The dark and serious musical of today is lean and besotted, a sort of operetta comedy.

One cannot read the musical's history, then, without understanding the difference between the two forms—especially in the 1920s, operetta's golden age. Yet while every theatregoer knows a musical comedy when he sees one—*Anything Goes* or *Guys and Dolls*, for instance—operetta can be slippery, ambiguous. Is *South Pacific* an operetta? What, with those horny seabees grunting out "There Is Nothing Like a Dame" and a heroine who sings bass and does a drag act? Is *My Fair Lady* an operetta? Why, because the heroine reaches two high G's and "You Did It" has a concerted final section? Did you notice that the leading man can get through the entire score on *Sprechstimme?* That's an operetta?

Even operetta in its infancy, when it was known as "comic opera," can be deceptive. It sometimes seems as though writers assume operetta is anything with a soprano in it, or anything set outside the United States, or anything not by George M. Cohan.

However, operetta in the 1920s is fairly easy to identify, for it had reached its high noon as a fully developed and unique genre yet had not begun its collaborative dialogue with musical comedy. Twenties operetta fielded more solid voices than musical comedy, liked exotic settings and historical periods, favored antique diction ("nigh," "betide"), placed a harp in the pit rather than musical comedy's piano, made use of martial airs and a ton of waltz, isolated the humor in one or two eccentric characters rather than let it seep out of the general company, and celebrated a crisis in the love plot with a gala confrontation in song where musical comedy might treat it in a few spoken lines. Mainly, operetta was passionate, and musical comedy was satiric. Or: operetta was "Indian Love Call" and musical comedy was a New Dance Sensation.

Operetta was also German or Austro-Hungarian, at least since *The Merry Widow* (1907), whose extraordinary vogue made Broadway a nesting place for not only Franz Lehár but Leo Fall, Emmerich Kálmán, Oscar Straus, Edmund Eysler, and others. Then came World War I and a national prejudice against anything connected to the Central Powers; even sauerkraut became "liberty cabbage." Suddenly, operetta of German origin—and by extension *any* operetta—was a dead show walking.

There were other factors. Operetta's collapse coincided with the rise of dance, and operetta's structure narrates almost entirely in music and dialogue. Dance is excrescent, perhaps a waltz at a ball or a Ländler by some handy peasants. Then, too, there had been a glut of operettas in the *Widow*'s wake. But, by 1918, not a single operetta opened on Broadway.

So *Apple Blossoms* (1919) could be called daring. It was set in contemporary Manhattan, struck a worldly attitude, and included the latest word in dance—the Astaires, barely out of their teens and in their first book show after a childhood spent in vaudeville and, lately, revue.* Nonetheless, producer Charles Dillingham boldly called *Apple Blossoms* "an operetta," and, while the book and lyrics were by Illinois's own William LeBaron, the music was the work of violin virtuoso Fritz Kreisler and Victor Jacobi, very much in the middle-European tradition. There

---

* Adele was billed as Molly and Fred as Johnny in the program, though they had no spoken or sung lines—no parts per se. They simply appeared after other people's numbers and danced.

were some snazzy rhythm numbers, true—the slithery, syncopated "A Widow," or the breathless "A Girl, a Man, a Night, a Dance." But the music abounds in the waltzes and marches that operetta traditionally doted upon, and *what* music! In its advanced harmony, intricate orchestration, and sheer outpouring of melody, *Apple Blossoms* stands among the greatest of Broadway's forgotten scores. The plot, about a forced marriage between a schoolgirl and a rake who eventually decide they are in love, was routine; the script itself delivered this tale no more than capably. What made *Apple Blossoms* a hit was its score: the enchanting waltz "Brothers" (*elegante e ritmato*, Jacobi directs), on passing off boy friends as relatives; Kreisler's "Who Can Tell," the show's sole enduring hit when it became popular in the Grace Moore film *The King Steps Out* as "Stars in My Eyes"; the heroine's exquisite "Letter Song" (by Kreisler), an operetta convention made special when the girls' chorus takes the main melody in cascading three-part harmony under the soprano's soaring obbligato; the hero's trumpeting "Little Girls, Good Bye!" (by Jacobi); and especially the "reverse" love duet just after the marriage, Jacobi's "You Are Free," in which the couple propose a platonic arrangement in music of supreme sensuality, as if they already know that, as operetta revels in romantic endings, this man and wife *must* fall in love.

Producer Dillingham did not content himself with Good Enough. Joseph Urban, Ziegfeld's pet designer, planned the sets, and in the leads were operatic baritone John Charles Thomas and the admired Broadway diva Wilda Bennett. Critic Alexander Woollcott thought she, at least, would improve "when she is not saying to herself, 'I am singing songs by the great Fritz Kreisler and there he is in the seventh row on the aisle. I think I'm going to faint.'"

Hailed as a find, *Apple Blossoms* played 256 performances, a very solid run for the day. Thomas even recorded two of his numbers, an unusual honor. Dillingham promptly readied an *Apple Blossoms* imitation, *The Love Letter* (1921), bringing back LeBaron and Jacobi, Urban, director Edward Royce, Thomas, and the Astaires. The show did not go over, but it was remembered—by the Astaires, at any rate—as the work in which their signature "oompah trot" was devised, under Royce's guidance, while improvising in rehearsal.*

The Love Letter's failure did not mean that operetta was still a bad bet. Less than a year earlier, the Shuberts had unveiled not only an op-

---

* See page 4 for a description.

eretta but a brazenly middle-European one, based upon a German original, composed by Europeans, and set in old Vienna. Yet, when it closed, this show not only set a record at 592 performances as the third-longest-running musical in Broadway history but lived on in (brief) New York revivals and (endless) road tours for twenty-five years, getting increasingly decrepit and becoming a kind of running gag: *Blossom Time* (1921).

This piece has a confusing history. It began in 1916 as *Das Dreimäderlhaus* (The Home of the Three Girls), the text by A. M. Willner and Heinz Reichert and the music drawn by Heinrich Berté, with nearly note-perfect fidelity, from Franz Schubert's vocal and dance music. The story concerns Schubert, in fact, for one of the three girls—sisters Hannerl, Haiderl, and Hederl Tschöll—is his secret love. Asking a handsome friend to "speak" for him (actually to sing "Ungeduld," from the song cycle *Die Schöne Müllerin,* as a courtship offering), Schubert unwittingly throws the two together romantically and must renounce love to live for music.

The show was a sensation, but the War kept it from travelling far at first. (A German troupe toured it through the United States in the original, after hostilities had ceased, playing small, out-of-the-way theatres for the then still-sizable German-speaking community.) Finally, France received it rapturously as *Chanson d'Amour* (Song of Love), wherein the three girls are Annette, Jeannette, and Nanette; and Italy knew it as *La Casa delle Tre Ragazze,* a literal translation of the title. Indeed, all Continental versions were virtually translations of Willner and Reichert with Berté's arrangements more or less intact. Even the rewritten English version, *Lilac Time* (1922), does not stray far from Berté.

Meanwhile, Mr. J. J. Shubert caught *Das Dreimäderlhaus* on his annual European scouting trip, bought the American rights, commissioned a translation of the original* for his American adaptors, Dorothy Donnelly and Sigmund Romberg, and gave them a free hand. Here is where *Das Dreimäderlhaus*'s fortunes take a sharp turn. While respecting the original story,† Donnelly larded the script with Broadway "fun," especially in her treatment of the girls' father, Herr Kranz, the comic part.

---

* This was standard procedure for American adaptations of European musicals, but the English-language *Dreimäderlhaus* script is one of the few to survive, in the Shubert Archives. The translator took his work literally, allowing the song lyrics to follow German sentence structure so that some of them sing as pure dada.

† *Blossom Time* enthusiasts will need to know what names the girls take this time around: Mitzi, Kitzi, and Fritzi Kranz. "Eyes that dance," they explain in their introductory trio, to the G Major *Andantino* from *Rosamunde,* "feet that prance."

Chasing after his daughters, who have gone to the Prater to flirt, he pauses at a tavern:

> KRANZ: Are there three young girls in this hostelry?
> KUPPELWEISER: Oh, you wicked old man!

Then, upon finding the girls:

> MITZI: Why, papa, is that you?
> KRANZ: It has been for years.

Kranz is the kind of role that *has* to have a drunk scene:

> KRANZ: *(to his wife)* Mother, I could think of a thousand reasons
>   why I shouldn't drink, and I can't think of one of them!
> FRAU KRANZ: Well, you've already had enough.
> KRANZ: I didn't think you *could* have enough.

To top it off, *Blossom Time* is the show that introduced—or, at least, popularized—a line that served as a staple of every really terrible musical for a generation: "Marriage is a wonderful institution. But who wants to live in an institution?"

For his part, Romberg recomposed much of the score, not only fiddling with Schubert but adding in plenty of Romberg. Mr. J. J. didn't mind; he liked to get his money's worth. Besides, in readying Walter Kollo's *Wie Einst im Mai* (As Once in May, 1913) for Broadway, Romberg threw out the *entire* score, wrote his own music to Rida Johnson Young's lyrics, and gave Mr. J. J. one of his biggest hits, *Maytime* (1917). Still, some of Romberg's Schubertiade gives pause. Simple tact led Berté to omit Schubert's "Ave Maria" as too spiritual a piece for a musical; Romberg included it. He also turned a wonderful tune in $\frac{3}{4}$ into a snappy gavotte in $\frac{4}{4}$ and trivialized the famous G Major theme of the Unfinished Symphony—which Berté had discreetly quoted, and only in the orchestra—into a waltz ditty, not only sung but swung:

> You are my song of love,
> Melody immortal.
> Echo of paradise,
> Heard through heaven's portal.

All this made *Blossom Time* a joke among intellectuals. Even the name of the original Broadway Schubert, Bertram Peacock, invited giggles. "Oh dear," says Mitzi when she meets him, "he doesn't look very romantic, does he?" One critic thought he looked like Harold Lloyd. But critics heaped scorn upon the Kranz. Because operetta's joke roles gave no scope to a star comic, they tended to go to second-raters. Ralph Herz, the original Kranz, died during the tryout and was replaced by William Danforth, but it seems not to have mattered who played the role—they all pushed too hard trying to wring laughs out of Donnelly's soggy lines. "He grimaces and hisses and gurgles and lucubrates and perspires," complained Arthur Pollock of Danforth, in the *Brooklyn Eagle*. "Let loose to do his worst," was Alan Dale's report.

They loved Danforth on the road, however, and that's where *Blossom Time* really lived. A second company in Chicago outgrossed New York, and three other touring outfits took the show across the nation, one of them breaking Philadelphia's long-run record for a musical, thirty-four weeks. As the years went on, Mr. J. J. took to mounting cheesy revivals, running them for a week in town, then advertising the tour as "Direct from Broadway!" One such production proclaimed, in the ads, "Symphony Orchestra of Twenty." That big, eh?

However. On the last of these revivals, in 1943, George Jean Nathan wrote, "The music still stubbornly dreams itself into a theatre, and the romantic audience mind suspends realistic judgment, and the angels are again in heaven." Because the simple truth of it is that, for all Romberg's tinkering, most of *Blossom Time* is pure Schubert. What show ever had a better composer? "At last a musical comedy is musical," Arthur Pollock had declared back in 1921, despite his distaste for Danforth. That has always been the secret of *Das Dreimäderlhaus*, in all its forms: the music. It's an elusive secret, for Mr. J. J. several times sought to retrieve *Blossom Time*'s success with shows on the life and work of a great composer—*The Love Song* (1925), out of Offenbach, *White Lilacs* (1928), out of Chopin. Neither worked.

One might have expected a deluge of operettas after *Blossom Time*, but the form's advance remained cautious. Oscar Hammerstein II admitted that *Wildflower* (1923) was "a timid attempt to bring back operetta, but still keeping enough of Cinderella and her dancing chorus [i.e., the feel of contemporary musical comedy] to compromise with the public." Hammerstein, grandson of the cigar magnate and vaudeville and opera impresario Oscar I, had launched his career as lyricist and librettist at the start of the decade, working in musical comedy, mainly with co-wordsmith Otto Harbach and composer Herbert Stothart and for producer Arthur Hammerstein, Oscar's uncle. Now this team was proposing to blend musical comedy sass with the musicality of operetta in a piece about an Italian termagant who, in another of those legacy-with-a-catch plots, must keep her temper for six months in order to inherit.

Arthur wanted to complete this circle of old comrades by bringing in composer Rudolf Friml to work with Stothart; Friml had composed Arthur's first show, the extraordinarily successful *The Firefly* (1912), and the two had·gone on to six more titles together. But Friml saw no reason to collaborate with another composer, and Arthur turned to Vincent Youmans, little more than a fledgling with one minor success, *Two Little Girls in Blue* (1921), cocomposed with Paul Lannin. Youmans was so unestablished that his last job had been as rehearsal pianist for Victor Herbert's *Orange Blossoms*.

From our modern viewpoint in the age when each musical has at most one book writer, one composer, and one lyricist,* we should halt for a moment and consider the highly collaborative nature of authorship in the twenties musical. One reason was the constant use of interpolated songs to juice up a tired score, even during the run or the tour. A foreign show needs jazzing up, Jolson's hollering for a novelty, Marie Cahill doesn't like her entrance number: so call in some outsiders for contributions. In such an atmosphere, there could be no concept of integrity of composition. Then, too, the shows' loose structure allowed composers to reuse tunes rescued from flops or discarded before the premiere— *Sally* billed Clifford Grey as its lyricist, but there were actually four lyricists, mostly because of songs slipped in from other shows. Furthermore, producers felt that bringing together specialists of different kinds would strengthen the entertainment, as when Ziegfeld hired Victor Herbert solely for Sally's "Butterfly Ballet." It was buying prestige.

Well, it was buying Herbert Stothart, anyway. Always ready to take the supplementary position in these composer duos, Stothart went from Youmans-Stothart to Friml-Stothart, Gershwin-Stothart, Kálmán-Stothart, thence to Hollywood and his most distinguished collaboration, Tchaikofsky-Stothart, in the opera pastiche *Tsaritsa,* culled from the Fifth Symphony, in the Jeanette MacDonald–Nelson Eddy *Maytime.* Otto Harbach, too, was a resolute team player. In his early years on Broadway, in the 1910s, when he was billed under his family name of Hauerbach, he often worked alone. But writing with Hammerstein—at once his protégé and his animator—so engaged Harbach that, from the very start of the 1920s almost to the end of his career, he seldom wrote either book or lyrics by himself.

Wildflower, which rehearsed as *Whisperin' Blossoms* and tried out as

* The scarce exceptions only prove the rule, such as Betty Comden and Adolph Green, who got their start more than fifty years ago with *On the Town.* At that time, book-writing duos were common. Herbert and Dorothy Fields and Howard Lindsay and Russel Crouse were active, Guy Bolton was *still* working with Fred Thompson, and George Abbott was a perennial collaborator when he wrote as well as directed.

The Wild Flower, came in to generally enthusiastic reviews and wide-spread popularity. It looked even better in comparison with the competition that season—the redundant *Sally, Irene and Mary;* the uninspired *Orange Blossoms* and *Little Nellie Kelly;* the tawdry *Gingham Girl;* the drab Nora Bayes vehicle *Queen O'Hearts* (1922), about a marriage broker, and of which Oscar Hammerstein was a coauthor; the one-joke *Up She Goes* (1922), about a gigantic family comically impeding the building of a couple's honeymoon cottage, with a score by *Irene's* Harry Tierney and Joseph McCarthy, fresh out of tunes; and *Helen of Troy, New York* (1923), yet another Cinderella show, with a smart book by George S. Kaufman and Marc Connelly but an insipid score by Bert Kalmar and Harry Ruby.

Not that *Wildflower* was faultless. Like so many other shows of the time, it dragged in exotic dancers whenever the action flagged—here Marion and Martinez Randall, there Cortez and Peggy. Its characters were poured from the mold, from the tempestuous heroine and her amiable boyfriend to the scheming lawyer and the man-chasing older woman. Set in Lombardy, *Wildflower* made much of local color, especially in Charles LeMaire's costumes; like Ziegfeld and Dillingham, Arthur Hammerstein believed that producers had to spend money to make money. So there was a feast for the eyes—but very little plot. In Act One, we meet the principals and learn the terms of the will. In Act Two . . . well, nothing happens in Act Two till the last minute, when heroine and boy friend quarrel and a mean cousin tries and fails to get the heroine to lose her temper. In Act Three, the quarrel is resolved.

Nor was the comedy anything for the anthologies. Where Bolton and Wodehouse preferred humor born of character and where the younger book writers such as Herbert Fields depended on a sardonic Prohibition-era sarcasm, Hammerstein and Harbach loved corn, hoke, the good old stuff. This is especially true of the older woman and her vis-à-vis, a peasant called Gabby.* Lucrezia is avid, Gabby unimpressed:

> LUCREZIA: I know I'm only an average sort of girl.
> GABBY: Who promoted you?

Two acts later, she's still working on him:

> LUCREZIA: Can't you be tempted?
> GABBY: I can be tempted. But it takes an expert.

---

* This is short for "Gabrielle," though that's still not an Italian name. Nor is the woman's: Lucrezia La Roche. Where are we, Bordeaux? The London production corrected her surname to "Larotta."

Still, by the day's standards, Hammerstein and Harbach had done their job, providing a frame for the music, the dance, and the performing talent. This last came down to the heroine, Edith Day, making her entrance on a donkey cart, adorably losing her temper in a come-and-go Italian accent, and utterly dominating the score, as in the second-act finale, when the quarrel with her boy friend and the end of her six months of forced good behavior coincided and Day sang a repeated "I hate him!" on ever higher notes, finally reaching a B.

It was the score, mainly, that made *Wildflower*. Though none of its tunes has survived as a standard, it did produce a few seasonal hits, especially "Bambalina," cued in when Day plans her birthday celebration, with all the suppressed excitement and idiotic statements one expects before a Big Number:

> NINA: After the party, can we have a dance?
> LUIGI: I've sent for some music. We'll have grand dancing.
> NINA: We'll dance the Bambalina.
> ALL: The Bambalina!

The orchestra strikes up, the boys and girls spread out grinning, and Day takes stage to sing—no, not a New Dance Sensation, but a salute to Bambalina himself, "a fiddler man by trade, both beloved by man and maid," who has the odd habit of cutting off his playing right in the middle of the dance. (Memo to choreographer: arrange for comical misadventures when orchestra suddenly goes silent during dance section.)

Interestingly, though it was Arthur Hammerstein's belief that Herbert Stothart was useful in bolstering the work of the ballad masters with those all-important comic numbers, *Wildflower*'s score is truly half-and-half, with Youmans useful in some of the silliness and Stothart supplying two of the love songs, "April Blossoms" and the hero's heartbroken "Good Bye Little Rosebud." Indeed, *Wildflower*'s operetta and musical comedy strains were so nicely blended that no critic noticed that this was virtually a genre masquerade. "A real musical comedy," said the *World*. "One of those 'here-come-the-girls-and-boys-now' operettas," remarked the *Daily News*.

Wildflower is an operetta. The score tells us so: in the *spiccato* violin solo that nuances the "April Blossoms" dance; in the mean cousin's role, a very high soprano; in the many *tenuti, Luftpausen,* and other musical niceties that stud the score; even in the heroine's leitmotif, a supple triplet phrase introduced in the verse to the title song, carried over in a choral antiphon against the main strain, then heard in snatches throughout the show. One way of understanding operetta is to see it as musical comedy guided by a powerful musical intelligence.

That definition surely identifies a pair of out-and-out operettas that arrived about two years after *Wildflower,* two of the most enduring works of the decade, *Rose-Marie* (1924) and *The Student Prince in Heidelberg* (1924). These are prime exhibits in the study of operetta: produced by parish honchos Arthur Hammerstein and Mr. J. J. Shubert, respectively; bringing in the very summoning names of twenties operetta, Rudolf Friml and Sigmund Romberg; invoking operetta's fondness for picturesque locales and gallant attitudes; and stuffing the theatre with music. *Rose-Marie! The Student Prince!* The twenties musical was many, many things, from the Astaires to the Fairbanks Twins, from "I'm Just Wild About Harry" to "Diga Diga Do," from the *Follies* to the intimate revue. But what we most recall of this age is the flowering of operetta, for it occurred in the early 1920s, disclosed a trove of wonderful scores that ring yet today, and was over by 1930. If anything was by, of, and entirely for this era, it was operetta.

First, *Rose-Marie,* "a romance of the Canadian Rockies." Arthur Hammerstein, so legend tells, had heard about a Canadian winter carnival and sent nephew Oscar north to investigate, for the carnival was to feature a melting ice palace that Arthur wanted to build his show on. However, this can't be; twenties stage technology couldn't have managed it, and Arthur knew it. But Oscar did indeed trek to Canada, and he returned with an idea for a show involving a lot of French-Canadian savor—Mounties, Indians, Québeçois, and, at the center, a "half-breed"* beauty whose Anglo lover is falsely accused of murder.

Oscar and Otto Harbach would do the book and lyrics, and Arthur had the perfect team for the music—Friml and Stothart. Why the producer felt that Friml couldn't pull it off by himself is a puzzle, especially as, in the end, all the *Rose-Marie* hits are Friml's and all the duds are Stothart's. Besides Friml was as capable in musical comedy as in the grander reaches of operetta. *The Blue Kitten* (1922), from a French farce, shows Friml at his most versatile, fox trotting in "Cutie (whose beauty are you?)" and "I've Found a Bud Among the Roses," devilish in

---

* Rose-Marie la Flamme is part-French, part-Indian. Much as I deplore judgmental adjectives that pretend to be merely descriptive, such as "half-breed," we must consider the extremely racist nature of twenties theatre in order to appreciate how quickly a sensitive racial awareness developed in this same decade. More about this later.

the comic waltz "A Twelve O'Clock Girl in a Nine O'Clock Town," trendily sarcastic in "Blue Kitten Blues," then mounting to the broad line in "When I Waltz With You." And Arthur produced it, so he should know.

But Arthur was adamant about Stothart, and Friml hadn't had a hit in years. He gave in and came up with "Indian Love Call," the title song, the hefty male chorus "The Mounties," the rhythm spectacle "Totem Tom-Tom," danced by forty-five girls dressed as totem poles, Rose-Marie's two character songs "Lak Jeem" (about her light of love, Jim Kenyon) and "Pretty Things," and Friml's own favorite, "The Door of My Dreams," a big eleven-o'clock waltz number that never caught on. Many reprises—a feature more of operetta than of musical comedy—virtually indoctrinated the public in *Rose-Marie*'s score, and Arthur even found two romantic leads who actually became stars in this very show, Mary Ellis and Dennis King.

Ellis stood in the line of Edith Day and Jeanette MacDonald: plangent, fiery, a little bizarre. But King was something new in operetta, a real man. English, trained in Shakespeare, an active here from 1921 on, King controlled a matinee idol's looks and a powerful baritone. Yet he had an elegant side. He was virile, but he was poetry, just what operetta needed. The rest of the principals were no more than types—the stolid Mountie, various villains. As usual in operetta, the humor was segregated, entirely in the hands of the "Dutch" (i.e., Jewish dialect) comic, Hard-Boiled Herman, and Lady Jane, a haughty dame who lives to push Herman around.

Still, the authors told a good story, with the elements of song, dance, comedy, and dramatic tension all in balance. In fact, they were so impressed with their own work that they refused to cite the full table of musical numbers in the program "as separate episodes" (so they said) because they are "such an integral part of the action."

This is fraud. *Rose-Marie* pulled off some interesting musical coups—in the opening barroom scene, a jumble of vocal bits and dance pieces designed to reflect the feeling of a rough crowd on a boozy spree; and in the murder scene, performed entirely in mime as the orchestra commented, silent-movie style. There were leitmotifs, too, for the Mounties and the love plot, for instance. And, all right, Hard-Boiled Herman's entrance number comes to an abrupt discordant stop rather than to the usual tonic close. Still, *Rose-Marie*'s score was no more "integral" than that of many an operetta, even many a musical comedy.

Of course, *Rose-Marie* did have a full-scale mixture of song and dialogue, tautly bent to narrative ends, in the finale of Act One: but then, every musical did. This was the so-called "finaletto," the "little finale" that is actually the big one, for a musical's *real* finale, at the evening's end, was a quick reprise of a hit tune or two by the full cast, over and out. (*Rose-Marie* ended more daringly, with just the two lovers and a last go-through of "Indian Love Call.")

But the *first*-act finale (and sometimes also the second, in a three-act layout, or even simply the close of a major scene) actually pursued the story in a combination of speech and song, in a tradition running back through Gilbert and Sullivan and Offenbach to the comic opera of Rossini's day and even considerably earlier. Think of *The Mikado*'s first-act finale, which considers the complications attendant upon Nanki-Poo's marriage to Yum-Yum, celebrates with a chorus of joy, gives Poo-Bah a solo with an elaborate cadenza, drums up the vindictive Katisha to threaten the marriage, and even finds room for an arietta for her while keeping vital the confrontation between her and everyone else, all this to a continually shifting texture of recitative, solos, and ensembles.

By the early 1900s, the American musical had developed the finaletto into a commercial as well as a delineative feature: along with one new melody, usually for the chorus, to launch the scene, we get a number of tune-plugging reprises, often with new lyrics to suit the action, all this interspersed with underscored dialogue. The finaletto became so generic that even shows of the most rudimentary musicality would sport them, though ambitious composers and lyricists liked to play around with the form. For example, *Sally*'s first-act finale is tightly controlled, to strike one important note, that of Sally's anticipation of her Cinderella ball. Kern quotes "On with the Dance" (with new lyrics) and "You Can't Keep a Good Girl Down," closing with the last third of "Look for the Silver Lining," and, just as the curtain falls, giving a fanfare to a brace of toy trumpets. But *Sally*'s second-act finale, happening upon Sally's quarrel with the hero, is a far more expansive and dramatic affair, punctuated by Marilyn Miller's dance breaks, now defiant, now desperate, and using a great deal of heated dialogue between the sung lines.

To pick another example, *Lady, Be Good!*'s first-act finale is more typical of the era, the model of a fast-moving, efficient curtain scene. The chorus starts it off with a merry new tune. A bit of plot development, and the tune is heard again, now—as I mentioned before—in dramatic counterpoint to a solo from the heroine. More dialogue, a snatch of "Oh, Lady Be Good," *more* dialogue of dire import to the plot, Fred and Adele Astaire get to bickering, and, to his cry of "Why is it, every time we are having a good fight, somebody has to *play that tune?*," the stage erupts in a full-out choral reprise of "Fascinating Rhythm." Thus, the

story has rolled along to a suspenseful cliffhanger, all necessary principals have been worked into the scene, a few of the best melodies heard
so far have been heard again, and, most important, the audience is left
with a goodly taste of Gershwin jazz.

Perhaps it was the more intricate finalettos in *Rose-Marie* that led its
authors to disdain listing song titles in the program. Songs were what
Al Jolson sang; *Rose-Marie* was opera, at least during its finales. Or not
opera—music theatre, for these scenes glide so fluently from song to
speech and back that they create their own genre. It is as if both the
word men and the musicians have become impatient with the musical's
relentless alternation of dialogue scenes with song-and-dance scenes.
They want to wring music out of the spoken lines, bend the music into
drama.

In *Rose-Marie*'s first-act finale, characters sing barely a line before
they are pleading or shouting; tense spoken exchanges suddenly take
wing in song. It's dizzying, thrilling. The Mounties are hunting for Rose-
Marie's boy friend, Jim, and her evil brother will tell them where Jim is
hiding if Rose-Marie doesn't agree to a hateful arranged marriage. The
music begins when Jim gives Rose-Marie a ring (underscoring: title song
and "Lak Jeem"). Jim leaves as the brother and the rival suitor bring her
to earth. Instantly, we are plunged into a Quarrel Trio—no, here's the
dialogue again, to further underscoring of themes both new and old.
Rose-Marie dips into a reprise—no, she is cut off by a commotion off
stage. (Underscoring: "The Mounties," *fortissimo*.) "They've got their
man!" the chorus carols, to Rose-Marie's horror. Employing an old stage
trick, the Mounties drag in the culprit all the way upstage, obscured by
the crowd. Not till the last minute do they reveal him—it's the *comic*,
Hard-Boiled Herman, who has a dialogue with the head Mountie, spoken in rhythm to Herman's entrance number.

"Now to get down to business," says the head Mountie. Herman
isn't the murderer—Jim is. Who knows his whereabouts? The head
Mountie sings this part of the scene; everyone else speaks it. Rose-
Marie's brother starts to give Jim away—and Rose-Marie at last must
agree to the marriage to save her Jim. Tosca, upon surrendering to
Scarpia to save Cavaradossi, sings "Vissi d'Arte"; Rose-Marie, in the
same position, goes into a reprise of "Indian Love Call," the only sustained piece of singing in the whole finale. But this is a reprise with a
twist. Rose-Marie presents it as a betrothal hymn to her hated suitor,
but Jim will hear it, according to their private code, as a signal to cross
the border into America and safety. With the chorus joining in, the en-

semble builds to a climax as Rose-Marie rises to two high B Flats, a B, and a top C. Friml (or is it Stothart?) bangs out the altered chords he associates with Indian music, and the curtain falls.

The finale scene underwent an important historical change during the 1920s. Even as operettas invested it with ever more strength of purpose, musical comedy found it too quaint for a jazz age and began to trim it to a few lines of dialogue and a restatement of one (or even part of one) song.

However, musicals of both kinds found the finaletto's mixture of dialogue and song useful in the new "musical scene," such as we observed in Kern's *Good Morning, Dearie*. This scene would come to full maturity with Rodgers and Hammerstein in the 1940s, in such numbers as "The Surrey with the Fringe on Top" and "If I Loved You." But *The Student Prince,* which arrived on Broadway exactly three months after *Rose-Marie,* seems to be the first show that truly exploited the musical scene.

In fact, *The Student Prince* is virtually made of musical scenes, all the more surprising in that neither its composer, Sigmund Romberg, nor its librettist, Dorothy Donnelly, was particularly enterprising in tackling this age-old question of how to balance the words with the music. Romberg took so little interest in the textual side of the musical that he once blew a bridge hand when Kern, trying to signal him to bid one heart, whistled "One Alone" (from Romberg's *The Desert Song*), yet couldn't get through to him. Later, Kern asked Romberg why he hadn't picked up on the tune. Of course he had, Romberg replied. "One of my best."

"But why didn't you bid *one heart?*" Kern persisted. "*One* Alone?"

"Who knows from lyrics?" said Romberg.

Nevertheless, he and Donnelly created one of the most intense relationships between the words and music to be found in *any* twenties musical, and that in one of the most risible stories of the decade: Prince Karl Franz attends Heidelberg University, falls in love with waitress Kathie, abandons university life to inherit the throne, then returns nostalgically only to renounce Kathie as unsuitable for court life. Worse yet, *The Student Prince* develops all of operetta's conventional drawbacks into outright disasters. The usual comic figure, Lutz, the prince's valet, is a pretentious clod who calls the roistering students "Zulus," which is supposed to heave us into the aisles, roaring with laughter, holding our stomachs and begging for mercy. (There's also a comic duchess in the inevitable ball scene, who gets helplessly wedged into chairs.) In the opening is a quartet of footmen who start solemnly, then rush around in a tizzy, detailing court gossip as if they were Walter Winchell's henchmen. The love plot gets into "Deep In My Heart, Dear (I have a dream of you)" literally minutes after Karl Franz and Kathie have met.

Still, all this is nothing next to the sweep of Romberg's melody. Besides indicating numerous instrumental nuances and fighting Mr. J. J. on the number of male choristers in the student numbers—"Forty, or I pull my score!"—Romberg gave splendid opportunities to the singers. These are *big* tunes with a *wide* range. Kathie has nineteen high A's, four B flats, two B's, and sixteen C's. The Prince has six A's, four B flats, and two C's. Second tenor Detlef (a student) has eleven A's and one B but countless G's and A flats. This is not to mention the encores, freely granted, that were prevalent in the days before cast album recordings, when audiences could hear theatre music as it was meant to be heard only in a theatre. Critics had begun to complain about encores as showstoppers in the worse sense. Enough was enough, especially given the reprises that *The Student Prince* in particular is stuffed with. The end of Act Three, when the Prince, back at court, hears the siren song of Heidelberg, is very like the "New York sequence" in *Brigadoon,* twenty-three years later, when, again, the hero suffers visions (read "rehearings of all the hit tunes") of the magical land he left behind. *Brigadoon's* Tommy Albright says, "I want to go back to Scotland!" The student prince cries, "I'll go back to Heidelberg!"

The show was drawn from Rudolf Bleichman's play *Old Heidelberg,* which was *The Student Prince's* tryout title. Bleichman built his text on a German original by Wilhelm Meyer-Foerster, which Richard Mansfield first played in 1903 at the age of forty-nine. Yet the whole thing is about youth, about enjoying life and love when one is in one's fresh prime. Romberg's prince and waitress throw off spectacular high-flying phrases the way kids do yo-yo tricks. "Youth is king of Spring" is one line; there are plenty of others such. Yet the score dances past one several times before one grasps the dippy story's sorrowful interior: happiness is for the young only. Age brings on responsibility, regret. Old people turn into Doctor Engel, the bass role of Karl Franz's tutor and, throughout, a partisan of but never a partner in the lovely innocence of college, its carefree independence. True, he's included among the roistering crew in the "Student Life" number, but it is frankly embarrassing to see this old codger alcoholically gamboling with the youngsters. But what notice did anyone take of this pathetic figure in the first place? *The Student Prince* was all Karl Franz and Kathie and caroling undergrads, and it struck a chord of such resonance that it ran almost eighteen months, the record among musicals of the 1920s.*

Note that, where *Rose-Marie* claimed to be unprecedentedly integrated, *The Student Prince* actually *was*, breaking into song not only to make love and spread joy but to conduct plot business. The show was virtually made of finalettos, with a bit of script slipped in here and there. Interestingly, when the two shows went to London (*Rose-Marie* in 1925 and *The Student Prince* in 1926), *Rose-Marie* filled Drury Lane for more than two years to become the longest-running West End musical of the decade, while *The Student Prince* flopped. The critics savaged it, possibly because of a postwar resistance to stories about love and fun in Germany, possibly also because of a xenophobic resentment of the production, a replica of Broadway's, with the same director, designers, conductor, and Kathie, Ilse Marvenga, not to mention several minor players. (An English tour, however, did excellent business, and the show quickly became a classic there as here.)

Operetta, by 1919 musical comedy's poor relation, has become by 1924 its rich uncle. These shows can be a season's biggest hit, sell tons of sheet music, and go to Europe. They don't even have to be ambitious about the storytelling, like *Rose-Marie*, or ambitious about the musical construction, like *The Student Prince*. They can be *The Vagabond King* (1925).

This must be the least attractive of the decade's famous operettas, the one that not only is never revived but that no one wants to see revived. *The Vagabond King* is the ultimate operetta—most replete with archaic diction, most elaborately historical in setting (Paris under Louis XI), opening in a tavern and closing on the gibbet where the hero will get a last-minute pardon, introducing its heroine in a dream vision, and counting its dramatis personae as one-third whores and thieves, one-third scurvy law officers, one-third wily courtiers, and François Villon. It sounds like a spoof.

Russell Janney, the show's producer and colibrettist (with Brian Hooker and W. H. Post; Hooker wrote the lyrics) apparently had a thing about

* This is as good a place as any for the top-ten long-run totals of twenties musicals: *The Student Prince*, 608; *Blossom Time*, 592; *Show Boat*, 575; *Sally*, 570; *Rose-Marie*, 557; *Good News!*, 551; *Blackbirds of 1928*, 518; *Sunny*, 517; *The Vagabond King*, 511; *The New Moon*, 509. Remember, though, that *Irene*, which opened in late 1919, spent most of its run in the 1920s and, at 670 performances, would dominate the lineup. Who wants to know Number Eleven on the list? *Shuffle Along*, at 504 performances.

Justin Huntley McCarthy's play *If I Were King* ever since seeing an amateur production produced by the Benjamin School for Girls drama club
in 1923, with a score by Rodgers and Hart and starring Dorothy Fields
as Villon. Janney's Villon was Dennis King, looking like death raw as the
bandit poet and like an order of ice-cream cake to go in his transformation as the "king for a day" and putting over the rousing "Song of the
Vagabonds" with immense conviction. In King's Villon we find perhaps
the closest the musical ever got to what the young idealistic John Barrymore could do in drama, and surely it was King and Rudolf Friml's
vapidly tuneful score that made *The Vagabond King* a hit. To be fair, it
was a hit in London, too, with a far from electrifying Villon, the one-
time Savoyard tenor Derek Oldham (who had played the Dennis King
role in London's *Rose-Marie*). Nevertheless, despite its success, *The
Vagabond King*'s over-the-top attitude seemed to set a limit to how far
operetta could go—just about up to 1930, when the form imploded on
its own extravagance. The 1920s is famous for its cluster of operetta
classics, but this is, after all, the Jazz Age.

Hooray for Captain Spalding

THE STAR COMIC

The American musical has undergone four ages of development. The First, taking it from obscure origins to the end of the nineteenth century, is the primitive age. The Second Age, a flowering under distinctly European influences, comprised the first two decades of the twentieth century. The golden age lasts from 1920 to 1970, and the present, Fourth Age, that of the dark musical play, when joyous musical comedies seem like throwbacks and when the tourist-attraction pop operas from England threaten to monopolize Broadway real estate with endless runs, is still under way.

Various generic elements have been more significant in some ages than in other ages. For instance, the girls of the "beauty chorus," often seminude and more pretty than talented, essential in the first two ages and in much of the golden age, have almost entirely vanished. The value of a strong score was incidental in the first age but has been basic ever since. Spectacle and beauty of design have been appreciated in all four ages but have not been central to any one of them. The director-choreographer, or closely bonded director-and-choreographer team, of absolute importance in the last fifty years, was utterly unknown before.

In fact, when we consider the components of the twenties show, whether musical comedy, operetta, or revue, we find only one that was

53

absolutely crucial right from the dawn of the First Age: the star comic. By this, I mean not any actor who plays a lead comic part but a comic actor so renowned for his individual style that he becomes the reason the public attends a given show.

The star comic was the musical's first headliner, in a time when there was no equivalent for a Marilyn Miller* or even a Dennis King, when dance was rudimentary or built of stock items from the ballet trunk, when scores were routinely cobbled out of everything from Von Suppé to folk tunes.

Who *were* the musical's first stars? From 1850 to 1890, a span of two generations, they were George L. Fox, Edward Harrigan and Tony Hart, Henry E. Dixey, Francis Wilson, Lillian Russell, De Wolf Hopper, and Fay Templeton: but for the two women, all comics. In the Second Age, that of Victor Herbert and George M. Cohan, the composer comes into prominence, but so does the producer, as Ziegfeld, Dillingham, and Arthur Hammerstein begin their ascent. Late in the age, Wodehouse arrives, and the lyricist is discovered. But notice that, throughout the 1920s, the star comic retains his or her power: Ed Wynn, W. C. Fields, Willie and Eugene Howard, Eddie Cantor, Joe Cook, the Marx Brothers, Fanny Brice, Leon Errol, Will Rogers, Victor Moore, Ray Dooley, Bobby Clark, Bert Lahr, Jimmy Durante.

Some of them are vital today through their movies (Fields and the Marxes especially). Others are presences, such as Fanny Brice (not least in the Streisand version), or Names, like Durante and Rogers. Lahr, at least, lucked into the film that everyone raised in America sees sixteen or seventeen times, minimum, *The Wizard of Oz.* Some, like Dooley and Cook, are forgotten. Still, all of them helped define the primacy of this virtually prehistoric figure in an epoch when the musical was in furious development—a development that would, in the 1940s, begin to restrict the star comic's freedom and, in the 1960s, hunt him from the stage.

---

* This seems a questionable statement in the light of Lillian Russell's national fame, and those with a long historical perspective will think of Lydia Thompson. But much of Russell's appeal as the "Queen of Comic Opera" stemmed from her introduction to America of shows composed by Offenbach, Cellier, Audran, and Lecocq at a time when these were greatly superior to the home product. Nor was Russell an all-around talent like Miller; nor were shows conceived as Russell showcases, as they were for Miller. As for Thompson, her brief novelty vogue around 1870 (with sporadic appearances thereafter) is not comparable to Miller's star reign, from the *Ziegfeld Follies of 1919* to *As Thousands Cheer* in 1933—a reign, moreover, ended only by Miller's death.

There are no star comics in musicals today. When was the last such performance? Bert Lahr in *Foxy* (1964)?*

Let's start with Fred Stone, beyond debate the most old-fashioned of the comics active in the 1920s and thus a link to the progenitors of the type. Stone's genre of choice was extravaganza, derived from the English "pantomime" and, in essence, a very loosely integrated fairy tale designed as family fare, especially dependent on spectacular stage effects and the often improvised antics of the star comic. Other identifying features—the "principal boy" (a young woman in tights playing the hero), the animal (*Gypsy*'s dancing cow is an hommage), a prologue in which some fairyland figure officially initiates the proceedings, and the interpolation of songs that cover some current cultural craze or news item at any time during a show's run—came and went. The genre prospered in the first age but was moribund by 1900, when suddenly the unknown Fred Stone and his partner, Dave Montgomery, played the Scarecrow and Tin Woodman in *The Wizard of Oz* (1903), the only musical of its decade to outrun (in national tours) *The Merry Widow*. An imitation, *Babes in Toyland* (1903), was not as successful but had the advantage of a score composed by Victor Herbert (whereas that of *The Wizard* was a compendium of interpolations) and thus has outlived *The Wizard*.

In any case, Montgomery and Stone's universal popularity put some kick back into extravaganza. Though the team appeared in other kinds of musicals, most notably Victor Herbert's musical comedy *The Red Mill* (1906), by Montgomery's death in 1917 he and Stone had become the force that alone kept extravaganza not only alive but very blue-chip. Luckily, the passing of Montgomery, a pallid foil to the vigorous Stone, did not hurt Stone's career, and he continued to play extravaganza through the 1920s.

Is't possible? The plot of *The Stepping Stones* (1923) suggests something from 1886 or so, and this just a year before *Lady, Be Good!*: in the prologue, young Richard and Mary hear the tale of Little Red Rid-

---

* Some might think of Nathan Lane's Pseudolus in the 1996 revival of *A Funny Thing Happened on the Way to the Forum*. True, this is a star comic's part, conceived for Phil Silvers, the last of the genuine star comics. And, also true, when the show was produced in 1962, Zero Mostel played the role with all the gauche knickknacks of the freewheeling loony of old. But Lane is an actor, changing his approach from role to role as the script demands, and thus nothing like the star comic, who applies *his* set character to every part. But there's something about this part that brings out the improviser: midway through the run, Lane began to fool around a bit. The show needs it.

ing Hood and wonder what happened after. Radiola, the fairy of the radio, appears and introduces the requested sequel, performed by puppets. Stone makes his entrance, as Peter Plug, a plumber. It is his mission to win the Radio Purse and take it to Rougette Hood in the Sweet Shop run by her mother, Violet Hood. There is a villain, of course, one De Wolfe, and a swain for the heroine, Prince Silvio. The action moves from one picturesque set to another, and everything ends in joy, weddings, and typical extravaganza it's-only-a-play corn:

> DE WOLFE: Do you poor fools think you have cured me of me villainy?
> PETER: I should say not! Come around tomorrow night [or: afternoon] and we'll start all over again!

Charles Dillingham had been Stone's producer since *The Red Mill*, and he maintained a virtual Fred Stone stock company—Stone's performer wife, Allene Crater, villain Oscar Ragland, many supporting players, and even chorus members, all under the supervision of director-librettist R. H. Burnside. Thus, the company could play a long New York run (Stone's shows were invariably hits), tour for a year or two, take the summer off, then reunite for the next show. Anne Caldwell had been the house lyricist for more than a decade, but the composers varied; this time out it was Jerome Kern.

Extravaganza did not usually attract major composers, but Dillingham, remember, was a major producer. He gave Stone Victor Herbert on *The Lady of the Slipper* (1912), the now forgotten but then eminent Ivan Caryll for *Chin-Chin* (1914), *Jack O'Lantern* (1917), and *Tip-Top* (1920), and, on Caryll's death, turned to their most apparent successor, Kern. Clearly, the Stone shows were imposing productions, so Stone was not keeping extravaganza alive singlehandedly. But *The Stepping Stones* was extra-special. As the title implies, this one was a real family outing, marking the debut, as Rougette Hood, of Stone's seventeen-year-old daughter, Dorothy.

She was a darling, and when she and Stone duetted on "Wonderful Dad," "Dear Little Peter Pan" (in cunning Peter Pan outfits), and, especially, "Raggedy Ann" (as exact replicas of the Johnny Gruelle characters, his pants rising almost to the armpits and her apron almost covering her dress), their public went all gooey. Stone truly had a public, a separate one from theatregoers trying out the jazzy new urban musical comedy or the risqué revue. Many Stone fans had been taken to *The Wizard of Oz* as children for their first theatre trip and were now taking their kids to *The Stepping Stones,* which made the graduation of

Dorothy into the ranks all the more fitting. This is why this particular series of extravaganzas lasted—it addressed folks across the generation line.

Then, too, Stone was the goods. Not a great singer or comic, but wonderful company; and he *was* a great acrobat.* The circus was where he got his start, and Stone brought more than a taste of it to his roles, so his audience could always count on a trick entrance and at least one wild physical stunt in each show. In *The Red Mill*, Stone fell backwards down the length of an eighteen-foot ladder. "The Punch Bowl Glide," in *The Lady of the Slipper*, was a dance performed on hidden trampolines so that Stone appeared to bounce giddily off the floor and furniture. In *Chin-Chin*'s circus scene, as Madame Falloffski, Stone used a revolving derrick to perform stunts while riding a real horse.

Stone did not introduce any acrobatics into *The Stepping Stones*, in order to keep Dorothy at stage center. Otherwise, the piece observed the conventions of the Extravaganza According to Stone. There were the puns so beloved of the nineteenth century, as when Violet explains why she needs a new bus boy: "He thought he was a big gun, so I fired him." There was Stone as street-corner philosopher, when a fortune teller is mentioned: "I wonder if she could tell why a taxi clock [i.e., the meter] always jumps ten cents just as you get out." There were many such anachronisms—references to Prohibition, Charlie Chaplin, Calvin Coolidge (who had succeeded the late Warren G. Harding as President three months before *The Stepping Stones* opened). There were the self-contained sketches (Stone did a hypnotic mind-reading act) and the songs plopped in from nowhere (for instance, "Pie," Stone's absolutely unmotivated salute to the American national dessert, which rattles off the names of twenty-five kinds and ends with a college cheer; and the "Raggedy Ann" number, central to the piece because an authentic Gruelle depiction of it formed the show's poster, turns up on the lame excuse that the two children in the prologue had Raggedy dolls).

Nevertheless, the score as sheer music is a delight. Freed by the very looseness of extravaganza to write about anything at all, Kern and Caldwell created numbers unlike anything in other musicals. They also attended to the plot, as in Dorothy Stone's entrance scene, a dizzy choral fantasia that quiets down for her solo, "(Everybody calls me) Little Red Riding Hood." But the authors were happiest just summoning the fairy-

* The curious can catch Stone at the end of his career, in the 1935 RKO film *Alice Adams*, as Katharine Hepburn's despairing dreamer of a father. It's a brilliant performance, though it shows nothing of the cavorting daredevil of Stone's Broadway prime.

tale magic. "Wonderful Dad" has a timeless, cross-generational charm, yet its sound is very contemporary, with insistent syncopations and blue harmony, while "In Love With Love" has the lively verse and tactfully limpid chorus that might have graced a Princess show.

A hit even at an unusual $5.50 top (raised to $7.70 when the show reached sellout level), *The Stepping Stones* played 241 times in town and toured into 1926. Dillingham decided to hold the company together yet again for *Criss Cross* (1926), a thriller with an Arabian setting. Dillingham added Otto Harbach to the mix to assist Anne Caldwell on book and lyrics, but otherwise it was more Dorothy, more Kern, and good old Stone.

The show's prologue, set in Wonderland, was stuffed with allusions to earlier Stone shows back to *The Wizard of Oz*. Stone, unseen in voiceover, claimed to want *new* things tonight, as if making a slight kowtow to the general feeling along Broadway that the 1920s had launched the next Epoch in theatre history—in the rise of off-Broadway, the Theatre Guild, Eugene O'Neill, bold new approaches to previously taboo subject matter, advances in lighting and design, expressionism. Yes, Stone noted, Broadway was new all over. Why, "Next year, they're going to play *Abie's Irish Rose* in modern dress.* Then Dorothy turned up in Cinderella garb for an extravaganza convention, the "travel scene," riding her coach to the ball. But she dismissed her coachmen: "I'm a 1927 model—*I drive my own!*"

Criss Cross was, in all, the same show Stone had been playing for twenty-three years. He delighted in fancy costumes and, as aviator Criss Cross, found one reason after another (and sometimes no reason) to present himself as: an Italian music master complete with Don Basilio† hat, in Argentinian and Russian costumes for a travel number, in drag as a ballerina and again as an older woman in a chador, as a sheik, as a French officer. Stone donned eight outfits altogether—and Dorothy wore ten. As for the sets, there were four in Act One and eight in Act Two, a Stone record even in a genre famous for lavish visuals. He also revived an extravaganza tradition that even he had forgotten, the danc-

---

* (Informed theatre buffs please skip this footnote.) Anne Nichols's *Abie's Irish Rose,* a comedy about the romance of a Jewish boy and an Irish girl, opened in 1922 and was still playing when *Criss Cross* opened, some four years later, an unthinkable run for a play that the intelligentsia thought meretricious. Stone's joke turns on the notion that *Abie* was so old it could have been a costume drama. Compare this line with Robert Benchley, getting mischievous about *Abie* in *The New Yorker's* theatre listings: "An interesting revival of one of America's old favorites."

† In Rossini's opera *The Barber of Seville.*

ing animal, in this case two men as a camel named Susie. There were the usual social notes:

> CHRIS (*disguised as a Moslem woman, in falsetto*): You still wear the veil.
> COUNTESS (*Allene*): They say Oriental women are taking them off, to be like American girls.
> CHRIS (*his voice dropping about three octaves*): They'll have to take off more than a veil, dearie.

And there was the Stone acrobatic stunt: at the end of Act One, Stone, rescuing Dorothy from a hideous forced marriage, literally flew on in a tiny airplane, grabbed her, and shot off as the curtain fell and the audience went mad.

The *Criss Cross* score is dismayingly uninteresting—this was Kern one year before *Show Boat*? It didn't hurt the show, yet it must be said that the twenties public was increasingly music-conscious, if only because radio was making American pop music abundant in the home. The day when a musical could triumph on a comic personality and solid showshop techniques was ending. If the star comic was the essential element in the primitive American musical, a vital score would become the essential element of the mature American musical.

Another antique theatre trope was the "blackface" performer, a white turning himself into a stereotyped black presence and singing songs about life in Dixie. Blackface work derived from the minstrel show, an hour of jokes, songs, dances, and comic sketches; some of this lasted long enough to work its way into the first film musicals, and moderns take it in utterly bewildered. Why would anyone *do* that? It's offensive and fraudulent. Besides, we never learn what actually happens in Dixie other than the ceaseless production of picnics. What is the *content* of blackface?

The three most prominent blackface comics on Broadway in the early 1920s were, in progressive order of birth, Frank Tinney, Al Jolson, and Eddie Cantor. Tinney is not even a statistic today, partly because he made no commemorative talkies and also because his reputation was shattered in an adulterous scandal.* Like every star comic, Tinney had a trademark, a tendency to drift in and out of the action, improvising shtick and conversing with the conductor. Obviously, Tinney was a natural in revue, but he liked book shows, because there his unpredictable

---

* The married Tinney got involved in 1924 with a *Follies* showgirl, Imogene Wilson, who pressed charges against him for physical assault. The headlines destroyed his career and gave hers a boost.

behavior presented an enjoyable tension between what the audience expected (a story) and what it actually got (chaos). Oddly, Tinney's use of blackface was purely cosmetic, for once he made up he went about his business without reference to his complexion in either intonation or material. It was as if Tinney saw his shows as parties and himself as an uninvited guest, showing up in the wrong outfit and not knowing his host. Typically, in both his twenties titles, *Tickle Me* (1920) and *Daffy Dill* (1922), Tinney's character was billed in the programs as "Frank Tinney." He participated in plot scenes and musical numbers but, mainly, would redevise his material from night to night.

Al Jolson's reign on Broadway began the same year as Tinney's, in the same format, in 1911 in a Shubert Winter Garden variety evening, Jolson in *La Belle Paree* and Tinney later that year in *The Revue of Revues*. However, virtually from the first, Jolson's star shot far higher than Tinney's, or anyone else's. He was known less as a comic than as a singer, of course, but among his "cheer up" ditties and odes to southern life were countless comic novelties such as "Where Did Robinson Crusoe Go with Friday on Saturday Night?," "Now He's Got a Beautiful Girl (but he's worried to death all the time)," and "Tillie Titwillow," all from *Robinson Crusoe, Jr.* (1916). Moreover, Jolson's postwar shows, mostly staged at the Winter Garden—after *Crusoe* they were *Sinbad* (1918), *Bombo* (1921), and *Big Boy* (1925)—were structured like star-comic vehicles. They had to be, for there were no singing male stars in the musical then, except for the Irish-to-a-fault Chauncey Olcott, who was near retirement when Jolson debuted.

The Question of Jolson is something that every historian of the musical must face, for the man was the giant of his day.* He was a troll, his voice itself lacked beauty, his persona was that of the aggressive, know-nothing urban opportunist, his casting couch made Ziegfeld look like Squirrel Nutkin, he blackmailed songwriters into giving him co-author credit (and therefore royalties) for the privilege of having Jolson introduce their song, and his bedazzled media contacts perforce advertised him as "The World's Greatest Entertainer," the press release as mythopoeia.

---

* This was, roughly, 1911 to 1925 on Broadway; then Jolson played the lead in the breakthrough sound film, *The Jazz Singer* (1927), and became perhaps the biggest star in the Western world till his films began to fail in the early middle 1930s. He hung on in a bit of this and a bit of that, on radio, in film, even in a Broadway return, till he supplied his own voice (for actor Larry Parks) in the amazingly successful film *The Jolson Story* (1946), and Jolson was a king recrowned. He died in 1950.

But his shows were mints, and his recordings sold so well that Columbia could issue them with Jolson on one side and filler artists on the other, to double sales. And surely Hollywood's crashing of the sound barrier might have been compromised without that man in that role at that time. Clearly, Jolson had Something.

Let's sit in on one of his Winter Garden specials, *Big Boy*. The title refers to a horse, not to Jolson, who was playing his usual character, Gus, in blackface throughout the evening. Gus is a stableboy just promoted to jockey for the Kentucky Derby. (The climactic race will be shown us with the use of treadmills; the critics will declare it a hoot.) The company will be one of the most dreary ever assembled—as a rule, or Jolson will have them fired, as he once did hoofer (but later major producer) George White. "There's only one star in a Jolson show," he is reported to have said, many a time. "And that's Jolson!"

We should not concern ourselves with the score, because only the interpolations mattered. (*Big Boy* offered, among others, the pep-talk ballad "Keep Smiling at Trouble," the rhythm number "Miami," and the inevitable southern paean "Hello, 'Tucky.") In fact, Harold Atteridge's *Big Boy* script indicates how generically lumpen the nominal score in a Jolson show really was: as Atteridge reaches a song cue, he gives the vaguest of directions to the songwriters. For the Act One curtain-raiser he requests "'Down Old Kentucky Way' or some other title." A flashback to 1870 in which the principals play their own ancestors should begin, Atteridge says, with "'Old Plantation Days' or some other title." Yet another number is to be "along type of 'Jump, Jim Crow.'"*

At least *Big Boy*'s script does focus on the story at hand; Jolson's shows more typically wandered from one fantastical setting to another, like an Oz book. But the script is a bore, because all its subject is how wonderful Jolson is. There is the star entrance, with offstage horse noises, the stamping of hooves, and cries of "Whoa! Whoa!" till a grinning Jolson leads in Big Boy. There's the taking down of the pompous, such as an English jockey:

> LESLIE: Now, let me see . . . where was I? I picked up . . .
> GUS: Your niblick.
> LESLIE: I picked up my n—That's not right. What was I saying?
>   Right now, my mind's a blank.
> GUS: Ah, you're back to normalcy.

---

* The antique minstrel-show number in Romberg's *Maytime*, modeled on a song of the same title popularized in the early middle nineteenth century by the white blackface star T. D. Rice.

There's the comic monologue, a very Jolsonesque moment in that he has the entire stage to himself, except for Big Boy. Jolson rambles on in near-stream-of-consciousness fashion and tells of searching for employment:

> GUS: I walked into a little town called Pittsfield, the most un-
> healthy town you ever saw. It was so unhealthy that everyone
> in town owned their own personal hearse. I saw a sign in the
> window, it said, "Man wanted to work in the Eagle Laundry."
> I didn't take it. What do I know about washing an eagle?

There's the silliness, basic to virtually every comic of the day. The Englishman turns out to be a fake—he's from Mobile, Alabama, Gus's home town. In fact, the two suddenly realize that they were boyhood friends, throw their arms around each other, and sing the old school song, a salute to Heidelberg. (*The Student Prince* had opened a month before.) Ah, but *that* reminds Gus of his Alabamy youth, and he plunges into another interpolated special, one that could change by the week, at Jolson's whim. "California, Here I Come" was in *Big Boy* for a time, as was "If You Knew Susie (like I know Susie)," though for some reason Jolson quickly tired of it and passed it on to our third great blackface specialist, Eddie Cantor.

Cantor compares interestingly with Jolson. First, where Jolson's ever-present Gus was an underling in control of everybody, the tiny Cantor played a fragile yet intense man in terror of bullies, forever going into anxiety attacks, narcoleptic interludes, and assorted cringing and alibiing. Jolson is brash; Cantor is wary. When a critic chided Eddie Buzzell for playing the hero of *The Gingham Girl* "in a Winter Garden manner," we hear "He's as pushy as Jolson."

Cantor isn't pushy: Cantor is worried. Both he and Jolson joked almost obsessively about sex, but Jolson chased women and Cantor was chased by them, running all the way. Their approach to blackface, too, differed, for Cantor reserved it for a specialty number (typically an interpolation), prancing and clapping and wagging his head, blackface as a cultural doodad, whereas Jolson used the makeup without really using it, blackface as wallpaper.

In fact, there was no reason for either of these two (or Tinney, for that matter) to pretend to be Negroes. None of their shows needed an Afro-American character, and nothing in the music spoke to Afro-American culture. The minstrel show's popularity had waned in the late nineteenth century; by 1900 minstrelsy's very performing traditions had virtually died out. The blackface entertainers of the 1920s were not the last of the line: the line had already ended. But we notice that most of the prominent blackface artists of the decade were Jewish. Could they have revived the makeup to turn a sly trick on American racism?

The major difference between Jolson and Cantor lies in the quality of their shows. Jolson's producer, Mr. J. J. Shubert, was content to surround his star with the nobodies that Jolson preferred: less expensive. But Cantor worked for the Shuberts only when he was feuding with his *real* producer, Florenz Ziegfeld, and Ziegfeld liked to stuff his shows with talent: more profitable. You spend money to make money. Ziegfeld's musicals were chaotically conceived as a rule, but by the time they opened they were like Chinese boxes, intricately elaborate. The notion of Cantor dismissing the "help" in the middle of a performance to hog the stage and give the public what it *really* wanted—a Cantor songfest— is unthinkable. The notion of *any* Broadway star doing this is unthinkable. Wouldn't there be problems with Equity (after 1919, of course)? Wouldn't the orchestra need parts to play from? Wouldn't the audience rather hear how the story comes out?

Yet this is what legend (and even the best historians) tell us that Jolson did, especially during the run of *Big Boy*. If this is true, it had to be partly because Jolson's shows, as shows, were terrible and partly because he really was that good a singer. It's not that there was only one star in a Jolson show. It's that there was only one Jolson in the world.

Cantor's shows were better than Jolson's because you didn't need to be a Cantor fan to enjoy them. Sure, Cantor had the star entrance, the taking down of the pompous, the monologue, the silliness. The Jolson stuff. But Cantor's Ziegfeld hit *Kid Boots* (1923), "the musical comedy of Palm Beach and golf," also had Mary Eaton, Ziegfeld's intended successor to Marilyn Miller; and personable love interests for Cantor and Eaton; and Harland Dixon, one of the most popular of twenties supporting players (we last met him as gangster "Chesty" Costello in *Good Morning, Dearie*), playing a buttinsky gossip columnist; and the six-foot-three comedienne Jobyna Howland, brilliant in zany grande-dame parts; and George Olsen's band in the pit; and a host of the usual Ziegfeld kibitzers, specialty acts, and showgirls.

Jolson would have had them all fired; and what would he have thought of William Anthony McGuire and Otto Harbach's book, tailored to Cantor's style but letting *all* the characters in on the fun? Granted, Cantor, as a country-club caddie master, has the best lines, and he's as sharp as ever. Is someone unintelligent?

CANTOR: They had to burn down the schoolhouse to get him out
    of the second grade.

Or, after Howland's round of golf, Cantor asks her what her score was. "Seventy-one," she says. "Seventy-one," he echoes, to make sure the audience registered it. "Why, that's phenomenal." After a perfectly timed pause, he adds, "And the second hole?"

Then, of course, there are the set pieces, virtually as self-contained as revue sketches: Cantor giving a wacky golf lesson; Cantor enduring Dr. Howland's punishing physical exam; Cantor the impedient clerk in the club shop; Cantor doing riffs on that trendy concept of psychoanalysis.

Kid Boots's plot, following socialite Mary Eaton's romance with an apparently penniless golf champ, is conventional but far livelier than anything Jolson ever got (or wanted) from the Shuberts. Like so many twenties musicals, it builds up to a Big Something—a Big *Follies* Debut, a Big Race, a Big Game, or, as here, a Big Golf Tournament. The score, too, strikes usual attitudes. It was the work of Harry Tierney and Joseph McCarthy, who unfortunately had peaked in their first collaboration, *Irene*. (No problem: in went the interpolation, Harry Akst, Sam Lewis, and Joe Young's "Dinah," for Cantor's blackface sequence.)

A curiosity of the day was that star comic vehicles generally made do with dreary scores. The excitement crazing out of the orchestra pit of *Lady, Be Good!* or the rhapsody of *The Student Prince* was foreign to the structure of the comedy show. This was the reason comic singers like Jolson and Cantor were always sneaking in sure-thing interpolations—but these had nothing to do with their role or situation. The idea that a comic character might require comic songs written specifically for that character—such as "I Cain't Say No" or "Always True To You in My Fashion"—was yet to come.

Then, too, most of the star comics were not natural singers. W. C. Fields juggled and played zany pool in the *Follies*, where no one expected him to sing, but he became a star carefully edging his way around the songs as "Professor" Eustace McGargle in the smash hit *Poppy* (1923). Another Cinderella tale, this one had a circus background that gave full scope to Fields's side-show specialities—not only the juggling and pool but also the shell-game touting, snake-oil selling, card sharking, and all-around light-fingered conniving. It was in *Poppy*, apparently, that Fields introduced the pale, banded stovepipe hat, the checked trousers and the coat with gigantic buttons, the full and fluffy cravat, the matching set of white spats and gloves that were to define his eccentric and antique worldview, vivified in the flavorfully Victorian speech patterns he favored. Most of Fields's part (written not by Dorothy Donnelly, *Poppy*'s official librettist, but by Howard Dietz) comes off as a revival of commercial newpaper copy of the 1880s. Nothing is merely stated; everything is apotheosized. Evil is "the toils of Beelzebub," death "the man in the bright nightgown." Yet let one of his victims accuse him of cheating, and Fields is quick to understate. At length, he is called out for a forger, a seducer, a vile, inhuman reprobate, and he replies, "This is no time for idle twitting."

Poppy sounds like Fields's vehicle. On the contrary, it was a stroke of luck, for the show was written before Fields was hired. His name wasn't even above the title: Madge Kennedy's was, for she played the title role as Fields's foster daughter, who falls in love with a society boy and turns out to be an heiress herself. Yet the critics hailed Fields as the show's real content. "He carried everything away from everybody," wrote Alan Dale. Before *Poppy*'s New York run was over, Fields's name had made it to above-the-title billing on the theatre marquee.

Now comes an irony of history. D. W. Griffith wanted to film *Poppy*, as a showcase for his current inspiration, Carol Dempster—yet with Fields in his original role. This is a double irony, for the result, *Sally of the Sawdust* (1925), is of course a silent film: songs couldn't have mattered less to the story now. At the same time, we lose the very sound of Fields. Still, because so much of Griffith's work was preserved, we of today can see Fields at work in *Poppy*, more or less. (This is a third irony, for, except for his first one-reeler, *Pool Sharks* [1915], all of Fields's vast catalogue of silent films has vanished.) True, in the mid-1930s, Fields's movie studio, Paramount, bought *Poppy*, this time, finally, as a vehicle for Fields from start to finish. But consider yet a fourth irony in this paragraph of ironies, for the talkie *Poppy* finds a strangely underpowered Fields, possibly ailing but, in any case, no more than a shadow of the Eustace McGargle of 1925. We even suspect the use of a double in long shots, and we lament Fields's absence for long periods that busy themselves with the likes of Rochelle Hudson.

Ed Wynn was another comic who got to preserve a single Broadway role, that of Crickets in *Manhattan Mary* (1927), in the film version, *Follow the Leader* (1930). But Wynn maintained a deeper relationship with musical comedy than Fields did. What other comic sang Rudolf Friml, De Sylva, Brown, and Henderson, Rodgers and Hart, and Harburg and Arlen in story shows? (Yes, Friml—in *Some Time* [1918], which also featured Mae West.) It's an odd credit for a jester who was no more able a vocalist than Fields. But Broadway observed a venerable tradition

of comics rhythmically talking their way through songs. Besides, Wynn
had surprising musical resources. His aggressive role in the 1919 Actors' Strike got him blacklisted, so he decided to produce the show himself. Okay; but word on The Street had it that any performer or writer
who worked with Wynn would be blacklisted, too. So he decided to hire
only nothing-to-lose vaudevillians and write his own show, *score and all.*
Okay; but who would give him a theatre?

Luckily, the producers who most hated Wynn were the Shuberts, who
could not forgive his walking out of *The Shubert Gaieties of 1919* to
honor the strike. Luckily: because no one hated the Shuberts more than
Abe Erlanger, for it was the Shuberts who had bested Erlanger's mo-
nopolistic hold on the national theatre scene—the "Syndicate," as it was
known. So Erlanger gave Wynn the New Amsterdam Theatre, just to be
sure the Shuberts noticed: the flagship of the Broadway fleet, the place
of Ziegfeld and Marilyn Miller. There Wynn unveiled his "entertainment" (Wynn avoided the term "revue" as too limiting) titled *The Ed
Wynn Carnival* (1920). Proving how quickly the enmities of 1919 were
fading, Wynn found for his succeeding entertainments homes in theatres owned by George M. Cohan (bitterest of the managers) and
Charles Dillingham and gave Broadway *The Perfect Fool* (1921) and *The
Grab Bag* (1924).

Here we see Wynn at his most characteristic: funny-looking, freak-
ishly dressed, bearing a never-ending assortment of ridiculous inventions (such as the typewriter for eating corn on the cob), utterly sappy,
yet strangely in charge of it all. Other comics dominated shows; Wynn
ran them, interfering with the other acts, remarking to the audience on
the show's progress, spinning out an introduction to such lengths that
the announced performer got no time in which to perform, chatting
up the theatregoers in the lobby. Wynn was a sort of wit's end, a last
word—the Perfect Fool, indeed: for so was he known.

Aspects of Wynn's persona recall that of Joe Cook, similarly given to
wild inventions, though Cook's were more elaborate, usually Rube Gold-
berg-like contraptions involving gears, props, actors, and an amazing
amount of energy through which, finally, a balloon was punctured or a
walnut cracked. Both were more absurd than funny—Cook's signature
shtick was his oft-repeated failure to imitate four "Hywoyans," a ram-
bling and eternally reimprovised speech about why he could very well
imitate *three* Hawaiians but had good and sufficient reason to desist at
that point. *Four Hawaiians?* Ridiculous! Moreover, both Wynn and
Cook were critics' darlings, even when the critics hated a particular show.

Brooks Atkinson wrote of Cook in terms usually reserved for Charlie Chaplin: "He has the divine spark of madness."

That mad spark enlivened all these twenties comics. Onstage, some of them seemed confident, like Jolson or Fanny Brice; or dazed, not entirely whole, like Cook or the wanly fey Victor Moore. But all of them had it in common that they were more pixie than human. They were not actors speaking humorous lines but case studies taking their demented premises to logical extremes. Anything could happen. In *The Ramblers* (1926), playing two small-time con men who for reasons not worth going into now must bid farewell to a movie company on location, the comic team of Bobby Clark and Paul McCullough found itself actually caught up in the music. It's a "so long" number, the chorus tearfully taking leave as the two jokers pump their hands, clap their shoulders, wet various handkerchiefs, bellow snatches of Tosti's old chestnut "Goodbye Forever," and finally work their way off stage left. Moments later, they're back again, stage *right*, for more; at last they clamber over the orchestra pit to get into the auditorium to bid the public goodbye, too.

Beatrice Lillie posed an arresting question—what do you do with a musical comedy heroine who is simply too silly to support (or abide) a love plot? Fanny Brice solved the problem by sticking almost entirely to the naturally plotless revue, Lillie's own haunt in the West End for the first ten years of her career, save the secondary (and highly comic) lead in *Oh, Joy!* (1919), the London version of Kern's *Oh, Boy!* In 1924, producer André Charlot brought to Broadway an English cast to perform the best bits of several variety shows. Led by Lillie, Gertrude Lawrence, and Jack Buchanan, the company, as *André Charlot's Revue,* was a sensation.

The off-the-wall comedy, lyrical wit, and wispy sensuality of the English style (to know that some of the songs were by Noël Coward is to know all) seemed, next to the pushy American revues, blithe and smart. Charlot presented Lawrence in Harlequin costume playing a beribboned guitar to sing Coward's "Parisian Pierrot," and Lillie's spotlight number, "March with Me!," a ridiculous affair meant as a takeoff on the old *marche militaire* showgirl displays, veritably stormed the critics. The three stars returned to New York in 1925 for *The Charlot Revue of 1926,* and the two women promptly went into book shows after it closed half a year later. For the almost grotesquely enchanting Lawrence, the book show was a classic twenties exhibit, *Oh, Kay!* (1926): rumrunners, a nice guy about to marry a stick, farcical masquerade, tuxedoed chorus boys surrounding the heroine to articulate the public's own fascination ("Oh,

Kay! You're okay with me!"), a Gershwin score, and, at the center, Lawrence singing "Someone to Watch Over Me" to a rag doll in her signature quavery style.

But then, Lawrence was lovable. Lillie was a zany. She could hardly have used an *Oh, Kay!* and, in "Someone to Watch Over Me," would have started doing extremely curious things to the doll. All these comics had their through-line, their character hook: W. C. Fields blended frustrated dishonesty with misanthropy; Ed Wynn worked an enlightened lunacy. Lillie used oxymoron—the grande dame on roller skates, the Girl Guide making life hazardous for innocents, the star sneaking onstage disguised as one of the ensemble in a Geisha Number till she solos on "It's better with your shoes off!": and the entire house does a take.

This is great fun, and it must have seemed a dream notion to Charles Dillingham to star Lillie as an actress who raids the home of the bluenose who closed her show. New York City's attorney general, Joab H. Banton, had been grabbing headlines by threatening (and even closing) shows with unconventional subject matter that same year, 1926. So Dillingham would corral the star of the hour in the topic of the hour: Lillie invades bluenose's home, bluenose's wife shows up, suspicion, wonder, subterfuge—a hit.

There is a touch in all this of *No, No, Nanette,* the superhit of the previous year. Moreover, Dillingham hired *Nanette's* Charles Winninger as the bluenose and also *Nanette's* coauthor Otto Harbach (working here with Anne Caldwell) and composer Vincent Youmans. The result, *Oh, Please!* (1926), was not a hit. First, it lacked *Nanette's* structural cohesion, which Dillingham tried to cover by billing *Oh, Please!* as a "farce revue." Then, too, Youmans failed to duplicate *Nanette's* extraordinarily tuneful score, one of the few of the era to become popular almost as a whole rather than for a few titles.

At least Lillie was a self-starter. She found all sorts of places to clown around in—especially the love scenes. "When the plot betrays her," Brooks Atkinson wrote, "into warbling the usual love bathos with Charles Purcell at the usual close range she manages with some difficulty to keep a straight face." But, from then on, "she ridicules every traditional staple of musical comedy, every one in the cast, every one in the audience, and nearly everything she does herself."

Oh, Please! flopped. So did *She's My Baby* (1928). From then on, Lillie stuck with revue till, seventy and glowing, she accepted the character role of Madame Arcati in the musical version of Noël Coward's *Blithe Spirit, High Spirits* (1964). Now the only love bathos she had to warble was "Talking To You," a duet more or less, with her ouija board.

Lillie's difficulties in the book show typify one aspect of the twenties musical. The increasing interest in replacing generic plots with one-of-a-kind plots began to force star comics into a secondary status, a self-destructive paradox. The star comic can't be secondary; he owns the show. But one-of-a-kind plots don't take well to the autonomous performer. He functions well in anarchy, not in plots. If I had to synopsize the twenties musical in a phrase, I'd say, "From *Sally* to *Show Boat*"—that is, from a loosely integrated show that is about how wonderful Marilyn Miller and Leon Errol are to a tightly integrated show that is about American life.

Let's consider what can go wrong in a star comic's vehicle by looking at Leon Errol's *Louie the 14th* (1925). No, pardon me, Sigmund Romberg and Arthur Wimperis's *Louie the 14th*. Even Florenz Ziegfeld's *Louie the 14th*. Romberg had finally been graduated into regular operetta production with the decisive success of *The Student Prince* the year before and was not overjoyed to return to musical comedy. His next shows were *Princess Flavia* (from *The Prisoner of Zenda*) and *The Desert Song*, which tells us where his head was at this time. His music sounds it, capably ordinary dance and comic pieces surrounding ballads that would not have been out of place in old Heidelberg. For his part, Ziegfeld lavished his famous good taste on the show—a Joan of Arc pageant to end Act One, a real cordon bleu dinner served on the actual gold plate of Russia's Romanofs for the second-act banquet. But he foolishly booked the piece into the Cosmopolitan Theatre in Columbus Circle, far north of the at-the-time still vital walk-in business of last-minute theatregoers that could mean the difference between a "make house" and a "break house."

Louie the 14th itself was not without promise. The scene was France about a year after the Armistice, and Errol played one Louie Ketchup, cook of a regiment of American doughboys eager to go home. One of them loves a local French girl, which provisions the ballads. Errol has a romance of his own with the daughter (Ethel Shutta) of American parvenus residing in a fifteenth-century castle. Father parvenu kicks in the action when he has only thirteen guests for his fancy dinner and gets Louie to posh up as a rajah to grace the table with glamor and good luck.

Of course, we all know that Errol will make a superbly asinine rajah, do his funny weak-leg-fall-down routine (at first when a sergeant grabs the rifle Errol has been leaning on), pull off a drunk scene, and install a running gag on the name of his host. (It's Trapmann; so Errol calls him "Trashman," "Trashmouse," and so on.) There are novelties, too: a surprise entrance for the star when, after singing and drilling to "The Regimental Band," the soldiers march off, leaving Errol behind, though we had never noticed his entrance. (Director Edward Royce slyly sneaked him onstage during the drill, when two lines of men stretched from wing to wing. Distracting the audience with the sergeant's barking commands at stage right, Royce had Errol slip in to join the upstage line at stage left.)

Then, too, the rajah scene is better than it should be, for corn can be caviar when the jester is inspired. Will the rajah favor the company with a speech?

A FRENCH OIL TYCOON: We are all anxious to hear your address.
LOUIS: Fifty-eight West Seventy-Second Street.

Or take this exchange with a well-traveled countess:

LOUIE: Where did you go from Seringapatem?
COUNTESS: Columbo.
LOUIE: He discovered America.

There are problems, though. As the entire show is virtually a show-case for Ziegfeld's showgirls, Ziegfeld's spectacle, and one of Ziegfeld's favorite comics, why should we sympathize with the soldier boy-French girl love story? They're there partly to spell the hard-working Errol and partly because book musicals in this age absolutely had to contain a pretty pair singing pretty tunes. These two aren't really lovers: they're furniture.

There's another problem. This is the year in which—to choose but one of several possible examples—Rodgers and Hart unveiled in *Dearest Enemy* a story score so built into its story that most of the numbers would be jarring in any other show. Remember, this is only two years before *Show Boat*. Yet Romberg and Wimperis gave *Louie the 14th* a flatly generic score, as if there was too much clowning and too little actual character for them to find anything to sing of. The jaunty march "Follow the Rajah" at least salutes Errol's second-act disguise, and the authors tweak the New Dance Sensation with a *French* version for once, the "Rin Tin Tin" (which, Ziegfeld's chorus carefully informs us, is pronounced "Ran Tan Tan"). But the first-act curtain flies up on "Market Day," an opening chorus of the Jurassic Era. Such other numbers as "Little Peach," the Gershwinesque tango "Pep," "Edelweiss" (that's right; you can't copyright song titles), "Moon Flower," "Give a Little (get a little) Kiss," and Shutta's hotcha spot, "Don't Let Anybody Vamp Your Man," could have gone into any routine musical without a single lyric

change. Besides the tango and Shutta's number, Romberg's sole concession to contemporary American popular music was his playing of the
waltz duet "Sweetheart of Mine" as a fox trot on its second chorus, a
favorite Romberg stunt. In any event, the number was dropped before
the premiere and turned up the following year in *The Desert Song*, with
new lyrics, as "I Want a Kiss."

However. We have to see the era's entertainment *through the era's eyes*
(emphasis mine), and this era does not see the musical as we do. Today, of a new show, we may ask, What unique attitude does it strike?
How does the staging concept further nuance this attitude? Is the score
Sondheim or anti-Sondheim? How does the absurdly varying height of
the players, from Gargantua to Hop O' My Thumb, enlighten our
pensive gaze? Who, this time, are the postmodern commentative semi-
chorus? Ghosts? Crows? Caribbean islanders waiting out a storm? Is it
through-sung? Will a jazz combo eventually undertake a reading of the
principal melodies, bringing us perhaps far from text but nearer the secret truth?

Back in the 1920s, they asked, "Who's in it?" They just might have
added, "Who produced?," thinking of the magnificence of Ziegfeld,
Dillingham, Arthur Hammerstein. And, although I'm getting a little
ahead of myself, in the *late* 1920s, they would certainly ask, "Who wrote
the songs?" Because by then, with Kern and Berlin already placed, and
with the Gershwins and Vincent Youmans having joined them, to be followed by Rodgers and Hart, Cole Porter, and De Sylva, Brown, and Henderson, the public realized that something special was happening to the
music.

So, ultimately, our analysis of *Louie the 14th* as a musical is wrong-
headed. It should properly be analyzed as a Leon Errol show: not how
was the composition but how was Errol?; and Errol was fine. But maybe
Romberg should have bolstered his score with an audience take-home
hit. And maybe that off-the-track theatre was a bad idea. And maybe—
just *maybe*—star comic vehicles that were empty as compositions were
starting to look somewhat Second Age for the 1920s: *Louie the 14th* was
a failure.

On the other hand, just before *Louie* opened, in the spring of 1924,
the Marx brothers showed up on Broadway, and if ever there was proof
that a comedians' vehicle shouldn't go, *I'll Say She Is!* was exhibitive.
Joe Adamson, in his book *Groucho, Harpo, Chico, and Sometimes Zeppo,* calls this piece "an underground production thrown together out of
spit and desperation." The Marxes had been blacklisted in vaudeville,
and this was all that was offered them: "financed [Adamson continues]

by a pretzel-salt manufacturer whose concubine . . . had no talent and wanted a chance to prove it."

A hodgepodge of variety acts plus the Marxes' old vaudeville routines, set off by cheesecloth sets and charity-shop costumes, *I'll Say She Is!* toured for a year while its producer, James P. Beury, tried to decide whether or not to dare The Street. A little history is made here: the "Four Marx Brothers," as they were billed on the road, became simply "the Marx Brothers,"* and by a neat coincidence they were able to make their Broadway debut in the Casino Theatre.

Here was a house! It had been built in 1883, on the most glamorous block in all Broadway, directly across from the brand-new Metropolitan Opera. (And the Casino stole the headlines by opening one night before its rival.) As the Met was to be a temple of opera, the Casino was to be a temple of the musical—literally, in its Moorish architecture, and symbolically, because it was the first theatre raised specifically to house musicals. Thus, the Casino dates from just about the time when the musical was finding its place ontologically in American show business: when the musical started to matter. In its own way, the Casino was even more important than the New Amsterdam that Ziegfeld was so fond of. True, it was a bit south of the Main Drag by 1924, but it still bore a proud name and would never have hosted a ragbag of a show like *I'll Say She Is!*—never, that is, until the previous tenant suddenly closed. That was *Paradise Alley* (1924), a backstager with book by Charles W. Bell and Edward Clark, lyrics by Howard Johnson, music by Carle Carleton (also the show's producer; this is seldom an encouraging sign), Harry Archer, and one A. Otros, and featuring Helen Shipman, Ida May Chadwick, and Charles Derickson. Except for Harry Archer,† this is a depressingly obscure lineup, but they did make a major contribution to American comedy: for if *Paradise Alley* hadn't gone under, persuading Beury to bring *I'll Say She Is!* into New York, where he scored a tremendous success with it, the Marxes might never have gone to Hollywood. In fact, while Beury was considering what to do with the show, the

---

* As Shelley Winters, playing their agent mother, says in *Minnie's Boys* (1970), a musical based on the brothers' early years, "What'sa matter, the audience can't count?"

† The startlingly ungifted Archer lucked into what they call a "sleeper" when his and Harlan Thompson's *Little Jessie James* (1923) became the hit of the season, partly because its running costs were minuscule (there was one set and a tiny cast with little chorus) and mainly because the monotonous "I Love You (I love you)" caught on with dance bands. Don't let the title mislead you: the show, set in a New York apartment, tells of Jessie's pursuit of a boy friend.

brothers were considering breaking up the act and getting out of show business.

So in came *I'll Say She Is!* and out went the critics on a wave of delight. They wrote as if they'd never seen anything like these four crazies—and they hadn't. We know what the boys do, and they were already doing it at this time. The evening's best and final sketch saw Groucho, as Napoleon, taking leave of Josephine. Napoleon keeps returning on various pretexts, but mainly because the room is filled with hidden lovers (the other three Marxes) who, naturally, keep surging out and rehiding. Napoleon presently catches on; then a trumpet sounds "The Marseillaise." "The Mayonnaise!" he cries. "The Army must be dressing! I'm off!" Out of the side of his mouth, while rolling his eyes, he adds, "And if I leave you here alone, I *must* be off!" At length, he pulls out a snuffbox to toss out helpings here and there. Chico and Zeppo crash into view, Etnas of sneeze. Harpo appears in a gas mask, but he, too, goes down in a hail of snuff. "I am true to the French army," Josephine announces. "Thank God we have no navy!" retorts Napoleon. Blackout.

In the 1920s, as before and for four decades after, when a new star (or stars) showed up, a new show would instantly be built around that star, and the Marxes' next piece was Broadway Bigtime: Sam Harris produced, Irving Berlin wrote the score, and George S. Kaufman (and an unbilled Morrie Ryskind) wrote the book. The subject was Florida landgrabbing, fresh from the headlines, for the musical had become very trend-conscious. Surely it was the public's growing interest in aviation during World War I, and in the flying ace in particular, that led to Louis Hirsch, Otto Harbach, and James Montgomery's *Going Up* (1917), in which the alleged ace has never been in the air. The musical also responded to early airings of the feminist worldview with *Marjorie* (1924), a shapeless mess by Herbert Stothart, Fred Thompson, Clifford Grey, and a pair of nobodies that at least tried to give Elizabeth Hines a heroine role of some self-willing power. It was as if the musical wanted to establish a dialogue with the culture, not only to exploit but to address issues as they arose: what was the appeal of flying? How much is a woman allowed to demand of men?

And what about this Florida, where northerners would arrive to visit the plot of land they had bought only to find it part of a swamp? Florida was capitalism's latest playground, so rich and corrupt that Bertolt Brecht seems to have taken it as a model for Mahagonny City, the evil setting of his and Kurt Weill's opera *Aufstieg und Fall der Stadt Mahagonny* in 1930. We have seen Florida already, in Eddie Cantor's vehi-

cle *Kid Boots*, but that was the Florida of country clubs and golf. As the
Marxes' personas thrived in an atmosphere of chicanery, their Florida
would be that of real estate deals and shady entrepreneurs.

The "Cocoanuts" (1925) bears an odd resemblance to yet another
Florida musical that opened but a month before—*Florida Girl* (1925),
which found Vivienne Segal in Coral Gables. Both shows dealt with
stolen jewels, and both featured a comic sibling act, though *Florida
Girl's* Ritz Brothers lacked the Marxes' distinguishing identities—Groucho's shyster, Chico's Italian grifter, Harpo's silent imp, Zeppo's straight
man—that gave content to their anarchy. Anyway, one show flopped, and
one made a hit. Or: one show vanished, and one survives, because it
was filmed. Or: *Florida Girl* was just another musical comedy, and *The
"Cocoanuts"* was just another musical comedy containing the Marx
Brothers.

The last verb is questionable. More fairly, the Marx Brothers con-
tained *The "Cocoanuts"*. For *I'll Say She Is!*, brothers Tom Johnstone and
Will B. Johnstone simply wrote songs, any they could think of. Irving
Berlin actually tried to work the Brothers into the *"Cocoanuts"* score,
but they really do come with their own music in Chico's piano and Harpo's harp. Groucho will talk through a patter song (here, "Why Am I a
Hit with the Ladies?"), and Zeppo will sing ballads ("Florida By the
Sea"), always eying the audience as if it might boo him for not being
funny. (In movie revival houses, before the age of the VCR, Zeppo's appearance in the opening credits invariably occasioned a storm of scorn.)

In the end, Berlin was stymied. A look at *The "Cocoanuts"'s* tune-
stack* reveals a musical whose songs are edging around the stars rather
than using them. One notes the conventional numbers—the Opening
Chorus (Zeppo leads the Cocoanut Grove Girls and Boys) and the dance
of the Sixteen Stepping Bellhops (mostly women in drag), which follows.
There's the New Dance Sensation, the "Monkey Doodle Doo," introduced by Frances Williams. There's the first-act finaletto. There are the
other dance numbers, "Five O'Clock Tea" (specialty by the De Marcos)
and "They're Blaming the Charleston," in which this ubiquitous dance
is tried out in English, Spanish, "Lenox Avenue" (i.e., Afro-American),
and Russian styles. Frances Williams again presents the vocal, suggesting a role that is more practical than dramatic. Janet Velie, the ingenue,
gets "Minstrel Days," bringing in a lengthy minstrel-show sequence de-

---

* This recent neologism refers to the listing of tracks on a CD and, by my arrogant extrapolation, to any listing of a show's songs, including those in playbills from
the 1920s. We have needed such a term for over a century.

signed to fill out a somewhat less than plot-filled evening. Something called "Tango Melody" calls back the De Marcos. There are songs for the lovers, Jack Barker and Mabel Withee: "Family Reputation" (because she's "above" him), "Lucky Boy," "We Should Care," and the obvious hit ballad—though it never caught on—"A Little Bungalow (an hour or so from anywhere)."

Where are the Marxes in all this music? It doesn't matter: they dominate the show in *their* way. It's not Vivienne Segal's or Eddie Cantor's way, but they weren't making rules in those days for how a musical is supposed to behave, on whether the music pumps through the story or simply punctuates it. Besides, it was fun to see the Brothers trash their own show with ad libs and complots. As the piece entered a long run, Henry W. Schlemmer (Groucho), Willie the Wop (Chico), Silent Sam (Harpo), and, to a greatly lesser extent, Jamison (Zeppo) enlivened the scene with new fun, sometimes setting it up moments earlier to surprise each other. *The "Cocoanuts"* is the show in which, notoriously, Harpo asked a chorus girl to run across the stage, Harpo giving chase, during one of Groucho's speeches. Screams from the public as the two zip past; but Groucho doesn't miss a note:

GROUCHO: *(checking his watch)* Well, the 9:20's right on time tonight.

Ironically, *the* comedy musical hit of the 1920s—without question the most successful musical comedy of the decade and also the most enduring even as I write—was no star vehicle but an ensemble show, a virtual pride of comic actors sticking to a script. It started as May Edginton's novel *Oh, James* and went to Broadway as *My Lady Friends* (1919), adapted by Emil Nyitray and Frank Mandel and starring Clifton Crawford as a rich Bible publisher whose innocent philanthropies in setting up "deserving" (read "pretty") young women with clothes and apartments implicate him in adultery. Postwar Broadway loved slick, coy diversion: is he or is he not guilty? (A Bible man, at that!) The play never tells, for, though the protagonist *says* that he's innocent, he is all the same keeping women.

Crawford, a singer and songwriter, blessed *My Lady Friends* with a couple of tunes, and by the time that the company had finished the road tour its producer, H. H. Frazee, visualized it as a full-fledged musical. Frazee was a producer of the old school—buy cheap, sell dear, and screw the world. (His most characteristic move was purchasing the Boston Red Sox, selling off their best players—including Babe Ruth, to the Yankees—then dumping the crippled team on some less wise investor.)

Frazee easily might have reimagined *My Lady Friends* as a vehicle for a star—W. C. Fields, perhaps, just after his emergence in *Poppy*. Any other producer would have, for this was an age of shows built for comics as the Capitol was built for Congress. Frazee, luckily, preferred the simpler route: if it ain't broke, don't fix it. Mandel and a new collaborator, Otto Harbach, were simply to retool the old script for a score by Vincent Youmans and Harbach and Irving Caesar, meanwhile building up two minor players for the typical musical comedy love plot. One might argue that Mandel and Harbach's major work lay in renaming *My Lady Friends*'s characters. The Bible magnate remained Jimmy Smith, but his wife went from Catherine to Sue. Jimmy's lawyer, Edward Early (originally played by Frank Morgan), became Billy Early, whose wife Lucille serves as a spendthrift foil to Sue, "a saving little woman," the new script tells us, "who can get a full meal out of a soupbone." The Smiths' ward, Eva, turned into Nanette (cuter), though her beau remained Tom Trainor; and the indispensable comic maid, Hilda, became Pauline. A more sweeping change involved Jimmy's three grasping protégées, Norah, Gwendoleyn, and Julia, who turned into "Betty from Boston," "Winnie from Washington," and "Flora from Frisco."

Why these finicky alterations in a text that was otherwise simply cut down and reshaped to allow the insertion of songs—especially when the authors retained the original's three-acts-one-set-per-act breakdown, which, by very early 1924, when the musical was written, had almost overnight become old hat? The spectacular revues of Florenz Ziegfeld, George White, and Earl Carroll had proved that stage technology could manage multiple changes of decor by alternating big sets with small scenes played before the so-called "traveller" curtain. In other words, Will Rogers might do his monologue "in one" while the stage hands prepared the elaborate "Trans-Atlantic Love" number, on a gigantic map with the girls costumed as telephones; then Van and Schenk might do their twelve minutes in one while the next big number was readied; and so on throughout the evening. Among other book musicals of 1924, *Lady, Be Good!* seemed trendy with its three sets in each of two acts (big set, little set, big set); the more expensive *Rose-Marie* fitted five sets into each of its two acts. By comparison, *No, No, Nanette* seems stodgy.

But Frazee's show had a supportive sense of proportion. With so many principals, Act One is not merely an extended exposition but a delightful string of numbers introducing the characters—the dourly eccentric maid, the amiable Billy, the flip but secretly sensitive Lucille, the doting Nanette and Tom, the all-loving Jimmy, and then the suddenly *re-*

bellious Nanette, bridling at the way everyone appears to take her for granted.

There is a trap in all this: with so many important characters, one needs a strong ensemble cast, something that a Broadway raised on the star system had trouble accommodating. Certainly, Frazee had trouble. He had to replace key players when the Detroit, Cincinnati, and Chicago tryout stands lost money. The new Nanette was Louise Groody, known to us as *Good Morning, Dearie*'s heroine; the new Earlys were Bernard Granville and the gala vaudeville star Blanche Ring; and Charles Winninger was now Jimmy, so pure yet so compromised.

I still say W. C. Fields would have been a gem in the part; but Fields couldn't sing. Moreover, Winninger was an unusual talent in that he fitted his comic business *into* the characters he played rather than fitting characters into his business. He wasn't a star comic, but rather a comic who starred, and that protected *No, No, Nanette*: from the mad delight but also the egomaniacal disorder of a star comic's vehicle. It utterly elucidates Winninger that—unlike Fields or Eddie Cantor or Ed Wynn—he never truly headlined in anything, yet played the central role in the most perennial of all American musicals, *Show Boat*.

And *this* show, *No, No, Nanette* (1925), won such success that it swept the world from South America to China. This had never happened before, not with Gilbert and Sullivan (popular only in Anglophile lands, though *The Mikado* travels), not with Victor Herbert (a failure even in England), not with *Sally, Irene,* or *Mary*. Letting the newly cast and now popular Chicago *Nanette* continue there on an open run, Frazee organized an American tour and a London premiere (for which Youmans composed a new ballad, "I've Confessed To the Breeze," and socked in a dance number, "Take a Little One Step," salvaged from *Lollipop* [1924]). So New York didn't see Nanette till the Chicago cast came in and "Tea For Two" and "I Want To Be Happy" had been irritatingly overplayed. The London stay—behind only *Rose-Marie* and *Bitter Sweet* as London's longest-running twenties musicals—lasted a bit more than twice that of New York, even with a flawed ensemble. (The Tom, Seymour Beard, sang like a fiftyish capon, and everyone else save the heroine, Binnie Hale, was a bit off, one way or another.)

Paris adored the show, for the French were just floating into a wave of sexy musicals, such as Maurice Yvain's *Ta Bouche* (1922), *Là-Haut* (1923), and *Pas Sur la Bouche* (1925). Indeed, *Nanette*'s adaptation, by Roger Ferréol and Robert de Simone, with lyrics by Paul Colline and Georges Mergy, subsumed *Nanette* into the *opérette* style, moving the setting from New York City and Chicadee Cottage in Atlantic City to Paris and the resort town of Paris-Plage, on the Strait of Dover. Similarly, the West End Nanette took its characters from London to the French Riviera, a scene plot typical of English musicals for over a generation. Thus, the American second-act finale's breathless refrain of "She spent the night in Trenton" became "She spent the night in Brighton," losing Harbach's sly choice of New Jersey's most innocent town to be suddenly caught up in controversy.

Frazee produced a *Nanette* rip-off in *Yes, Yes, Yvette* (1927), with Caesar and Winninger again on board. A flop. But *Nanette* stayed famous, if unperformed. The score, with its two super hits, "Tea" and "Happy," was ever in the ear. Hollywood utterly betrayed the piece—First National's 1930 version surrounded the plot with irrelevant backstage sequences and threw out all the songs but the two hits; and Warner Brothers' *Tea For Two* (1950), a Doris Day picture, threw out the plot. Yet *Nanette* hung on as a Famous Twenties Memory, from its opening parade of pretty young things ringing the doorbell, strutting onstage, and breaking into "Flappers Are We" to Lucille's torch song, known both as "Who's the Who" and the "'Where Has My Hubby Gone?' Blues." "Flappers" is conventional, but the torch number is distinguished by the first note of the refrain, a plaintively stinging dissonance—which, oddly, shows up as the *second* note of the refrain of the title song, with exactly the same harmony but now sounding querulous and bossy.

Perhaps this is why the 1971 Broadway revival did not tamper all that much with the score: in some dim way, it had a sort of inviolable integrity. True, "Flappers Are We," much of the first- and second-act finalettos, "Fight Over Me," and Pauline's two numbers were dropped. Lucille's keys were lowered from the original soprano to accommodate Helen Gallagher's belt range. Then, too, director Burt Shevelove streamlined the book; and Ralph Burns's orchestrations gave the show an anachronistic brassiness, even a grandeur. This is not even to consider the heavy nostalgia trip that the production presented, featuring as it did the comebacks of Ruby Keeler and Patsy Kelly and the imprimatur, at least, of a past-it Busby Berkeley, billed as the "supervisor" of the whole but in fact nothing but a Name rented for authentication.*

* Berkeley, of course, was celebrated for his high-tech stagings of numbers in the Warner Brothers backstager cycle—a thirties rather than a twenties resonance. But he in fact got his start playing a comic lead in one of *Irene*'s original touring companies and rose as a choreographer in the late 1920s, taking in *A Connecticut Yankee* (1927), the 1928 edition of the *Earl Carroll Vanities*, *Good Boy* (1928), and *Rainbow* (1928), among other shows.

This was *No, No, Nanette* as pastiche, then, part revival and part time travel. Still, it *was* indeed *No, No, Nanette*. And how else to revisit a conventional twenties musical in the season that also saw the premiere of Stephen Sondheim's *Follies* than in a knowing spirit? Designer Raoul Pène du Bois's raging pastels seconded Burns's arrangements in blowing a simple farce into a display piece, and choreographer Donald Saddler set the girls on giant beach balls for the "Peach on the Beach" number. Here was a *big* show, all the more because it became a surprise smash.

Well, it *was* stylish, after all—not twenties style, but with a kind of overeager fifties feeling. Then, too, it was a *dancing* show at a time when musicals were just starting to be acted and directed more than choreographed. There was a "back to the source" feeling here, a sense that, whether more or less faithful to the 1925 *Nanette*, the revival was faithful to the tenets of the mid-twenties musical: laugh, sing, and *dance*. As the Earlys, Helen Gallagher and Bobby Van made a specialty out of "You Can Dance with Any Girl at All," running through the Maxixe, a hesitation waltz, a polka, and a two-step; and of course there was Ruby Keeler, sixty-two years old and . . . well, as everyone in the audience wondered, *could* she?

"I Want To Be Happy" was her first time back in tap shoes in who knew how long. (She had retired after filming *Sweetheart of the Campus* in 1941.) Keeler entered after the vocal (by others), coming downstairs with the boys in their dizzingly colorful "twenties" sweaters, pulled up her skirt with one hand, and began to hoof ever so lightly. *Well,* the public thought. She's just going to ham-and-egg her way through it. Then came the second chorus, *allegro,* and Keeler and the boys went for it with such abandon that at one point Keeler had to slip offstage momentarily for what critic Ken Mandelbaum has referred to as "the oxygen break." It was probably while applauding this number, right then, at that moment, that a public long weaned from the musical as three hours of nonstop fun realized what it had lost.

A replica of the New York revival played London's Drury's Lane in 1973 (with Anna Neagle in Keeler's part), failing to duplicate the American success. Still, *Nanette* was relaunched and now stands on the short list of America's very old yet still active musicals. Classics are loved for their scores primarily, but *Nanette* has a surprisingly good book. In fact, it's one of the few twenties musicals that is really about something: money.

Only one song, "Pay Day Pauline," deals with the subject, but every principal, without exception, is obsessed with or at length offers firm opinions on it. Maybe this is why *My Lady Friends* was not retooled for a star comic: he would have disturbed the authors' concentration. From the curtain's rise, the idea of money as a medium of self-esteem, as power, as, even, a weapon in domestic life, is strongly felt. Nanette, the Smiths' orphaned ward, feels like a prisoner because she is penniless, Lucille uses her shopping bills to keep her husband tethered to her, and Jimmy's wealth makes him too free, a borderline adulterer. "I think everyone should spend every cent he can get his hands on," he explains: money buys happiness. Lucille agrees:

> LUCILLE: I lost fifty dollars at bridge and I felt so blue I just had to go out and do some shopping.

Lucille wants to bring Sue into the gender party line:

> LUCILLE: (*to Sue*) You, with a husband worth a million! It's a perfect outrage that you won't go out and . . . You're not a natural woman!
>
> SUE: But Jimmy isn't a millionaire!
>
> LUCILLE: He's liable to be, the way you're acting!

Lucille's no opportunist. She's a philosopher:

> LUCILLE: The only way to keep a husband straight is to keep him broke.

This view of money as society's cure-all so permeates the dialogue that it has the unity of a Bolton and Wodehouse Princess script. When Jimmy, spreading his sunshine, hands Nanette two hundred-dollar bills, she feels so empowered that the social structure is imperiled:

> TOM: (*aghast*) No good woman *has* two hundred dollars!*

By the evening's end, virtually everyone is blackmailing, bribing, looting. "Money, money, money, money, money, money," runs a lyric in "Pay

---

* Burt Shevelove's 1971 edit heightened the oppression latent in this line by changing "good" to "decent," as if suggesting that young women with money must be prostitutes. Unfortunately, Shevelove otherwise pruned the text of many of its references to the power of gold in defining human character, turning a jaggedly worldly entertainment into a smooth, brainless one. The 1971 version is the one offered today for production, but the 1925 original has survived and is very performable, as John McGlinn's 1986 New York concert staging demonstrated. Again, Jimmy was a comic actor rather than a star comic, Robert Nichols; but Judy Kaye's stunning Lucille centered the event, reminding us that, with Sue almost a nonsinging part and Nanette an ingenue, Lucille is the diva role.

Day Pauline." And "gimmee, gimmee, gimmee, gimmee, gimmee, gimmee." Finally, Sue is convinced:

> SUE: Hereinafter, my sole premise is life will be to spend, spend, spend!

Ironically, this is the happy ending—the one character who had been immune to the lure of riches accepts that to resist being a member of a corrupt society is by its destabilizing nonconformity a form of corruption itself. Mid-twenties musical comedies, in the post-Cinderella era, were generally cynical. But few of them had a genuine point of view. *Nanette* surely didn't begin with Frank Mandel nudging Otto Harbach and saying, "Let's give them something commentative, for a change." Yet there it is: a 1925 musical comedy with a *Weltanschauung*.

One cannot love twenties musicals without loving *No, No, Nanette*. Call *The Student Prince* a royalist absurdity, *Lady, Be Good!* songs without a story, *Sally* a besotted producer's ode to his girlfriend. But *Nanette* is so elementally of its day in the way the irresistible score holds together the contrived plot that Sandy Wilson used the show as the template for his twenties pastiche, *The Boy Friend* (1954).

This show, originally a sketch for London's Players Club, was expanded and moved to the West End and then to Broadway (where Paul McGrane and his Bearcats played Ted Royal and Charles L. Cooke's orchestrations, as opposed to the duo-piano pit that Wilson stubbornly maintained for *The Boy Friend*'s five-year London run) and was even filmed for MGM, in 1972, by Ken Russell. Popular also in high schools and summer stock and occasionally given major revivals, it has misled many about the nature of the twenties musical. Wilson's crystal-clear plotting has none of the Byzantine involutions that musical comedy second (or third) acts often got into, and he makes do without a proper chorus: almost everyone on stage is a principal. Nevertheless, *No, No, Nanette* was clearly in his mind from the start: in the setting on the French Riviera (as in the London *Nanette*'s second and third acts); in the three-act layout; in the raising of the curtain on the maid, followed by the entrance of four girls to sing "Perfect Young Ladies" (an echo of "Flappers Are We" right down to the similar introductory music); in the use of the key word "happy" in the hit tune ("I Want To Be Happy": "I Could Be Happy with You"); in the second-act opening of beachside frolicking, Wilson's "Sur la Plage" using the same syncopated descending line as Nanette's second-act lead-in, a reprise of "The Call of the Sea"; in the "other" heroine's courtship songs, Lucille's "Too Many Rings

Around Rosie" reversed in Maisie's "Safety in Numbers"; and in "The 'You-Don't-Want-To-Play-With-Me' Blues," a snappier version of Lucille's "'Where Has My Hubby Gone?' Blues."

True, in its title *The Boy Friend* recalls a forgotten Rodgers and Hart show, *The Girl Friend* (1926); builds its title song around *that* show's title song both melodically and harmonically; bases "A Room in Blooms-bury" on a twenties genre of song that *Nanette* didn't include; and features in a New Dance Sensation, "The Riviera," a salute to *Good News!*'s "Varsity Drag" so sharply pointed that *The Boy Friend*'s New York co-producer, Cy Feuer, himself recomposed the A strains, retaining Wilson's original release, to avoid legal trouble.

Still, *The Boy Friend* would seem to be where the twenties musical came to rest, if only because of a popular perception of this sleek and tidy modern piece as a replica of an old style. Not so. The twenties musical was noisy and sloppy, or grand and passionate, or wicked and wily. The twenties musical was *The Stepping Stones* but also *The "Cocoanuts"*; *The Rise of Rosie O'Reilly* but also *The Student Prince*; the Ziegfeld *Follies* but also Ziegfeld's *Show Boat*. The twenties musical has no one matrix, no one issue, no one memory. In fact, somewhat near half the total output of twenties musicals belonged to a form that is now not only dead but forgotten: the revue.

The Girls of My Dreams

THE VARIETY SHOW

Just as the 1920s must be seen, on one level, as a time of confrontation between musical comedy and operetta, in which the two forms learn from and imitate each other even as they pull further apart, with *Rose-Marie* over here and *Lady, Be Good!* over there, so must the 1920s also be seen as the climax of the long war between the musical in general and its nemesis, parasite, and major provider of fresh talent—vaudeville.

As only true thespians would tell you, vaudeville played to a different class of audience than the theatre did. Theatre was Shakespeare, Mrs. Fiske, Victor Herbert. Vaudeville was dog acts.

Actually, vaudeville was a mixed grill of vast diversity—animal acts, yes, and singers and comics and family acts and short plays and recitations (including Shakespeare) and magicians and acrobats and the untalented notorious who leaped out of the headlines into vaudeville to be gaped at. For many, such as George M. Cohan, Fred Stone, the Astaires, Marilyn Miller, W. C. Fields, and the Marx Brothers, vaudeville was a training ground. For many unknown others, it was a cemetery. For the audience, it was a number of worthless acts followed by some okay acts, building to the headliner (in the glorious "next to closing" spot), topped off or, rather, punctuated, by the "chaser," one final worthless act to shoo the public out and free seats for the next show.

Vaudeville's strength lay not only in its variety but in its emphasis on personality. Unusual or unique talents that might have been limited in a story show were liberated by vaudeville's string of unrelated appearances. Vaudeville's weakness lay in its very structure: those worthless acts. True, at the great urban theatres, such as, in New York, Hammerstein's Victoria or the absurdly overfabled Palace, the public licked up the cream of the industry, along with some grade-B talents and a few chance schmengies. But, in most places, even the headliner was grade C, and the rest of the bill was one tomato-baiting horror after another. At the time of vaudeville's prominence, roughly from 1890 to its sudden collapse in 1930, vaudeville was without question the least consistent of the popular arts.

Yet that liberation of talent kept beckoning to the story musical. Marilyn Miller's knockout beauty is irresistible: stuff her into a show! Those Marxes blow the roof off: can they sustain an entire evening? This always enriched the musical, though it could impede its maturing process, as when the Astaires' dancing merely decorated *Apple Blossoms.* Thus vaudeville and the musical maintained a wary truce, Broadway ever siphoning off vaudeville's discoveries and vaudeville giving Broadway regulars a berth when no show came through for them.

How long the two might have continued the arrangement one cannot say, as the movies, then radio, then particularly the talking picture lured vaudeville's audience away, and Joseph P. Kennedy's takeover in 1928 of the merged Keith-Albee-Orpheum corporate structure that had held vaudeville together absolutely destroyed vaudeville as an economic entity. Still, as early as the 1910s, Broadway had already begun to subsume vaudeville: in the revue.

It's an old form. It was spelled "review" in the late nineteenth century, when, as the word suggests, it "looked back upon" the season, the year, the times, typically with a satiric attitude. The modern revue may be dated from *The Passing Show* (1894), very much in this style but with the added elements of sumptuous production and an outstanding line of chorus girls, or from the Joe Weber and Lew Fields "burlesque" shows at the turn of the century, spoofs of the latest hit play mated with a variety show composed entirely of worthy acts. There is also the colossal Hippodrome to consider, though it was as much circus as revue and may not suit the parameters of this book.*

---

* The Hippodrome, opened in 1905 on Sixth Avenue between Forty-third and Forty-fourth streets, was the biggest theatre in history, seating more than six thousand and employing four hundred stagehands. The shows ran twice daily, six days a

Perhaps the best place to start is with the *Ziegfeld Follies,* for here is where we see how surely the revue replaced vaudeville by raising it to the highest power. At the series' founding, as the *Follies of 1907,* it appears to have been conceived by librettist Harry B. Smith and director Julian Mitchell as a takeoff on current events, rather like Smith's newspaper column, "The Follies of the Day." Pocahontas and John Smith, as emcees, took a smart look at such figures as John D. Rockefeller, Theodore Roosevelt, John Philip Sousa, Commodore Perry, actress Edna May, bluenose Anthony Comstock, Ziegfeld's own attraction Sandow the strong man; at the automobile, the Gibson Girl, and the "opera war" between the Met and Oscar Hammerstein's Manhattan Opera House. There were showgirls, apparently at the suggestion of Ziegfeld's wife, Anna Held. But, in successive editions—annual from 1907 into the mid-1920s, sporadically thereafter—Ziegfeld revealed *his* conception of the revue: the girls, spectacular sets and costumes, and vaudeville with nothing but headline acts.

Such a concentration of stars was unknown on Broadway. The most important shows offered a single star or team, like Montgomery and Stone. The *Ziegfeld Follies of 1915* offered W. C. Fields, Bert Williams, Ina Claire, Ed Wynn, Ann Pennington, Mae Murray, and Leon Errol, all top-liners at the time, along with the not-yet-established George White and Carl Randall and such Ziegfeldian beauties as Kay Laurell, Justine Johnstone, and Olive Thomas. This was the *Follies* that introduced designer Joseph Urban, a key player in Ziegfeld's game because of the unprecedented finesse of his color schemes, his unexpected perspectives, and his pointillistic painting style, as in an "Arabian nights" setting for the *Follies of 1927,* the trees executed in speckles of green, yellow, and brown and the sky a vast mosaic of splotches in shades of blue, from aquamarine to navy.

Giuseppe Verdi called the Paris Opera "la grande boutique," and that's

---

week, ten months a year. Built by Frederic Thompson and Elmer S. Dundy, who owned Coney Island's Luna Park, the Hippodrome was another such: theatre as amusement park with stationary visitors. Water sports, battles, opera, clowns, animal shows, and all sorts of spectacles were combined into mixed-bill programs, year after year, each bill running more or less for the entire ten months. The Shuberts took control in 1909, Charles Dillingham in 1915. The house went over to vaudeville in 1923, ironically when thousand-seat vaudeville houses were struggling and fifteen-hundred-seat houses were going under. Cinema took over in 1928, and producer Billy Rose brought the place back to its roots in 1935 with the Rodgers-Hart-Paul Whiteman-Jimmy Durante circus musical *Jumbo.* In 1939, the Hippodrome was demolished.

what Ziegfeld's *Follies* was: an entertainment shop. Ziegfeld himself called it "a national institution," and, starting with the 1922 edition, he proclaimed its purpose to be "glorifying the American girl." Here was a monument. Had there been many tourists then, it would have been a guidebook attraction, giving two shows daily ten months a year like the Hippodrome annuals. As it was, the *Follies* invariably made money, doing half a year's business in New York in fall and winter and another half on the road in spring.

The girls were lit and costumed very dramatically, and a never-ending flirtation with something near to nudity left the public breathless. Stars and material were dropped into and out of the shows so suddenly that attending was a real adventure, not to mention the fascination churned up when one of the girls became notorious overnight in another off-stage scandal. Then, think of the stars—Fanny Brice, Eddie Cantor, Will Rogers, singers, dancers, comics utterly let loose at their best. The spectacle, at a time when most book musicals offered one set per act, was kaleidoscopically nonstop. *Irene* cost $41,000; the *Ziegfeld Follies of 1919* that same year cost $170,000. Let there be light.

And let there be imitations. As vaudeville groaned with loss, Broadway began to fill with revues, both one-offs and series. George M. Cohan, Elsie Janis, Ed Wynn, and Raymond Hitchcock produced and appeared in essentially one-star revues in the late 1910s and early 1920s. The Shuberts presented a renovated version of *The Passing Show* almost yearly from 1912 to 1924, dropping it for the promisingly naughty-sounding *Artists and Models* from 1923 to 1930. Meanwhile, George White offered the *Scandals,* starting in 1919, and Earl Carroll the *Vanities,* from 1923. There was *Broadway Brevities of 1920,* the first (and last) of a series; there were ragbags like *The Broadway Whirl* (1921) and *The Mimic World* (1921); a bunch of veterans in *Some Party* (1922) and debutants in *The Newcomers* (1923); the Russian-French *Chauve Souris* (1922), famed for its droll emcee, Nikita Balieff, and its "Parade of the Wooden Soldiers"; *The 49ers* (1922), with sketches by the Algonquin Round Table; black revues, smart revues, silly revues, trendy revues, old-hat revues. Some seasons, there were as many revues as there were book shows.

The big series are interesting mainly for the light that they shed on the *Follies.* For instance, the *Passing Show*s followed the lead of that original 1894 *Passing Show* in emphasizing takeoffs on the hit plays and show-biz personalities of the previous season, as if the Shuberts wanted to challenge Ziegfeld's fame but not his format. Ziegfeld mostly scorned such spoofs. He preferred to develop his own ideas, commissioning, for instance, a Swing Song so les girls could swing out over the audience while tossing flowers or dreaming up a miniature revival of the old minstrel show, with Eddie Cantor as Tambo and Bert Williams as Mr. Bones, that suddenly opened up into an elaborate mustering of the full company on a pavillion of steps rising into the fly loft, all in tones of silver, pink, and white and built around Irving Berlin's irresistible pseudominstrel number "Mandy."

Then, too, the *Passing Shows* suffered from weak scores, though the main composer for most of them was Sigmund Romberg, a Shubert employee and typed by Mr. J. J. as a musical comedy tunesmith despite the success of Romberg's expansive *Maytime* musical in 1917. Historians hail *The Passing Show of 1915* as outstanding in the series, possibly because of a touch of Russian ballet from Theodore Kosloff and Madame (so-billed) Baldina and a pride of spoofs: Willie Howard doing Charlie Chaplin, "Lou Tellegram" (matinee idol Lou Tellegen) and Trilby (to brother Eugene's Svengali), Marilynn Miller as Clifton Crawford and Mary Pickford, along with bits on "Ruth Chatterteeth" (Ruth Chatterton) and "Belascoa Odile" (Frances Starr, heroine of David Belasco's latest hit, *Marie-Odile*).

Well, that may be a lot of fun, but a look at the score, mostly by Leo Edwards and Harold Atteridge, reveals lyrics so witless and music so dead they make *The Gingham Girl* feel like a Princess Show. We can forgive the ghastly "My Hula Maid" because of the hula craze that year. But why must there be *two* "ragging the classics" numbers—"Billy Shakespeare" and the miserably endless "Ragtime Overture of Grand Operas," a vocal medley? Ziegfeld was supposedly deaf to a good tune, but over the years the *Follies* introduced more than their share of good ones, from "Shine On, Harvest Moon" and "By the Light of the Silvery Moon" through "Row, Row, Row," and "A Pretty Girl Is Like a Melody" to "Second Hand Rose" and "Shaking the Blues Away."

From 1917 to 1920, Raymond Hitchcock presented New York with four *Hitchy Koo* revues that were utterly unlike the *Follies* and *Passing Shows*. In fact, Hitchcock pointed the way toward the "intimate" revue whose forte was strength of material rather than spectacle and trendiness. Not that Hitchcock's shows were first-rate. His homey, corny approach has its exasperating side, and he managed to hire the young Cole Porter (in 1919 and again in 1922 for an edition that closed out of town) at his most uneven and Jerome Kern (in 1920) in plain bad form. Still, Hitchcock could be thought of as an antidote to Ziegfeld's grandiosity, especially for the less sophisticated audiences, for Hitchcock could do almost as well on tour as George M. Cohan or Fred Stone.

Take *Hitchy Koo 1920,* with a script by Glen McDonough and lyrics by McDonough and Anne Caldwell to Kern's music. The director was Ned Wayburn, by then an old hand at revue—he had done both the *Follies* and the *Passing Shows.* For Hitchcock, Wayburn laid on the air of old-home week, bringing out all the nostalgia in the material. (The sketches included a mock old-time melodrama, a look at small-town life, where everything happens in the drugstore, and a daguerrotype recreation of Madison Square in 1884, when Lily Langtry and John L. Sullivan lead a torchlight parade in honor of President-elect Grover Cleveland.) The first scene was almost improvisatory, as Hitchcock ad-libbed, kidded the audience, and set about "preparing" the show. Would-be chorus girls, in the hoary tradition, are Iona Rolls, Maida Wood, and so on. Maida is going to audition with "The Gypsy's Warning."

> A BACKER: Isn't it interesting—some songs never die!
> HITCHCOCK: (*in his usual mild, even offhand manner*) No, they're very hard to kill. But Maida will do her best to that end.

Grace Moore sang, Florence O'Denishawn danced, Hitchcock played the druggist (and bootlegger) in the drugstore and then went sparking with Julia Sanderson in a "Buggy Riding" number. At length, in the finale, "The Star of Hitchy Koo," all debated just who that star might be till Sanderson awarded the honor to Hitchcock.

If you liked the bucolic, easygoing Hitchcock, this sort of art was refreshingly unpretentious. If you didn't, it was tiresome and self-indulgent—really, the "star" of *Hitchy Koo!* Who cared? It typifies the series that, as with the Princess shows, the 1920s killed them off. If the new musical comedy, such as *Lady, Be Good!,* pushed the old musical comedy, such as *Sally,* to the side, then, comparably, the twenties revue would be animated, sleek, know-it-all: the *Scandals.*

Ziegfeld, originally, was a promoter and the Shuberts were realtors, but George White was a dancer. A *Follies* dancer, even. How Ziegfeld must have laughed when he heard that his former hoofer was about to challenge him. White and another ex-Ziegfeld dancer, Ann Pennington, were nearly all that registered in the *Scandals of 1919;* the scornful Ziegfeld offered White $2,000 a week if he would return to the *Follies.* White countered with an offer of $3,000 a week for Ziegfeld and his actress wife, Billie Burke, to appear in the *Scandals.* Anyway, this was all PR frou-frou. White now had a take on Big Revue, based on this one *Scandals* experience: the public loved great dancing and was hungry for good songs. The *Scandals* dancing had worked, but the score was dull. White sought a good score for 1920.

Of all the producers of Big Revue, White had the keenest ear, and he hired George Gershwin for the next *Scandals* because Gershwin and Irving Caesar's "Swanee" was sweeping the country just then. Al Jolson recorded it on January 8, 1920, so the disc must have been released by mid-February. White would have hired his 1920 *Scandals* composer in February or March for an August opening. (Virtually all the annuals, Big or Little, opened in late summer or very early fall.)

White hired Gershwin, and that's good fast work. White could hear the nervous ambitious energy in "Swanee" for himself, while Ziegfeld greatly depended on the advice of his scouts, especially Gene Buck. It was Buck, not Ziegfeld, who found Joseph Urban, for instance. So how do we know that it was Ziegfeld who called for that Swing Number, and not *Follies* director Julian Mitchell? How do we know it wasn't Buck who heard Irving Berlin's "Mandy" in the all-soldier revue *Yip, Yip, Yaphank* (1918) and then dreamed up the minstrel spectacular for the *Follies of 1919*?

What *was* Ziegfeld? A traffic manager? White was a racing car. None of that Ziegfeldian tableau for *him*, the curtains parting on "Night in the Harem" with everybody posed just this side of the law, holding it, and the curtains shutting to; none of those stupendous showgirls parading around the stage, *andante, adagio, largo*. White's idea of Big Revue was some crazy ukelele guy like Tom Patricola singing a Charleston number, then zipping offstage as sixty girls raced on and danced the tune to pieces. *Animated.*

When Gershwin left the *Scandals* after the 1924 edition, White found lyricist Lew Brown and composer Ray Henderson and paired this already complete duo with "idea man" B. G. De Sylva, thus creating the consummate songwriting team of the 1920s: not the best, but the most timely, typical, redolent, so much so that when the decade ended, the trio broke up. It was in 1921 that White felt confident enough to put his name on the series as *The George White Scandals*, but it was in 1926 that White and his no-fail songwriting team, with vocalists Harry Richman, Frances Williams, and Tom Patricola, dancer Ann Pennington, comics Willie and Eugene Howard, and cuties the McCarthy Sisters and the Fairbanks Twins, brought forth the hallmark of the twenties revue.

Here, in 1926, was the first great revue score. "The Birth of the Blues" (featured in an elaborate battle between classical and pop music, with the girls costumed to represent, for example, the "St. Louis Blues" on one hand and Schumann's "Träumerai" on the other), "Black Bottom" (whose verse quotes Stephen Foster's "Swanee River" as if to unite a cultural tradition with the New Dance Sensation as a Great American Rhythm), and "Lucky Day" immediately became standards. The tender "The Girl Is You and the Boy Is Me" was the little ballad tucked away amid all the jazz, so humble yet so publishable. The witlessly bouncing "Sevilla (where senoritas dance around)" provisioned a typical ethnic episode, and there was the innocently knowing rhythm number, a De Sylva, Brown, and Henderson trademark, "Tweet-Tweet." Six hits for one revue? At 424 performances, this *Scandals* broke the revue record, and Ziegfeld was smoldering. Meanwhile, Earl Carroll had arrived.

Carroll's series was the *Vanities,* the closest thing to a *Follies* of all Ziegfeld's imitators. Closest in the emphasis upon skin and comics: burlesque in the modern sense, not Weber and Fields' chaste spoofs but the strippers and top bananas whose degraded art Mayor La Guardia eventually closed down. Notice, too, that while Carroll launched his series as Earl Carroll's *Vanities,* in the mid-1920s he changed it to *The Earl Carroll Vanities,* as if to ring more nearly like the *Ziegfeld Follies.*

Like Ziegfeld, Carroll was a skillful publicist. Like Ziegfeld, Carroll sought not fame but notoriety and blessed all his cohort with it; simply to attend a Carroll party was to give one's reputation an unseemly twist. They credit Walter Winchell with inventing "celebrity journalism," but Winchell only popularized it. Ziegfeld and Carroll pioneered it. Like Ziegfeld, Carroll opened a superlavish theatre bearing his name.* Like Ziegfeld, Carroll had brushes with the law, though, unlike Ziegfeld, Carroll did time in a federal penitentiary. And, like Ziegfeld, Carroll plumed himself on the Absolute Truth of His Girls. A Carroll publicity handout claimed that "the 'picking' of beauties is a ceremony almost as elaborate as the coronation of an Indian potentate. . . . Mr. Carroll takes the matter of selecting beauties very seriously and . . . he exercises the same care with each individual girl."

Why were the *Vanities* so terrible yet so successful? They were terrible because, as historian Cecil Smith wrote,

> they never developed a genuinely distinctive character. Carroll always seemed merely to elaborate needlessly upon themes already more than adequately taken care of in the *Follies, The Passing Show,* and the *Scandals.*

---

* Actually, Carroll opened two theatres, the first a modest house, in 1922. After Ziegfeld erected his eponymous showplace, Carroll followed suit with a Taj Mahal of a theatre on the same site as the old one. But for the Hippodrome and certain opera houses and cinemas, it was the largest playhouse in New York.

Smith also tells us why the *Vanities* were so successful:

> The *Vanities* were just the dish for the weary . . . seeker after
> beauty who could be satisfied by a finale in which 108 Vanities
> Girls stood on a revolving staircase and revolved.

Another reason was twenties revue fever in general, the nearly insatiable
demand for undemanding variety evenings. Besides, a publicity war
among Ziegfeld, White, and Carroll (and every so often the Shuberts
threw in a punch) kept these shows in the news.

The appeal of the *Vanities* certainly didn't lie in the music. In the
1930s, Carroll was to hire Harold Arlen and E. Y. Harburg, but during
the revue heyday in the 1920s Carroll's scores were almost as terrible
as the Shuberts'. Another press handout: "The name of EARL CARROLL
is almost as closely linked with melody as it is with feminine pulchri-
tude. . . . The solitude of his studio, or the darkness of his theatre are
the settings that the master showman chooses to select the music that,
later, is to set millions of hearts pulsating, millions of toes tingling. The
melody must be played a score of times in varying keys and tempos . . .
and if that abstract, uncanny something in the EARL CARROLL brain is
stirred, the song goes in the production."

First of all, *into* the production; second, what does Carroll think he
has here, *Show Boat*? The melody must be played a score of times?
Halfway through the first chorus, Ziegfeld would say, "Use it."

At least Ziegfeld and Carroll were as one in the emphasis on the girls.
But a Ziegfeld girl was someone fabulous, scandalous, how to marry a
millionaire. There was no such thing as an "Earl Carroll girl." For all
that, the Ziegfeld girls were hyped—"ballyhooed" is how they put it
then—beyond reason. Even normally skeptical critics like George Jean
Nathan insisted that Ziegfeld's models were nothing offstage and that
dress and lighting and Ziegfeld's direction changed them into an order
of sexdeath to go. The photographs say otherwise: these were truly beautiful women. Ziegfeld was the magnet, and Carroll took Ziegfeld's leav-
ings, adding to them a total lack of imagination and taste.

Was the showing of leg the mandate of the twenties revue? Well, more
or less: more with Ziegfeld and Carroll, less with the Shuberts and
George White. And one series did without skin altogether: the *Music
Box Revues,* named for the theatre they played in and limited to four
yearly editions, from 1921 to 1924.

If Ziegfeld contained multitudes and the *Scandals* were about dance
and Earl Carroll was about Ziegfeld, the Music Box shows were about
class. Here was the big-star revue that was lavish but not vulgar (unlike

the *Vanities*), that used its talent inventively instead of simply exploiting it (unlike the *Follies*), that preferred elegance to energy (unlike the *Scandals*). The sketches were on a higher than usual level. Two of them, Robert Benchley's fumbling "Treasurer's Report" and George S. Kaufman's "If Men Played Cards As Women Do," are probably the only nonmusical spots in all the decade's revues that may be called "classic." Director Hassard Short's special effects—"old faithful" gushes of steam, darts of flame, and elevators in a sequence set in "Satan's Palace," or a lone soprano singing the nostalgic "Crinoline Days" while slowly rising into the air as her hoop-skirt grows in size and length till it fills the stage—were the talk of the town. The performers—comics Sam Bernard, Willie Collier, Bobby Clark and Paul McCullough, Fanny Brice, Frank Tinney; singers Grace Moore, Wilda Bennett, John Steel; all-arounder Charlotte Greenwood; the Fairbanks Twins and the Brox Sisters—rivaled Ziegfeld's. (Some even *were* Ziegfeld's—not only, obviously, Brice but also John Steel, the top-hatted tenor who Brought on the Girls in Song, an avatar lovingly retrieved by Stephen Sondheim in the character of Roscoe in Sondheim's own *Follies* in 1971.) And the scores, all four exclusively by Irving Berlin, were nearly as good as De Sylva, Brown, and Henderson's 1926 *Scandals* numbers and better than anything else in the twenties revue.

"Say It with Music" was the advice of the chief ballad of the first *Music Box Revue*, which also contained the exhortative "Everybody Step": the quasi-Schubertian Berlin and the dance-frenzied Berlin at once, American Pop 101. Other revues had stars and special effects, but only this series had Berlin on a regular basis. True, the staging structure was Ziegfeldian—"An Orange Grove in California" saw Grace Moore and John Steel warbling in the indicated locale, followed by an orange light show during which citrus scent was sprayed into the auditorium. The level of composition in both songs and sketches, however, was beyond Ziegfeld. After all, that king of showmen had been purveying his ware for a generation; both in eye and ear he was a bit old by the 1920s. The *Follies* were by then an institution: the *Music Box Revues* were an invention. Not quite avant-garde, they were all the same state-of-the-art, ultra-1920s in Berlin's intense quest for the Hit Tune upon which, he believed, a hit show absolutely depended.

The pressure was on, then: even if Berlin was putting it on himself. Of course, a needy show could simply slot in an interpolation, but Berlin was above such field expedients. It was *he* they turned to for a last-minute hit, as Ziegfeld presently would when Rodgers and Hart disappointed him with their score for *Betsy* (1926) and Berlin tossed off "Blue Skies."

In the end, he never got much hit play out of the Music Box shows—the titles mentioned earlier, along with "Lady of the Evening," "Pack Up Your Sins and Go To the Devil" (in the "Satan's Palace" number, as a red-clad Charlotte Greenwood sent performers dressed as Ted Lewis, shimmy queen Gilda Gray, and other merchants of jazz to their hot Reward), "What'll I Do?," "All Alone," and "Tell Her in the Springtime" (with another perfume assault). Berlin didn't realize that the quality of his scores inhered in his overall tunefulness—the kind of thing that Jerome Kern seemed to find so easy in his Princess days—and not in the commercial rocketing of a specific title. That, really, was the distinguishing feature of the Music Box style in revue—a consistent level of entertainment in every department.

Naturally, Berlin wrote the Music Box scores—he owned the Music Box Theatre. It was George M. Cohan's doing. In the 1919 Actors' Strike, Cohan, half actor and half producer, felt betrayed by the walkout on a personal level. Couldn't they have come to him and said, "Georgie, we like *you*, but this is about *them*"? Thus Cohan ended his longtime producer partnership with Sam H. Harris because Harris had been the least anti-union of all the producers. So Harris turned to Berlin, an astute theatre businessman, and the pair built a theatre, this same Music Box, and opened it with a flourish, the first *Music Box Revue*, at the Ziegfeldian budget of $187,613 (for the show alone). Harris went on to produce not only the three Music Box successors but the next three Berlin musical comedies—the first book shows of Berlin's career, almost certainly at Harris's prodding.

So this was a historic partnership, just as Cohan and Harris had been. Harris's career takes us from deep in the Second Age of musical theatre, with *Little Johnny Jones* in 1904, through the Princess shows (in an imitation, by Louis Hirsch, Otto Harbach, and James Montgomery, *Going Up*, in 1917) and into the Third Age with the Gershwins (*Of Thee I Sing* and *Let 'Em Eat Cake*), Cole Porter (*Jubilee*), Rodgers and Hart (*I'd Rather Be Right*—with Cohan in his Great Role as Franklin Roosevelt), and Kurt Weill (*Lady in the Dark*, after which Harris died). Sam Harris thus stands forth as one of the musical's few founding figures* who neither died nor lost power during the 1920s. This man spanned eras. As we'll see, almost all the most influential mentors of the musical in the 1900s and 1910s were dead, retired, or failing by 1930—the

---

* There were of course major figures in the First Age (see note, page 4). But their long-range impact was, I think, marginal in that most of the forms they worked in were moribund by 1900 and in that their successors replaced the old styles rather than pursued them.

most prominent composer, Victor Herbert; the most prominent musical comedy *capocomico,* George M. Cohan; the most prominent librettist, Harry B. Smith; the most prominent producers, Florenz Ziegfeld, Charles Dillingham, and Arthur Hammerstein; and the most prominent directors, Julian Mitchell and Edward Royce.

Clearly, the 1920s marked a time of evolution, as such New People as the Gershwins, Rodgers and Hart, and Oscar Hammerstein swept in and the Old Names were blown away. A few who, like Harris, had their roots in the Second Age, lasted well into the Third: Kern, Berlin, the Shuberts, Victor Moore. Another of this company is less celebrated, because for all his genius he had the odd luck to choose all the wrong projects for a career that lasted from 1919 to 1953: John Murray Anderson.

A director, designer (sort of), and lyricist, but really a supervisor of *Gesamtkunstwerk,* Anderson invented the urbane revue, saw Rodgers and Hart through their first successful book show, conceived and directed the only brilliant film revue *(King of Jazz)* when Hollywood got into a revue cycle in 1929–30, played genius in water shows and nightclubs, staged the biggest book musical that ever lived, *Jumbo* (1935), which was really more a circus than a musical, and played a considerable part in the choosing and shaping of material in what were probably the last first-rate Third-Age revues, *New Faces of 1952* and *John Murray Anderson's Almanac* (1953).

This must have been a lot of fun—conquer Hollywood, outcircus P. T. Barnum, then churn up an Aquacade—but it didn't make for an enduring curriculum vitae. And, in between, Anderson got into such disasters as *Sunny River* (1941), Sigmund Romberg and Oscar Hammerstein's Cajun *bombe-surprise* of 36 performances; Kurt Weill's outlandish disaster *The Firebrand of Florence* (1945); and a Bette Davis musical— let's line up for tickets!—called *Two's Company* (1952).

Anderson's contribution to twenties revue was his invention, in 1919, of the *Greenwich Village Follies.* This was the bohemian annual, Sheridan Square's very small-scaled riposte to all that uptown bluster. It cost $35,000 to mount, one-fifth of what Ziegfeld spent on the 1919 *Follies,* and it got by on style, delicacy, and a touch of the grotesque. Anderson wrote the sketches and lyrics with Philip Bartholomae, to A. Baldwin Sloane's music, and they opened it downtown as *Greenwich Village Nights.* Word of mouth heralded a naughty, sophisticated, and unpredictable evening, a notion supported by the show's poster logo of a monocled gent, a Pierrot marionette, and three women wearing a few green ribbons, supported by a gigantic bed.

Then the authors changed the title to *Greenwich Village Follies.* Ziegfeld cried foul, but someone remembered producer H. G. Pellisier's *Follies* revue at London's Tivoli Music Hall in 1906, one year before Ziegfeld used the word. This was good publicity for the underdog show. Better yet, the Actors' Strike occurred two months after the little *Follies* opened. Because it was an off-Broadway exhibit, its management did not belong to the strictly uptown Producing Managers Association. The *Greenwich Village Follies* was thus exempted from the strike, and it enjoyed sellout weeks as one of the very few shows playing. To cap it all, the Shuberts moved it up to the Nora Bayes Theatre, a roof garden* atop the Forty-Fourth Street Theatre. The little *Follies* was in.

Like many revues, this one used a loose frame of a group (of Villagers) putting on a show. A chorine is auditioning:

> CHORINE: I see you have a bedroom set. That's all you need for a successful play nowadays.
> COMIC: Ours is a Greenwich Village play, so it's sure to be all about free love.
> CHORINE: Free love? Well, the Villagers won't like that. They don't want to see what they get at home all the time.

Her audition piece is that weird old song that begins, "Oh, do you remember Sweet Alice, Ben Bolt?" So, of course:

> COMIC: You know, I'm the guy who wrote "Sweet Alice Ben Bolt."
> But she never answered my letter.
> CHORINE: Now I know he's the comedian.

The "bed" theme recurs, as when the Ingenue and the Juvenile (so-billed) ponder the frequency of boudoir scenes in contemporary theatre:

> INGENUE: I hope there is one in ours.
> JUVENILE: Why?
> INGENUE: Because . . .

The orchestra chimes in, and she sings:

> In nearly every playhouse nowadays,
> You'll find there is a vogue for bedroom plays.
> And, as an antidote to gloom,
> You have been *Up in Mabel's Room*,
> A "No-Man's" land of frills and negligees . . .

---

* Nothing more than late-night dinner theatres for the cognoscenti, these long-vanished supper clubs were popular during the Second Age and were on their way out in the 1920s, when Prohibition's scofflaws popularized the more conventional night club.

The verse continues to cite the titles of risqué comedies—*She Walked in Her Sleep, Tumble In,* and so on. This could be a number in any revue, of any quality, sending out the usual topical signals. But then the chorus steals in to a wistfully long-lined melody that would not have disgraced Kern, a love song with ragtime hooks such as no other revue would have had the imagination to attempt, and we see the finesse of Anderson. His Prohibition number, "I'm the Hostess of a Bum Cabaret," is infinitely more appealing than the standard Prohibition numbers and even challenges Irving Berlin's "You Cannot Make Your Shimmy Shake on Tea," from the *Ziegfeld Follies of 1919.* A teasing bit of bizarrerie was "My Marionette," in which Bessie McCoy Davis recalled her early fame singing "Yama-Yama Man" in *Three Twins* (1908) by appearing as a white-faced puppet manipulated by strings from above the stage.

Like the 1919 edition, the 1920 *Follies* opened downtown but moved up, to the Shubert, where the 1921 edition *opened*—losing, some said, its outlander's freshness. But the 1922 edition, similarly unveiled at the Shubert, was possibly the best in the series, and not the least daring. First of all, there was wicked Reginald Marsh's show curtain, a panorama of Village habitués on parade along Fourteenth Street, down MacDougal Alley, on the platform of the Sixth Avenue elevated line, even on a truck—F. Scott Fitzgerald, Marcel Duchamp, Sinclair Lewis, Eugene O'Neill, John Barrymore and his wife, Michael Strange, John Dos Passos, Steven Vincent Benét, Mayor Hylan, and our own John Murray Anderson. Second, it was in 1922 that Anderson devised a subtle blend of song and dance for an adaptation of Oscar Wilde's poem "The Nightingale and the Rose," tactfully erotic, a sensation of the day, and generically so new that not for twenty-five years did anyone know what to call such pieces: "ballet ballads."*

Anderson stuffed this 1922 *Follies* with unique artists; the designers James Reynolds (whom Ziegfeld stole) and Erté were also on hand. But most Village of all in the series was the comedy team of Savoy and Brennan, who had first appeared in the 1920 edition. Jay Brennan was the straight man, and Bert Savoy was the drag queen—yes, they had them then, though the typical drag act would be Fred Stone going goofy in

---

* Composer Jerome Moross and lyricist John LaTouche employed Anderson's form in three one-acters produced on Broadway as *Ballet Ballads* (1948) and in *The Golden Apple* (1954). Historians routinely term "The Nightingale and the Rose" and its successor in the 1924 *Greenwich Village Follies,* "The Happy Prince" (also after Wilde), "ballet ballads." But in his autobiography Anderson clearly singles out his conception as "the forerunner of what *today* [my emphasis] are known as 'Ballet Ballads.'"

one of his many disguises or the suave Julian Eltinge, so tasteful in his portrayals that one wondered why he bothered. Bert Savoy was a drag act in the modern sense, wild, hissy, and tumultuously on the make. "He was bald, paunchy, middle-aged and blind in one eye," Anderson recalled. "But after an hour in his dressing room, when he had made up, been trussed into a corset by Agnes, his perspiring maid, adjusted his flaming wig and put on his form-fitting dress and spreading, feathered hat—he emerged a dashing, if slightly bawdy, fashion plate."

"You *mussst* come over," Savoy would insist. Mae West heard that. (So did Ziegfeld. His 1921 *Follies* included a number called "You Must Come Over," a concession to the power of Anderson's little revue; and a book musical, *Captain Jinks* [1925] cashed in with the "You Must Come Over Blues.") Another bit of Savoy business was reports on the doings of a friend named Margie. "*Oh*, that Margie," Savoy would groan, head a-shake. "The *trouble* with her gentlemen friends. Now, I *told* Margie . . . Didn't I?" she shouts at Brennan, posing with hand on hip.

"Yes, I believe you did," he replies, with a patient smile.

"I told her, if it's ten P.M. on a Saturday night, and the lights are out, and *he* suggests a taffy pull *without the taffy* . . . well! He's *no gentleman!*"

As the audience giggles, Savoy struts downstage, turns to profile, and adds, "You *mussst* come over!"

Anderson staged not only the *Greenwich Village Follies* in 1924 but also the last of the four *Music Box Revues*. A famous story connected with the latter gives us an insight into Anderson's talent. The show opened strongly, but the eternally nervous Berlin perceived that nothing in the score was looking like a hit, so he added one of his many non-show tunes, the recently published "All Alone (by the telephone)." Now the show had a hit, but the depleted budget gave director Anderson little to work with. So he thought small: Grace Moore in black velvet and Oscar Shaw in a tux at opposite sides of the stage in front of the black traveller curtain, each holding a telephone that bore a light attachment in the mouthpiece, the only illumination in the scene. It was the biggest thing in the show.

Berlin and Harris were smart to call off their series after this one, for the revue was exhausting itself with its own richness. Besides, the book shows had all the good music, because revues weren't about anything, and the better writers needed a launching pad—Sally's ambition, the student prince's first date. Consider this: Rodgers and Hart first won notice in revue, in two editions of the *Garrick Gaieties*. Yet all of their succeeding Broadway scores—twenty shows—were book musicals. Kern,

too, after *Hitchy Koo 1920,* and Gershwin after the *Scandals,* never
wrote another revue. It was not a stimulating environment for a distinctive songwriter. All alone by the telephone was not what these writers had in mind. They were going to dig into story and find new kinds
of songs, a new music, new characters. This was a *fast* time, heading
somewhere.

Just as the revue swallowed vaudeville, the book musical swallowed
the revue. Able performers became caught up in the storytelling; limited performers were driven out of the business. No, the revue did not
vanish in 1930. The annuals fitfully continued—George White produced a last *Scandals* in 1939, Earl Carroll a *Vanities* in 1940. And there
was a late flowering, of revues unified by a theme, as in *As Thousands
Cheer*'s newspaper format (each headline inspired a song or sketch) or
the travelogue of *At Home Abroad.* These were mid-1930s, all-star revues, much loved. But they were the end. By the 1940s, the revue had
devolved into chance agglomerations or a single star's glorified nightclub
act filled out with fiesta dancers and a clammy comic. The 1950s saw
a last stand, but television presented variety shows for free. By the
1970s, all that was left of revue was the songwriter anthology, an
evening of Fats Waller, Leonard Bernstein, Johnny Burke. These are not
variety shows.

But then the book musical, it turned out, could not coexist with the
variety show. The book musical needed variety talents, to use them,
however, in an orderly way. The rationalizing of the musical had begun;
the fiesta dancers were out of work. And the wonderful thing about the
story show is that it redeveloped the musical from a performer's medium into a performer's *and* writer's medium just when a generation
loaded with determined writers had appeared.

Yankee Doodle Rhythm

THE NEW MUSIC

On February 12, 1924, Paul Whiteman and his Palais Royale Orchestra gave a concert at New York's Aeolian Hall. Called "An Experiment in Modern Music," the offering was in fact a review of American pop, from "Livery Stable Blues" and "Yes, We Have No Bananas" to sizable new pieces by Victor Herbert and George Gershwin. But we should note that the concert hall was one typically given over to the classic European masters, that the extensive program notes discussed each composition as one might parse Beethoven, and that the audience included not only musicians Leopold Stokowski, Fritz Kreisler, Mary Garden, Syergyey Rachmaninof, Amelita Galli-Curci, Jascha Heifetz, and Deems Taylor, but many leaders of all the arts. This concert was the musical event of the season, written and talked about in extravagant terms, and ever after a date of historical denotation. Suddenly, Americans had discovered that pop had as much right to an ontology as did symphony or opera, that "jazz" was not a noise but an art, that all music was equal.

But not equally effective. Whiteman's guests patiently considered the many parts of jazz that were presented that day: in the offerings of novelty pianist Zez Confrey (including his "Kitten on the Keys"); in an arrangement for wind instruments of Jerome Kern's "Raggedy Ann" (from *The Stepping Stones*), whose plaintive wail suggested the Klezmer style of Jewish street music; in "Semi-Symphonic Arrangement[s] of

Popular Melodies" (all by Irving Berlin); and "Adaptation[s] of Standard Selections to Dance Rhythm." But surely the concert's strongest statement was made in the second half, when Herbert's *Suite of Serenades* faced off Gershwin's *Rhapsody in Blue*.

Just as in our comparison of the colossally dainty *Sally* and the lean, hip *Lady, Be Good!*, or in our noting of how quickly the Princess shows lost their appeal, we can see one era crumbling as another era asserts itself. Truly, an age is upon us—the golden Third Age of the musical's history. Herbert's four-movement suite is lovely and clever, from the perkily mysterious Spanish and haunting Chinese movements (the latter incorporating twee violin glissandos in imitation of an Asian instrument) to the sinuous Cuban and Oriental movements (ending in hilarious Middle Eastern "chase" music). It's easy to hear and just as easy to forget. Whiteman did his ample best to popularize it, but he was bucking the age. Herbert was over, and Gershwin was starting. From the *Rhapsody*'s first moments, when the clarinet playfully slides two-and-a-half octaves up to crown the B Flat Major chord that immediately hunkers chromatically down to A Flat Major diminished over a B Flat bass with the clarinet toying with triplets on A flat and G flat to create a Great American Discord, Gershwin put the Modern into music.*

Popular music has become arrogant, thought some; popular music has no limits, exulted others. Certainly, popular music had become self-conscious. It had a murky background but an ambitious future. First, though, someone was going to have to define the term "jazz."

Jazz was at once the center and the outskirts of the American sound in 1924, the most famous yet the most despised thing in the new music, a catch-all word that changed its meaning every time someone used it. Jazz was sinful, corrupt, lubricious; anything you could dance to, anything too loud, anything that wasn't a waltz or a polka; it ruined good music, it seduced good music, it *was* good music. In 1925 in Washington, D.C., the police sought to reactivate a disused law banning "indecent music." Was that jazz? "That tom-tommy sort of Oriental music that makes men forget home and babies," said one Mina Van Winkle, chief of policewomen. Oh, *drums*. "That hootchy-kootchy sort of intonation," added another official. Hmm. Sinuous, sensual music? *That's*

---

* Remember that this was not the juicelessly bloated symphonic version of the *Rhapsody* popularized over the years but the dance-band original, orchestrated by Ferde Grofé: just a solo piano backed by reeds and brass, timpani, piano, celesta, banjo, and eight violins. Besides the violinists and soloist Gershwin, Whiteman led no more than fifteen players. Call it *Concerto for Piano and a Broadway Pit*.

jazz? It was left to Sergeant Rhoda Milliken to specify conclusively: "Any music played on a saxophone is immoral."

The 1920s, of course, was called The Jazz Age, so the sound was everywhere. Funny that no two people could agree on what it was—no two composers, even, for, to Paul Whiteman, Victor Herbert and George Gershwin were equal parts of it. One knew what jazz wasn't—*The Student Prince*, "Alice Blue Gown," Brahms. But any of these could be jazzed: put into more or less fast-dance time by a smallish band of woods and brass (with maybe a piano) not only reproducing the piece but doing riffs and variations on it. In short: playing it on a saxophone.

Jazz would seem to be a uniquely limited form, obtrusive and self-interested. On the contrary, jazz traveled. Milhaud and Ravel used it on a symphonic scale. The Germans coined the term *Zeitoper* ("opera of the time," meaning "fad opera") because so many composers were writing jazz operas, or operas utilizing jazz, even operas about jazz, such as Ernst Křenek's *Jonny Spielt Auf* (1927), about a black American jazz violinst (so it *can* be done with strings!), who, as the title tells, Strikes Up the Band. This was Crossover a half century *avant la lettre*. John Alden Carpenter startled the music world with a ballet based on George Herriman's comic strip *Krazy Kat* (1921 as an orchestral piece; 1922 on stage), with the dancers completely hidden in Krazy, Ignatz, and Offisa Pup costumes and pop's sharp teeth combing the longhair sound style. Carpenter went on to *Skyscrapers* (1926), a "a ballet of modern American life" set, obviously, in a city because, as we know, the U.S.A. was now a city country, with city music. *That's* what jazz was: the opposite of Stephen Foster, "After the Ball," and the Women's Christian Temperance Union's hymn, "A Saloonless Nation in 1920."

While classical composers leaned into jazz, pop composers used it to expand. Cole Porter wrote the ballet *Within the Quota* (1923) to Gerald Murphy's satiric scenario, played against a blowup of a newspaper's front page with the headline "UNKNOWN BANKER BUYS ATLANTIC" and utilizing archetypes of American culture. An immigrant meets the Heiress, the Colored Gentleman, the Jazz-Baby, and the Cowboy, as a prudish character variously appearing as reformer, prohibition enforcer, religious zealot, and Wild West sheriff makes the times interesting. At length, the Sweetheart of the World (movie star Little Mary, of course) inducts the Immigrant into the marvels of show-biz fame.

The piece typifies the bohemian debunking style so much a part of the twenties worldview, but it's most unusual Porter, far more sophisticated than anything else he composed—contrapuntal, motivic, and opening and closing with a melody associated with the Sweetheart that is dreamy when first heard and apocalyptically cheesy at last. Commissioned by Les Ballets Suédois, the work was orchestrated by Charles Koechlin (later famous for his songs and tone poems *d'après* Kipling's *Jungle Book* stories), choreographed by Jean Borlin, and conducted by Vladimir Golschmann. It does not seem to have enjoyed a furor, though les Suédois toured it both here and abroad just before and even a bit after the Aeolian Hall concert. Perhaps *Within the Quota* was too classical to play carmagnole for the jazz revolution; the *Rhapsody in Blue* was, shall we say, just classical enough. In any case, when the Swedes disbanded, in 1924, Porter's score vanished. Not till the 1960s did it turn up, in an obscure museum in Stockholm that refused to allow it to be performed or even examined. In the 1980s the museum, under new management, released the document for performance.

Why all this modernist interest in such long-forgotten facets of American music? Original orchestrations with the banjo part intact, lost little ballets, Herbert versus Gershwin? Because all these bits of information combine to give us a comprehension of the very sound of the musical's Third Age, its great one and also the great one of American pop music as a whole, the century or so between "After the Ball" and rap. Where did this new sound come from, so rooted in the 1920s and its jazz, so vaguely defined yet so controversial? The question is not so much Who made jazz? as it is Who got Broadway out of generic plots punctuated by parlor ballads and vaudeville novelties and on to discovering the music latent in the individuality of each new story?

Proponents of the Great Man Theory would answer, "Jerome Kern." After all, it was he who made the greatest stylistic leap in the composition of musicals, from ditties to *Show Boat*. Yet George Gershwin made a greater leap, from musical comedy to *Porgy and Bess*, which is to American opera what *Show Boat* is to the musical: the best of all. And Cole Porter, on the basis of *Within the Quota*, was Kern's musical senior. Then, too, Richard Rodgers launched a second, extraordinarily influential career in his "musical plays" with Oscar Hammerstein but two years before Kern's death, making Rodgers perhaps the most enduring of all Third-Age composers.

But did not the generation of composers who made the 1920s a revolutionary era swear fealty to Kern the Master? (Only the soigné Cole Porter, so aloof and opaque, never mentioned Kern as a primary source. Porter's idea of a Master was Vincent D'Indy, at whose Schola Cantorum in Paris Porter briefly studied.) Does not every revolution begin with someone else's idea, just old enough to be new? And was not Kern the idea man, sparking the jazz in his younger colleagues?

Tolstoy, believe it or not, is illuminating here. At exactly the center of *War and Peace*, he says (in the classic Constance Garnett translation), "In historical events great men—so called—are but the labels that serve to give a name to an event. . . . Every action of theirs, that seems to them an act of their own free will, is in an historical sense not free at all, but in bondage to the whole course of previous history, and predestined from all eternity."

In other words, something was brewing in American music. Something was Going To Happen, no matter who in particular led the happening, and, because of his superiority to his coevals in sheer finesse and imagination, we label that something "Kern." But consider this: about fourteen weeks before the Whiteman evening, mezzo-soprano Eva Gauthier gave her own Aeolian Hall Concert, of "Ancient and Modern Music for Voice," taking in Purcell and Bellini, Milhaud and Schönberg (the Wood Dove's scene from *Gurrelieder*), Hindemith and Bartók . . . and a group of American songs: Kern, Berlin, and Gershwin (with the relentless George himself at the keyboard).

The juxtaposition of Kern, Berlin, and Gershwin could be coincidence. Maybe Gauthier simply liked Kern's "The Siren's Song," Berlin's "Everybody Step," and Gershwin's "Innocent Ingenue Baby" and "Swanee" and so programmed them. But one could argue that in 1923 *this* was what was brewing, these three names, soon to be joined by the others. Kern was the melodist, Berlin the ragtime bandleader, Gershwin the jazzman, each different. Still, very early Gershwin can imitate the sound of either of the two older men, and to study *their* work in the mid-1910s is to realize that Kern and Berlin were listening to each other and to the dance craze then prevalent and were actually starting to sound alike.

What, Kern the elegist and Berlin the cartoonist? It may seem so later; for about ten years during and after World War I the two can be said to, one, *sometimes* sound alike and, two, create American popular music. For instance, the song "Katy Did," from *Oh, I Say!* (1913) is pure Berlin in its ragtime piano part, simplistic harmony, and novelty lyric. But Kern wrote it (with lyricist Harry B. Smith). Or take "The Magic Melody," from the first Princess show, *Nobody Home*. Again, it's pure Berlin, especially in its view of the United States as a gigantic, giddy dance hall. ("Just so you'll know we'll show you All the late improvements in these syncopated movements.") The rather grand structure and the chording is also pure Berlin—and of course this one, too, is Kern's.

But then we press an ear to Berlin's *Stop! Look! Listen!* (1915) and hear the clean elegance of Kern's melodic line in "Teach Me How To

Love" and "I Love To Dance." More symbiotically, we notice in "Beautiful Faces (need beautiful clothes)" from *Broadway Brevities of 1920* a Kern-like melody on a distinctly Berlinesque notion. Looks, attire, the visual of who you appear to be at the moment someone glimpses you—this use of an objective-corelative in analyzing American cultural attitudes was Berlin territory. (Think of "A Pretty Girl Is Like a Melody" or "Top Hat, White Tie and Tails.") Neither Anne Caldwell nor B. G. De Sylva, Kern's lyricists at the time, would have thought of the lyrics. And, indeed, the song is Berlin's. But what is one to make of "They Call It Dancing," from the first *Music Box Revue* in 1921, which, again Berlin's, sounds like Kern *imitating* Berlin?

After 1920, the two went separate ways. And here we chart a revolutionary Kern, composer, unlike Berlin, of one story show after another. We want to unearth the seeds of *Show Boat*: the long melodic lines, the hugeness of gesture, the leitmotifs restated and developed for dramatic commentary, the music that draws a popular theatre into elite inventions. We have noted the arresting "musical scene" in *Good Morning, Dearie*—that mixture of underscored dialogue, stray vocal lines, and outright song that will so illuminate *Show Boat*. But none of the shows that followed *Good Morning, Dearie* suggests a deepening of Kern's musical instincts. There are two London collaborations with P. G. Wodehouse, *The Cabaret Girl* (1922) and *The Beauty Prize* (1923), with, back in New York, a Caldwell in between them, *The Bunch and Judy* (1923). They are charming, no more; and *The Stepping Stones*, the aforementioned Fred Stone vehicle of 1923, does not importantly amplify Kern's style, though it has some imaginative choral scenes. Then, in 1924, comes *Sitting Pretty*, the title that Kern-watchers inevitably cite as the Turning Point.

Sitting Pretty started as a project of Sam H. Harris. A Bolton-Wodehouse script with an Irving Berlin score was to be erected around Rosetta and Vivian Duncan, extremely popular vaudeville stars who had appeared on Broadway as a specialty act but had never attempted evening-length characterizations in a book show. Here they would play twin sisters—orphans, in fact, which sounded like box-office dynamite to all concerned.

Unfortunately, Harris and Berlin, tied up with business matters, were held up, and the Duncans took another engagement. Without them, Harris and Berlin withdrew, leaving Bolton and Wodehouse's script as orphaned as the sisters—till Kern read it. Charmed, he wanted to do the show no matter who played the sisters, and Princess manager R. Ray Comstock and his sometimes silent partner Morris Gest offered to produce it. Thus, some four years after *Zip! Goes a Million* died out of town, a last Princess show (albeit one booked into the larger Fulton Theatre) was readied for New York.

A word about the Duncan Sisters. They are a historian's despair, forever backing out of some truly worthy opportunity in order to play it safe in vaudeville, where they were truly beloved by—it was believed—the least discriminating public in the country. The simpering "Was that all right?" that one of them emits at the end of their recording of Kern's "The Bull Frog Patrol" clues us into the Duncan style—cutesy-poo, high-school-variety-night stuff. They were the models for the sister act in *The Broadway Melody* (1929), MGM's stupendously successful first all-talking, all-singing, all-dancing sound film, and they were actually offered the roles. So of course they were unavailable, doing their act in Kankakee, no doubt. Similarly, when *Sitting Pretty* was held up, the Duncans decided to realize a life's dream in playing the title roles in and writing the score to a musical version of *Uncle Tom's Cabin, Topsy and Eva* (1924). Rosetta, in blackface and gravity-defying braids, was Topsy. Critics in Chicago declared it the worst musical alive, but it ran a year there alone. ("A freak of the season," the *Tribune's* Frederick Donaghey called it. "A terrible thing.")

It was a terrible thing that the Duncans failed *Sitting Pretty*, because their charisma would have put the show over; without them, the lead roles proved uncastable, as Harris and Berlin had foreseen. True, the pleasing Queenie Smith played sister Dixie. But sister May was given to an actress who had to be replaced after the New York opening, and the other parts went to nobodies. Consider this: the juvenile, another of Bolton's likable crook characters, was played by Dwight Frye, known to cinema buffs because he played Renfield in Universal's *Dracula* film seven years later. You remember—the guy who goes nuts and eats spiders? This is not superb musical comedy juvenile material.

Sitting Pretty's plot is the usual Princess makeweight—a rich uncle, a disinherited nephew, a twist here and a lunge there, and reinstated nephew gets one sister while reformed crook gets the other. There were the typical Princess touches. The last spoken line is "Gee, Pop! When it comes to raising a family, you're sure *sitting pretty!*" As of old, the two acts each presented a single setting, though by 1924 this was old hat. Both acts were launched by the usual choral number, the first somewhat expository, with solos from four of the principals, and the second mere getting-the-audience-back-into-its-seats filler. There was even the characteristic Princess second-act trio for two men and one woman, "Ladies Are Present" (though this was dropped during tryouts).

However, Kern's music was truly out of some new drawer, particularly the expansive and very heartfelt ballads. Even the "southern hoedown" number, "Shufflin' Sam," enjoys a roomy structure that gives it surprising presence and body. Kern further expanded it by composing the release not as a contrasting melody but as a variation of the main strain, and laid in a touch of minor-key harmony rare in a cheer-up dance. In an era almost rotten with "keep steppin' to cure the blues" numbers, "Shufflin' Sam" is fresh, almost oddball. Orchestrator Robert Russell Bennett was so bemused that he laced it with an unmissable quotation of the spiritual "Goin' Home," adapted from the Largo of Dvořák's *New World* Symphony, thus pulling in both pop and classical allusions at one blow, a lovely touch.

One could go on cataloguing *Sitting Pretty*'s pleasures—the "tone poem" overture, not a medley of would-be hits but a replica of a railway trip based on the second act's hymn to suburban commuting, "The Enchanted Train." Startlingly, it ends, like the show's first act, on an unresolved dissonance on muted strings and harp. Or listen to "On a Desert Island with You," the sisters' one duet, made of wistful interlocking lines as they contemplate leaving a hostile world behind them; or the hero's "There Isn't One Girl (in the world for me)," a heaving lament that somehow finds poetry in loneliness.

The main thing is how far Kern, suddenly, could take himself with an altogether standard libretto. And he clearly knew he had something special, for he forbade the score's rendition "distorted by jazz orchestras," as he put it in a sweeping encyclical. The time had arrived, he said, "for the revival of the tuneful, melodious and mannerly musical play," and he cited by title the kind of plays he meant: Princess shows. *Mannerly,* as if the sweet naiveté of the old days could still the jazz. What Kern wanted were charm shows: but what was happening were *hot* shows, in the *Lady, Be Good!* style.

Sitting Pretty claims a modern, authentic recording, so the curious may investigate this almost time-traveling show, too ancien-régime to go over in 1924. Alas, the following *Dear Sir* later that year is unknown to all but historians. It tells of a couple reminiscent of Beatrice and Benedict who have to deal with their true feelings after he "wins" her as servant-for-a-week in a charity auction. The lyrics were by Howard Dietz (on his first Broadway assignment) and, again, Kern composed a lovely score, though it's hard to believe that the show's three stars, Oscar Shaw, Genevieve Tobin, and Walter Catlett, did it justice. In any case, *Dear Sir* collapsed in two weeks, at least partly because its producer,

Philip Goodman, had a feast-or-famine philosophy. Sure hits he pushed; anything else he closed Saturday night.

Kern's next show was a smash: *Sunny* (1925), another Marilyn Miller vehicle, this time for Charles Dillingham, because Miller was temporarily feuding with Ziegfeld. The score that has come down to us— led by "Who?," "D'ye Love me?," and the bouncy title song—suggests the earlier, unreconstructed Kern. But then, *Sunny* was a highly unreconstructed piece. It came about because Dillingham had Miller under contract, needed a show for her, and asked Kern, Otto Harbach, and Oscar Hammerstein to write one.

Harbach and Hammerstein had logged five shows together by then, but none with Dillingham or Kern. Kern, however, had forged much of his post-Princess career with Dillingham, and we may imagine that he coached the other two in How To Handle the Man.

"What do you have for me?" Dillingham asks them, at an early meeting.

"A circus, an ocean liner, a ladies' gymnasium, and a fox hunt," says Hammerstein, possibly making the whole thing up on the spot.

"And the hunt ball," adds Harbach.

"Excellent," replies Dillingham, visualizing the colorful sets, the girls' gym number in titillating sports togs, the brilliant hunt costumes. "Make sure Marilyn makes her entrance on a circus horse."

"As the crowd hails her," Kern offers, "in the burthen of her title song."

"Oh—you'll have to leave ten minutes for Cliff Edwards to do his specialty at ten o'clock," says Dillingham. "He'll be between club shows and that's the only—yes, and don't bother writing anything for him. He wants to do 'At the Hollywood Jazz Band Ball' and 'Townhouse Lulu.'"

"Fine," says Harbach.

"Interesting," says Hammerstein.

"Always," says Kern.

Sunny's book is every bit as perfunctory as that invented scene suggests. To escape an arranged marriage, Sunny, the queen of the circus, follows an old beau from England to America, is unmasked as a stowaway, and must marry in order to avoid jail time. But old beau is engaged to another! So Sunny marries his best friend . . . and so on. The plot meant so little to what *Sunny* represented as another spectacle glorifying Marilyn Miller that it was resolved one way on Broadway and another way in London.

Nor did Harbach and Hammerstein scruple to arrange their plot twists by bald contrivance. Sunny flees the circus in a clown costume. Okay, that's cute; and Miller looks resplendent in the photographs. But she gets stuck on the ship because she left her zither in a stateroom and the gangplank went up while she was retrieving it. Wait a minute: her *zither?* Then there was that old-time humor that both authors doted on:

> TOM: I don't believe in encouraging stowaways.
> JIM: They don't need encouragement. All they need is a boat and an ocean.

Yet Kern somehow heard enough between the lines to conceive a truly dramatic score—one, even, that strove to delineate a heroine more romantic than Sally, a dreamy waif with a jolly side and no glamor. (Miller, of course, would supply that.) Bits of the old Princess Kern flitted through the minor characters' music. "Two Little Blue Birds" and "Let's Say Good Night Till It's Morning" could have been written twelve years earlier, and "Sunshine" in fact was, to Harry B. Smith's lyrics for a salute to "Juana, by the Rio de la Plata" as "I Can't Forget Your Eyes" in *Oh, I Say!* Moreover, Clifton Webb's hoofer-cum-chorines special, "So's Your Old Man," echoes a dozen other such numbers in Princess-era shows, including *Oh, Boy!*'s "A Packet of Seeds."

But a trio for Sunny and her two main men, Tom and Jim, "It Won't Mean a Thing," gave Kern a chance to use counterpoint to juxtapose the characters' antagonistic yet perforce allied agendas—exactly what counterpoint itself is, together yet apart. Sunny's true love and his unappealing fiancée had a number called "Under the Sky" that exploited Kern's new-found freedom in the long-lined ballad. And, especially, a pair of gorgeous ballads for Sunny and Tom, "To Think That He Remembered Me" and "Dream a Dream," the two melodies carefully wrought to be sung simultaneously in reprise, vivified a love plot that, in the script, falls flat. Perhaps this was why Kern's younger colleagues found him so inspiring: his music didn't just enhance musical comedy. It redeemed musical comedy.

Unfortunately, all four numbers just mentioned were cut before the New York opening, three of them out of kindness to Miller, who ended up with six other numbers and numerous dances and was carrying the show in the first place. Even Ethel Merman lacked the energy to play the Sunny whom Kern had in mind, eight times a week. Was Kern rebelling against the idiotic nature of the subject matter of his show, trying to compose them into reason? Yet, all his life, he professed an overwhelming fondness for the old-school musicals he had enjoyed as a young man in London—tuneful, melodious, and mannerly, as he said, but never reasonable. Reasonable? In a show founded on a star turn, spectacular sets and costumes, and Cliff Edwards's ten o'clock cameo? Not to mention an old story that finds Kern playing his wondrous, characterful, dramatic score for Miller on the eve of rehearsals. When he finishes, all Miller says is, "But Mister Kern, when do I do my tap specialty?"

Whether or not Broadway was ready for it, something was stirring in Kern, and in his disciples as well. True, no one would have sensed the incipient composer of the Great American Opera in the George Gershwin of *Sunny*'s 1925. In that year, Gershwin unveiled yet another orchestral work, the (piano) Concerto in F, and produced three scores for Broadway, *Tell Me More*, "*Tip-Toes*," and *Song of the Flame*. But none of this elaborated on the excitement created by the *Rhapsody in Blue* or *Lady, Be Good!* of the previous year. Indeed, *Tell Me More* is dull music, lifted only by the lively "My Fair Lady" (the show's out-of-town title) and the typical Gershwinesque frolicking spiritual, all syncopation and flatted notes, "Kickin' the Clouds Away." Like *La, La Lucille*, *Tell Me More* was produced by Alfred E. Aarons (again, *not* by his son Alex A. Aarons, Vinton Freedley's partner). This probably explains the distinctly old-fashioned nature of the piece, whose lead comic, Lou Holtz, was the most archaic of the surviving "Dutch" comics. Holtz was in fact not yet thirty at the time, but his ultra-heavy Yiddish accent and outlandish mugging put audiences back into the Weber and Fields era. At 32 performances, *Tell Me More* had the shortest Broadway run of any of Gershwin's shows.

"*Tip-Toes*" (the heroine's nickname) brought Gershwin back to the high-energy Aarons-Freedley style, with more of the hot, driving sound that his reputation was based on: "Sweet and Low Down," "When Do We Dance?," "Nice Baby! (come to Papa!)." Gershwin further established the purity of his ballad style in "Looking For a Boy," a tune that teeters around a "blue" note with a lovely logic, and Ira revealed his satiric bent in "These Charming People" (the title drawn from Michael Arlen's novel of two years earlier), a spoof of hoity-toity attitudes. Ira was greatly to develop this aspect of his art in the political spoofs *Of Thee I Sing* (1931) and *Let 'Em Eat Cake* (1933), but his greatest gift was the transformation of vernacular American English into poetry. He said, "A good lyric should be rhymed conversation," and his best comedy songs are exactly that—two wary kids comparing their pet peeves in "I Don't Think I'll Fall in Love Today" from *Treasure Girl* (1928) or the slicker's courtship of the cowgirl in "Could You Use Me?" from *Girl Crazy* (1930).

Song of the Flame was an oddity for George, an Arthur Hammerstein operetta with a huge cast, spectacular Joseph Urban sets, an over-wrought plot about a woman rabble-rouser in love with a prince during the Russian Revolution . . . and the inevitable Herbert Stothart sharing the composing chores. Harbach and Hammerstein wrote the book and lyrics (this was the sole Gershwin show after *Lady, Be Good!* on which George didn't work with Ira), sometimes collaborating with both Gershwin and Stothart on a single number. "It took four men to write *that?*" asked Cole Porter, hearing the turgidly doleful "Cossack Love Song." In truth, *Song of the Flame* has a strong score, and Gershwin did try out a new voice for it, pseudo-Slavic rather than Manhattan-smart. "Midnight Bells," the heroine's big second-act solo, is a great lyrical anthem of a piece, like nothing Gershwin wrote before or after. Still, little in the show suggests that Gershwin had any affinity for music of real expressive power. What he was perceived to have was expertise in Aarons-Freedley razzle-dazzle.

There was plenty of that in *Oh, Kay!* (1926) and *Funny Face* (1927), which together represent the summit of what a "Gershwin show" meant in the 1920s. All the elements introduced in *Lady, Be Good!* were in place—duo-pianists Phil Ohman and Victor Arden superintending the Gershwin autograph sound in the pit; silly stories as thin as clothesline on which to hang song, dance, and comedy for the maximum decorative effect; first-class Aarons and Freedley productions—not spectacles, but sound, fully fleshed presentations; astonishingly tune-filled, even hit-filled scores, from *Oh, Kay!*'s "Someone to Watch Over Me," "Do, Do Do," "Clap Yo' Hands," "Maybe," and "Fidgety Feet" to *Funny Face's* "S'Wonderful," "My One and Only," "He Loves and She Loves," "The Babbitt and the Bromide," and the title song.

And there were the stars: Gertrude Lawrence and Victor Moore in *Oh, Kay!* and the Astaires plus more Moore in *Funny Face*. Gershwin's 1925 shows were notably poor in performing chemistry. Besides the obsolete Lou Holtz, *Tell Me More* offered Phyllis Cleveland (whose chief credential was getting fired in the title role of *No, No, Nanette* on its tryout the year before) and Alexander Gray (a baritone so wooden that, next to him, Nelson Eddy could be mistaken for Marcel Marceau). *"Tip-Toes"* at least boasted Queenie Smith's heroine and Jeanette MacDonald in a supporting role. But *Song of the Flame* brings us to the odd world of operetta casting, wherein voice is more important than personality. Hero Guy Robertson had his debonair side, to be sure, but the Flame, Tessa Kosta, was strictly a stand-and-deliver talent, stolid and blessed with the biggest voice on Broadway. (Herbert Stothart, conducing the show, loved to bring out the orchestra and swamp the singers. One day, Hammerstein ran backstage to take him to task for an especially Wagnerian Act One. "If I can't hear Kosta," Hammerstein fumed, "I can't hear anyone.")

The twenties musical wasn't about debonair Russian princes or ingenues who get fired in Chicago. It was about the Astaires and Gertrude Lawrence and Victor Moore, those captivating personalities on whom wonderful shows could be mounted. True, these were shows without any real content, which is the reason the entire Aarons-Freedley series constantly underwent changes of title from rehearsals to tryouts to New York. *Oh, Kay!* had been *Mayfair, Miss Mayfair,* and *Cheerio!* at various times. Any snappy title might do because the shows weren't stable, certain, substantial. It was the stars who gave them their character, and when Percy Hammond wrote of Lawrence's singing that she "wrung the withers of even the most hardhearted of those present," he was in effect praising her gifts as playwright: in defining the character that book writers Guy Bolton and P. G. Wodehouse had only hinted at. It was even the featured players who helped center the art—the indispensable Harland Dixon and the luscious Fairbanks Twins in *Oh, Kay!* and the crazed William Kent in *Funny Face* as . . . it doesn't matter. *Oh, Kay!* dealt with Prohibition rum-running and *Funny Face* with Fred Astaire's difficulties in controlling his flapper ward, Adele. But the plot in an Aarons-Freedley show was no more than a menu. Dinner was the talent.

It was, for instance, the way Gertrude Lawrence rendered *Oh, Kay!*'s "Someone To Watch Over Me" to that famous rag doll—George Gershwin's unique contribution to the show, as, some say, he ran out and bought the doll to help Lawrence dramatize the moment. It was a spot that might have occurred in any twenties musical: heroine wishes for hero. But the doll somehow unified Lawrence's wistfully uncertain soprano, gave that wavering voice something to concentrate on—or something for the audience to fix on as a little icon of Lawrence, of Gershwin ballads, of musical comedy heroines. The rest of *Oh, Kay!* gave Lawrence plenty of chances to reveal her aggressive comic style. (She finds herself in competition for the hero's favors with an undeserving heiress, wields a gun, and impersonates a bellicose maid.) But that rag doll and "Someone to Watch Over Me" revealed a vulnerable Lawrence—not Herbert- or Cohan-heroine vulnerable but jazz-vulnerable, a luscious paradox.

Funny Face's heroine, Adele Astaire, had a less rich range but a more pure style. Some preferred her to Marilyn Miller as an all-American sweetheart: Adele didn't need Gershwin balladry or a rag doll to invest her, divine her. Far more Adele's speed was the obligatory "runaround" number with Fred, "The Babbitt and the Bromide," in which they impersonate two leaden souls repeatedly meeting over the years and enthusiastically having nothing—and plenty of it—to say. It's a classic, not least because Fred and Gene Kelly preserved it in MGM's revue *The Ziegfeld Follies*. I find it a grueling misfire of a piece, made entirely of one unfunny joke. But *Funny Face* also gave us "High Hat," Fred's lesson in the art of handling a girl friend, and the very first occasion upon which this natural-born dapper Dan presented his all-dressed-up-and-on-the-town-with-the-men's-chorus number (though they were all in black tie, Fred sporting a buttonhole chrysanthemum, and not the tails that were to become Astaire's uniform).

There was a second Gershwin: Vincent Youmans. I call him that because the two had in common a taste for advanced harmony and rhythmic dexterity that distinguishes them from their coevals. And they were born a day apart in 1898. Also, each began around 1920 as a rehearsal pianist, rose to prominence as composer by the mid-1920s, and lost his career to illness by the mid-1930s (though Gershwin died in 1937 and a retired Youmans held on till 1946).

The trick that unites them most surely is the use of three-note melodic cells, in $\frac{4}{4}$ time, wherein each new measure accents a different pitch in the cell. Youmans did this most classically in the release of *Wildflower*'s title song, but my readers can hear a variation on the trick more easily in the main strain of Gershwin's "Fascinating Rhythm." Youmans also had his own trick of pursuing a melody right through the release, turning the standard AABA structure into AAAA, as in *No, No, Nanette*'s two big hits, "I Want To Be Happy" and "Tea For Two." (Think of "Nobody near us can see us or hear us"—it's the same tune as the first line of the refrain, raised in pitch and with a few more notes and words.)

Youmans never won the notice that Gershwin enjoyed. One reason was Youmans's lack of a regular lyricist partner. People tend to apprehend a *team*—George and Ira, Rodgers and Hart, De Sylva, Brown, and Henderson. Regularity breeds fame. Going show by show from his first, *Two Little Girls in Blue* (1921), we find Youmans leaving Ira Gershwin for Harbach and Hammerstein, moving on to William Carey Duncan and Hammerstein, thence to Zelda Sears, to Irving Caesar and Harbach (for *No, No, Nanette*), to Anne Caldwell, to Clifford Grey and Leo Robin.

That last collaboration, with Herbert Fields writing the book, produced a smash. This was the "nautical musical comedy" *Hit the Deck!* (1927), about the proprietress (Louise Groody) of a sailor's coffee bar who follows her gob boy friend (Charles King) to China to win his love. Why the Navy background? Well, it was a peculiarity of the twenties musical that, because of the relative sameness of the boy-loves-girl plots and the lack of strong character motivation, a novelty setting could give a show an individual tang—in decor, in topics for songs, and so on. Where would *Kid Boots* have been without its Palm Beach country-club background, *Big Boy* without horse racing, *The "Cocoanuts"* without Florida land-grabbing, *Song of the Flame* without Russia? How many legacy-with-a-catch or Cinderella plots could Broadway take? No wonder Charles Dillingham agreed to produce *Sunny* merely *after hearing where it was going to take place.*

One notices this exploitation of setting later in the decade especially, when authors got around a patent lack of story interest with such colorful matter as Texmex banditry (*Rio Rita,* 1927), a settlers-versus-Indians Arizona range war (Sigmund Romberg's *The Love Call,* 1927), old New Orleans (Romberg's *The New Moon,* 1928), boxing (*Hold Everything!,* 1928), Cardinal Richelieu's France (*The Red Robe,* 1928), more country-club golfing (*Follow Thru,* 1929), old Venice (*Fioretta,* 1929 with Leon Errol and Fanny Brice as old Venetians), and the Great War (*Sons O'Guns,* 1929).

Hit the Deck! is as guilty as any of these, and Youmans is no innocent, for he not only composed but produced it. (Coproduced, actually, with Lew Fields; but Youmans bought Fields out just after the New York opening.) Probably thanks more to Fields than to Youmans, *Hit the Deck!* was a sound piece of late-1920s showmanship on a modest scale. (It was one of the very few musicals to play the Belasco Theatre, which seats a thousand but offers very little stage or wing space.) There were no stars, the chorus count was much closer to the Princess size than to what Ziegfeld, Dillingham, or Arthur Hammerstein routinely employed, and the three sets in each of two acts was by 1927 considered on the stingy side. A just barely coherent script threaded the songs into the action whether they belonged there or not. "Sometimes I'm Happy" did and "Hallelujah" didn't, but no matter, for the pair* made *Hit the Deck!*'s fortune. And Youmans, Grey, and Robin did trouble to bring the

* Historians make much of the fact that both numbers were old work reclaimed, "Happy" from an out-of-town casualty, *A Night Out* (1925), and "Hallelujah" from Youmans's Navy stint during World War One. This reuse of old tunes as crucial to a show's success is somehow supposed to be quirky. However, songwriters of the 1920s habitually looted the trunk for material in the often headlong pace of composition and tryout tinkering. Youmans was second only to Jerome Kern in the replaying of old music, even music that had been heard in successful shows.

Navy into the music, in "Join the Navy," "Shore Leave" (the name of the play, by Hubert Osborne, on which *Hit the Deck!* was based), and even in a ballad, the metaphorical "The Harbor of My Heart."

All told, this may suggest an Aarons-Freedley show, the quick, brash, and freaky musical comedy that has everything but a story—except that Aarons and Freedley would have been unlikely to have cast Groody and King to carry a show. As Looloo Martin and "Bilge" Smith, the two were seasoned players; the thirty-year-old Groody was making her last musical comedy appearance, and King was shortly to help kick off the film musical in MGM's *The Broadway Melody*. There students can inspect King's style: more energy than talent, an overpowering New York accent, and a pudgy, long-in-the-tooth look. (He was in fact thirty-eight.) Nor would Aarons and Freedley have failed to fill the supporting cast with experts in the eccentric specialties that kept the audience tickled while the headliners were resting. In short, *Hit the Deck!*, for all its success (duplicated in London with Stanley Holloway in King's role), was more an also-ran than a champion, perhaps even a waste of Youmans's talents.

If Kern and Berlin marked the start of the new music some time before the 1920s, and if Gershwin and Youmans signaled the arrival of younger voices eager to develop the new style, still others arrived in their wake yet outstayed them by a wide margin. Richard Rodgers, of all these giants the last to continue as a working Broadway composer, presented his last show, *I Remember Mama*, forty-two years after Gershwin's death.

One other thing about Rodgers: he was the only major Third-Age composer who spent an entire generation working with a single lyricist, Lorenz Hart. As with the wandering Youmans, the names of Kern's and Romberg's collaborators would fill a paragraph; Rudolf Friml counted twelve lyricists on his twenty shows; and George Gershwin claimed a goodly number of partners before settling down with Ira (and even then slotted in Harbach and Hammerstein on *Song of the Flame*, teamed briefly with Howard Dietz on *Oh, Kay!* while Ira was in the hospital, worked equally with Gus Kahn and Ira on *Show Girl*, and let DuBose Heyward assist Ira on *Porgy and Bess*).

But "Rodgers and Hart" seemed so immutable, prolific, and unique that it was probably their work more than any Aeolian Hall manifestation that announced the arrival of a native art. The pair were comparable to what "Kern, Bolton, and Wodehouse" had signified in the late 1910s. Indeed, Rodgers and Hart had a house librettist in Herbert Fields, who wrote the book to six of their ten story shows staged on Broadway from 1925 to 1929.

The late 1920s could have been named after Rodgers and Hart; they never turned out fewer than two shows a year and, in 1926, came up with five, including one in London, *Lido Lady*. Oddly, their first professional credit dated back a full five years, to *Poor Little Ritz Girl* (1920). This strangely troubled piece, about a chorus girl who inadvertently rents an apartment occupied by a young bachelor, suffered one of the most remarkable tryouts in Broadway history. It opened in Boston (as the first attraction of the Wilbur Theatre) with a book by Henry B. Stillman and William J. O'Neil and the Rodgers and Hart score, with Victor Morley and Aileen Poe in the leads. Seven weeks later, in Stamford, Connecticut, Gertrude Vanderbilt was in the lead, and producer Lew Fields was commissioning some rewriting. After a week in Atlantic City, *Poor Little Ritz Girl* came in with Charles Purcell and Eleanor Griffith in the leads (Aileen Poe was still in the show, in a different role), with a book by George Campbell and Lew Fields and with a score by Sigmund Romberg and Alex Gerber *and* Rodgers and Hart (with one lyric, to Rodgers's music, by Herbert Fields, Lew's son). As Rodgers later put it, "Fields simply obeyed the ancient show-biz dictum that is still all too often followed today: If something is wrong, change *everything!*"

Rodgers was eighteen and Hart twenty-five, and if the surviving *Ritz Girl* songs seem a little raw, one nevertheless sees their style emerging, in Hart's slyly Freudian lyric to "You Can't Fool Your Dreams" or Rodgers's zestfully syncopated and artfully harmonized verse (just for fun, it jumps from D Major to the extremely foreign G Flat Major) to "Love's Intense in Tents." A kind of tryout for "Mountain Greenery," this last number also offers a Hart fairly bursting with wicked jest:

> My lady, pay your rent
> With love to your grand lord.
> I've a lease from Cupid, the landlord!

Oddly, Rodgers and Hart were virtually out of work for the next four years—this in a Broadway swelling with young talent and new ideas! It was the flash success of *The Garrick Gaieties* that saved the partnership in 1925. As so often with utterly unheralded shows, it dazzled critics wary of reputations and pretentiousness. The *Gaieties,* a semi-amateur benefit revue for the Theatre Guild put on by Guild underlings with an eleven-piece orchestra, had the air of a college entertainment. But "Manhattan" utterly proclaimed Rodgers and Hart. It was the cleverest lyric since Wodehouse's "Cleopatterer" in 1917, and Rodgers's sunbeam of a melody simply had not been heard before.

Three months after the *Gaieties* opened, the first Rodgers-Hart-Fields show, *Dearest Enemy* (1925), found the team on Broadway in a thoroughly professional staging. Better, the spotty *Gaieties* score had given way to a honeycomb of songs. "A baby-grand opera," Percy Hammond called it; also "a deluxe kindergarten." Burns Mantle found it "mannerly, melodious, sane and charming." E. W. Osborn praised it for lacking "even a touch of that heard-that-before feeling," and Arthur Hornblow thought it "very akin to a genuine comic opera."

Fresh. Tuneful. Enchanting. Perhaps the critics were disarmed because Rodgers' craftsmanship, Hart's twinkle, and Fields's earthy, even smutty attitude were serving a period piece. *Dearest Enemy* is set during the American Revolution, when colonial women loyal to the Cause detain English soldiers while Our Boys strategically regroup. The show had the air of a comedy of contemporary manners burlesquing a comedy of bygone manners, as when the aged General Tryon (Detmar Poppen) sings "Old Enough To Love" in defense of the seasoned campaigner ("Methusaleh could choose a *la petite* of twenty-two") or when he and Mrs. Robert Murray (Flavia Arcaro) make a flirtation out of "(What do all) The Hermits (do in springtime?)," complete with a Gilbert and Sullivanesque patter section and climaxing on "They can't hold a tree as you're holding me."

Dearest Enemy enjoyed a handsome production, partly because John Murray Anderson supervised it, bringing in his *Greenwich Village Follies* designers, Reginald Marsh and James Reynolds, but also because the star, Helen Ford, was sleeping with the producer—her husband, George Ford. Helen, who passed into legend by making her first entrance wearing only a barrel (she'd lost her clothes while swimming nude in the river), got in on the show's major ballads, "Here in My Arms," "Bye and Bye," and "Here's a Kiss," all duets with Charles Purcell as the English captain she loves. But her solo with the women's chorus, "I'd Like To Hide It," shows us the richness of Hart's view of love in all its ambiguities and discontents. Critics celebrate how, much later, Rodgers and Oscar Hammerstein avoided a straight-out love song by skewing the angle of approach, in "People Will Say We're in Love," "If I Loved You," or "We Kiss in a Shadow." But here's Hart already tapping an odd vein: that of a young woman as much alarmed as invigorated by her first romantic stirrings.

Dearest Enemy was a hit, and the very next Rodgers-Hart-Fields entry, *The Girl Friend* (1926), ran even longer. But *The Girl Friend* shows what can go wrong in its creators' particular format. *Dearest Enemy*'s strength was a good story, *Romeo and Juliet* with a wartime background. *The Girl Friend*'s strength was headliners, the married couple Sammy White and Eva Puck. *The Girl Friend* had no story. It had one of those

novelty backgrounds: the craze for six-day bicycle racing. White wants
to race, and Puck helps him do so. That's the plot. The score was fine,
featuring the title song and "Blue Room," both for the stars, along with
a comic waltz for Puck, "The Damsel Who Done All the Dirt," another
review of historical figures in modern terms. (Pharaoh made the He-
brews "pay the price" because he couldn't "make a date with Fanny
Brice.")

The Girl Friend seemed such an evocative twenties title to Sandy Wilson that, as I've said, he used it to certify *his* twenties musical, *The Boy
Friend*, in the 1950s. But it was only the original show's two hit songs
that had survived. *The Girl Friend* itself was by then long forgotten. In
fact, when it was first brought over to England, in 1927, the feckless
Herbert Fields script was simply junked. The producers substituted a
new book, based on one written for a musical called *Kitty's Kisses*, which
had opened on Broadway two months after *The Girl Friend*. The *Kitty's
Kisses* songs, by Con Conrad and Gus Kahn, were combined with those
of *The Girl Friend*. Bizarrely, a regional English tour of this pastiche in
the late 1980s (with yet another book, still based on *Kitty's Kisses*) advertised it as "Rodgers and Hart's *The Girl Friend*."

"Not even a furtive breath of jazz" was critic Frank Vreeland's comment on *Dearest Enemy*, and he meant it as a compliment. But "I Need
Some Cooling Off" is a cry raised in Rodgers and Hart's Bea Lillie vehicle, *She's My Baby* (1928). The song is prefabricated jazz, impervioius
to mauling by dance bands because it was *composed* mauled, a berserk
Charleston with a highly ambivalent message, for the more Hart begs
for respite, the more Rodgers jives. This, of course, was their unique
quality: Hart's anxieties enriching Rodgers's lyricism, Rodgers's merry
melody redeeming Hart's despair. Hart is a philosopher and Rodgers a
poet, yet both are ironists—that's where they meet. Let Rodgers compose a sprightly love tune, and Hart will fit something a little nervous
to it, as in "If I Were You," dropped during *She's My Baby*'s tryouts but
reinstated after the New York opening, for Irene Dunne and Jack Whiting. Another dropped number, "Morning Is Midnight," enjoys the seam-
less logic of a melody by Schubert but bears a lyric almost Schopen-
haurischly metaphysical.

But Rodgers and Hart could plunge into a comedy lyric with relish.
They'd have to, in a Bea Lillie show. "Whoopsie" catches her ability to
ridicule anything, even a positive attitude toward life, unfortunately in
a really rather awful number that must have taxed Lillie's powers.
"When I Go On the Stage," however, gave all three of them something
to work with: a no-talent scheming to become famous. Hart names the

great and near-great—Marilyn Miller, Marion Talley, Mae West, Ernestine Schumann-Heink, Gatti-Casazza, Irene Bordoni, Amelita Galli-Curci, producer Dillingham himself, and *Hit the Deck!*'s Charles King and Louise Groody (who'll "look like Punch and Judy"). This spendthrift cataloguing of celebrities, unheard of before the mid-1920s, was like a verbal jazz, improvisations by youngsters eager to blow their elders away. Hart used it best. Ira Gershwin thought it a little vulgar; his idea of celebrity was Heinrich Heine. Cole Porter was a thoroughly committed adherent, though he adulterated the mix by citing also his frou-frou society friends. Who was the Duke of Verdura, anyway?

Rodgers, at this time, was making his name as a founding member of Third-Age composition more consistently than any of his predecessors, including Kern. Both were supreme melodists, but Rodgers was also an astonishing harmonist. Let one example suffice. In *Spring Is Here* (1929), there is a torchy ballad sung by two sisters (Inez Courtney and Lillian Taiz), "Why Can't I?" Rodgers's tune is simple, even repetitive. But his harmonic structure is so dense that the chord breakdowns printed in the sheet music were beyond anything seen in pop music before, with a $B\flat\,{}^{7}_{-9}$ here and an $f\,{}^{7}_{-5}$ there. One chord, $\frac{b\flat 7}{E\flat}$, was so beyond the day's ken that it was marked without the bass, as if the editor had simply given up.

For his part, the mid- and late-1920s Hart would have to be called the most advanced lyricist since P. G. Wodehouse in his Princess prime. Cole Porter was his only rival, but Porter didn't really get going till the very end of the 1920s; and Ira Gershwin, stylistically somewhat close to Hart, never truly challenged Hart's brilliance, especially in exploring how closely one's self-esteem depends on one's success in love. One thinks of many famous titles—"Little Girl Blue," "It Never Entered My Mind," "Nobody's Heart," say. These are more than torch songs; the singer keens for confidence lost when romance rebuffs him or her. But an obscure number written for an unproduced project during Rodgers and Hart's Hollywood sojourn in the early 1930s recalls to us the true distinctiveness of Hart's worldview. "Tell Me I Know How To Love," the singer pleads, admitting to a poor self-image that love with someone admirable can improve. "Tell me I know how to love," the singer concludes, "and I'll know."

Ira develops forms; Hart creates them, as in *Heads Up!* (1929), an Aarons-and-Freedley Coast Guard-versus-rumrunners show. The inventions simply tumble over themselves: "Sky City," a tribute to New York in terms of its soaring architecture; "(I behave) As Though You Were There" (these two dropped during tryouts); "Knees," on the chorus girl's anatomy, laid out as a spoof of Rudyard Kipling's "Boots"; "Ongsay and

Anceday," in Pig Latin; the opening chorus, "You've Got To Surrender,"
which starts with an hommage to the opening chorus of Gilbert and Sullivan's *Patience;* "Mother Grows Younger," a battle among naval cadets
on the dance floor. And *Heads Up!*'s big ballad, the properly nautical "A
Ship Without a Sail," was the first torch song not only to pose but to
build on a metaphor—and, what's more, it went to the *man* in the case,
Jack Whiting. Despite the beauty of the refrain, the climax hits at the
second lead-in *verse*, where "You tell your grief to no girls" is despair-
ingly rhymed with "Your smile is like a show girl's."

Cole Porter is the odd man in this largely New York-centered, Jewish
group that took over the musical in the 1920s. Born to a rich midwest-
ern WASP family—Oscar Hammerstein's maternal grandfather made
milk punches and sketched; Porter's maternal grandfather thundered
and signed vast checks—and educated at Yale, Porter spent much of his
early adulthood sampling la dolce vita in Europe. When George Gershwin, Richard Rodgers, and Vincent Youmans were inhaling Princess music, Porter was throwing elaborate parties in the Venetian palazzo where
Robert Browning died. To say that Porter was sophisticated is putting it
mildly, but it does recall to us a time in American culture when there
were still taboos and secrets, when only a few people knew everything;
and Porter was one of those people. He was America's court jester, the
wit almost offically licensed to affront, seduce, deride. His work as a
whole could be viewed as a loving mockery of love and marriage among
the rich, unveiling with a wicked relish the hypocrisy behind the conventions. But he had a broad reach, and for all his classical study could
turn out the biggest song hits of the time. "Let's Do It (Let's Fall in
Love)," to give its full title, only swept the country. "Night and Day"
swept the world. It is no accident that, among the arrived masters, the
one who most encouraged Porter was that absolute populist Irving Berlin.

Porter had more trouble establishing himself than even Rodgers and
Hart. He had actually seen an early work, *See America First,* fold inside
of two weeks on Broadway in 1916. He wrote the scores to two *Hitchy
Koo*s and to the 1924 *Greenwich Village Follies,* though during the New
York run his songs were pulled one by one till the post-Broadway tour
lacked even the number that became Porter's first hit in Porter style,
"I'm in Love Again," possibly the jazziest number heard on a New York
stage in the entire decade* and a reminder that any Great Man Theo-

---

* Porter's first hit in *any* style, "An Old-Fashioned Garden," from the first *Hitchy
Koo,* is a bland trifle. "I'm in Love Again," like a number of Porter songs ("Begin the
Beguine" is the outstanding example) that took years to catch on, became a hit only
in 1927, when a number of recordings popularized it.

ry in American pop music obscures how much all the individuals had in common. "I'm in Love Again" is Gershwin in harmony but Porter in beat and melody, its chromatic line sleazy in its slithering glee. And even Gershwin, king of jazz, never challenged Porter's obsessively deceptive rhythmic sense, his pounding syncopations (especially in the climax of a release or in the last phrase of a chorus), his triplets kaleidoscopically dancing over a $\frac{4}{4}$ bass line, his constant flirtations with minor-key harmony. "I'll write Jewish tunes," Porter blithely told Rodgers at this time, meaning, There's something in this city music that all of us can use.

Porter also stood out for the intensely erotic nature of his lyrics. Think of it—that dear little Princess series was not ten years gone when Porter entitled a song "Let's *Do* It," meaning just what you thought he meant. And, unlike his sole gay colleague, Lorenz Hart, Porter frequently tossed out an Allusion To It right in front of everybody. He used the term "queen" in its nonroyal sense in "My Cozy Little Corner of the Ritz" in *Hitchy Koo 1919*; and while Noël Coward introduced the word "gay" in its sexual sense in the "Green Carnation" number in *Bitter Sweet* in July of 1929, Porter had already beaten him to it, using "lavender" (at the time a more common code word for "homosexual') in "The Gigolo" in *Wake Up and Dream*, which like *Bitter Sweet* premiered in London—in March of 1929.

Even the general outline and tone of Porter's shows were different from those of his colleagues. Aarons and Freedley had brought smarts to the musical—not just a know-it-all savvy, for that dates back at least to Cohan a generation before. No, twenties smarts were racy, worldly, appetitive. Adult. Rodgers and Hart fit right into this style, and Herbert Fields developed it in his books, edging the musical ever closer to what we might call "padlock art." For, remember, this was a decade in which censors turned tyrant on Broadway. It is notable that, around 1930, when Fields began to desert Rodgers and Hart, it was Cole Porter he left them for.

True, Porter's shows couldn't subvert all the conventions. He always dealt strictly in Boy meets Girl (or at least Lilo). It was not the centers of Porter's shows that challenged the standard cautions as it was the edges—*double entendres* in comedy songs, a chance line from a supporting character, as the demi-monde chuckled and others had something to wonder about. Sophisticated: hidden, shadowed, but beckoning. At bottom, the difference between Hart, the cleverest of Third-Age lyricists, and Porter, the funniest, is that Hart saw the love plot in the shows as something worthy, almost attainable, while Porter didn't see love at all. He saw tricking, marriage, prostitution, cheating, manipu-

lating, and whoring. He could never have written a lyric like that to
"With a Song in My Heart," from Rodgers and Hart's *Spring Is Here*
(1990): too pure. The odd fact is that, for all Hart's jesting and all
Porter's lyricism, Hart was a romantic and Porter a satirist.

We should note as well that Porter, alone among his colleagues, invented a major Third-Age musical genre, the "list song." "Let's Do It,"
he urges, citing as by-references the mating rituals of the animal kingdom. A year later, "Where Would You Get Your Coat" is even more dan-
gerous. This title is from Porter's "musical comedy tour of Paris" and his
first all-out book-musical smash hit, *Fifty Million Frenchmen* (1929).
Herbert Fields wrote the book, a now wry, now low-comic spoof of
American tourists abroad. Norman Bel Geddes's sets and James
Reynolds's costumes filled the eye in views of the Ritz bar, the American Express office, Longchamps racetrack, the Château Madrid, the
bookstalls along the Seine, and so on. But it was Fields and Porter who
supplied the atmosphere, Fields in a varied group of tourists—collegiate
Peter Forbes and his chums; the loud mid-American Carrolls, he crying,
"I'll buy it!" at every passing momenent and she hot to marry off her
daughter to European nobility; the daughter (and Peter's love interest),
Looloo; her pal Joyce, to sing snappy duets with one of Peter's cohorts;
the Rosens, a Jewish couple with an atrocious little boy; Violet Hildegarde, a spinster eager to sample that outrageous Gallic sensuality. (Violet gives the bookstall scene its *raison d'être* by trying to buy a copy of
the forbidden *Ulysses*.) The plot was a late-twenties twist on the old legacy-with-a-catch premise: the *wager* with a catch. Peter bets one of his
friends fifty thousand dollars that he can win Looloo without the Forbes
fortune. He must give up his letter of credit, subsist on his wits, and
court Looloo with nothing but his charm.

Fields manages to concentrate on the Peter-Looloo romance while
keeping the supplementary characters in play. Clearly, he had thrown
off the relative delicacy of his *Dearest Enemy* script:

> MRS. DE VERE: Do you know my little daughter May?
> PETER: I didn't, but thanks for the tip.*

Or try this throwaway line, as Peter shows Looloo the Café de la Paix:

> PETER: It was at one of these very tables that Charlotte Corday
> planned to kill Marat in his bath. She waited for months, but
> he finally took one, and she bumped him off.

---

* This became one of the most repeated couplets in musical comedy history. It
was still in use—and still getting laughs—in the 1985 revival of *Me and My Girl*.

It was, however, the score that singled out *Fifty Million Frenchmen*. All Porter's earlier scores had been spotty, with good things here and there but no through-line of excellence. Here, Porter reached consistency. It was also while writing this show that he initiated his habit of trying to improve himself, continually refilling a given song spot with yet another number, now of the same type but better, then of an entirely different type. Certain Porter scores—*Kiss Me, Kate* (1948) and *Can-Can* (1953) especially—are virtually two shows' worth of songs, as for instance Porter begins to find *Can-Can*'s second-act torch spot, "Who Said Gay Paree?," a little underpowered, decides to drop the torch component and compose something more positive, and comes in one day with "I Love Paris."

Fifty Million Frenchmen is one of those scores. At the New York opening, it had fifteen numbers, but at least eleven others, rejected before or during rehearsals or during the Boston tryout, have survived. These include "I Worship You," one of Porter's best ballads, and surely a candidate for the hit parade till it was replaced by the snappier "You Do Something To Me," the show's sole standard. Among the also-rans we should mention "Find Me a Primitive Man," Porter's salute to rough trade but couched in historical terms; the other list song, "You've Got That Thing"; and the heartbroken "You Don't Know Paree," distinguished by a stabbing major seventh discord in the first phrase of the main strain.

The forgotten titles, too, give us information about Porter's style. "The Happy Heaven of Harlem," a jiving specialty spot for a black jockey called Boule de Neige ("Snowball"), reminds us of Porter's awareness of the black subculture. There's a wonderful musical scene, "Do You Want To See Paris?," in which Peter plays guide to a group of Americans whose utterly insulated worldview makes Paris no more European than a Disneyland. Travel, to them, isn't broadening; on the contrary, it brings out the smallness in them. Yet it's a dashing number, neither cynical nor sarcastic: descriptive.

Among the dropped numbers, "That's Why I Love You" is a swinging duet that needs revival for its offbeat premise: I like you because your bad qualities are even worse in your rivals. An omitted ballet, "Snake in the Grass," involving a boy, a girl, and a snake charmer, recalls the Porter of *Within the Quota*. Better known today than some of the numbers that actually were heard in the show throughout its run is "The Tale of the Oyster." After queasy critics gagged, it was dropped, but it's a fine society-spoofing parable: an oyster rises on the social scale by being chosen to feed a Name, is thrown up during a rough yacht ride, and ends up philosophically wiser. In all this, Porter is wry, yes, but, more important, he is the voice of the age, the year, the minute. Does he typify Broadway's more adult attitude, or is he creating it? Imagine, in the time of *Sally*, a situation like the one outlined in "I'm Unlucky at Gambling": the girl takes a suspiciously unaggressive date to a John Gilbert movie, asks if he likes Gilbert, and discovers that he likes Gilbert all too well—definitively, in fact.

That Porter, Distingué. Risqué. But were there Broadway performers who could embody the attitudes Porter wrote about? *Paris* (1928), Porter's first Broadway hit, starred Irene Bordoni. You don't get more risqué than that. But *Fifty Million*'s Peter was William Gaxton, a restless, overweight clunker in a role that called for a late-twenties Howard McGillin. Oddly, Gaxton threaded his way through the Third-Age musical on nerve more than entitlement, and no one, apparently, objected. The rest of the show's cast were and remained unknown, except for Helen Broderick as Violet Hildegarde. Here was sound casting, for Broderick was one of the creators of this type: slightly older, slightly caustic, and slightly sex-starved. She runs around in *Fifty Million* begging to be insulted—where are all those Parisian bottom pinchers? When Peter, working as a guide, takes her on a tour of châteaux country, she learns that Mrs. Rosen had quite a different afternoon:

> MRS. ROSEN: We went to such a . . . innocent-looking place on the outside, but on the inside was a woman with nothing but . . . (*whispers in Miss Hildegarde's ear*) and six others came in and . . . (*whispers again*)
> MISS HILDEGARDE: (*turning to Peter in disgust*) You and your damn châteaux!

In a way, a Cole Porter musical was about the Broderick character, for his sympathy lay not with the Boy Meets Girl but with the smart yet alienated commentator who Knows What the World Is: Porter himself.

Kern, Berlin, the Gershwins, Rodgers and Hart, and Porter all worked well beyond the 1920s, but Bert Kalmar and Harry Ruby's Broadway career ended in 1929 (with an insignificant comeback in 1941), six years after it had started. Kalmar and Ruby have turned up in these pages already; the reader probably hasn't noticed them. Nobody did in the 1920s, either. Ruby, the composer, quite admired and was influenced by George Gershwin. One day, exasperated by Gershwin's infantile arrogance about his own talent, Ruby stopped speaking to him. When

Gershwin caught up with Ruby sometime later and asked for an explanation, Ruby reminded Gershwin that he had said, right to Ruby's face, that the two of them were not in the same class as composers.

"Why are you angry?" asked the baffled Gershwin. "It's true."

It was. Ruby and his lyricist partner Kalmar led the second rank, where we encounter such names as Harry Tierney and Joseph McCarthy, Harry Archer and Harlan Thompson, Lewis Gensler and his many lyricists, J. Fred Coots and Clifford Grey, James F. Hanley and Eddie Dowling, Dave Stamper and Gene Buck; to proceed would raise controversy over where the third rank begins.

To be fair, Kalmar and Ruby were no hacks. But they never quite discovered a unique style. Worse yet, the general public was confused by their versatility. Sometimes they wrote the score, sometimes they also wrote the book, and once they wrote *only* the book (to Rodgers and Hart's *She's My Baby*). Then, too, they tended to get lost in projects primarily associated with more imposing names—a Dillingham musical for a host of hot young talents (including Ruby Keeler), with some numbers by Jerome Kern and featuring the Paul Whiteman Orchestra: *Lucky* (1927); or a Marx Brothers musical, *Animal Crackers* (1928), the last place anyone would notice a score. Nor did Kalmar and Ruby once happen into one of those twenties titles whose resonance lingers long after the show itself is gone, a *Vagabond King* or *Good News!*

Yet the two logged plenty of song hits and had the honor of an MGM bio, *Three Little Words* (1950), with Fred Astaire as Kalmar and Red Skelton as Ruby. One of their shows was even revived on Broadway in recent years, *The 5 O'Clock Girl* (1927), and as this was not only their best but also their most typical show, here we shall pause.

The 5 O'Clock Girl was a "cinch" show, the kind that virtually writes itself, because Guy Bolton and Fred Thompson have an unusual brew (winsome laundry clerk calls society scion every day at five; love results), which the authors can fill out with the usual gargle (someone's pearls are stolen, of course; did Bolton ever write a script in which someone's pearls *weren't* stolen?), and meanwhile Kalmar and Ruby will find a way to fill it all out with . . . well, the same, only not different. The grand ballad is "Thinking of You," the rhythm ballad is "Up in the Clouds," and the cute ballad is "Who Did—You Did!" The vaudeville comic duo of Al Shaw and Sam Lee will get "We Want You," "Following in Father's Footsteps," and "Society Ladder," suiting their nobody-gets-out-of-here-alive comic style. There will be plenty of dancing, especially in the second half of Act Two, when a shortage of plot twists demands specialties by Shaw and Lee, juvenile Danny Dare, soubrette Pert Kelton, and title-role ingenue Mary Eaton. (The society beau, Oscar Shaw, doesn't dance.)

Kalmar and Ruby did their work well. The whole thing sings, with a certain sense of invention. "Up in the Clouds" begins its verse in the submediant minor, resolving in the second measure; the chorus, too, moves from the submediant seventh through an array of harmonies before hitting the tonic at the seventh measure. This is harmonic structure worthy of Gershwin. It should be noted, too, that lyricist Kalmar seems to strike a balance between Ira Gershwin and Lorenz Hart, borrowing the one's vernacular ease and the other's surprising wit. Even better is the socialite's accusing "*You* did!," followed by the heroine's challenging "*Who* did?" in their cute ballad. Kalmar and Ruby were the men who tried to rhyme "para*dise*" with "California *skies*" in *The Ramblers*, but *The 5 O'Clock Girl* found them in top form, virtually first rank—and, despite all the choreography, they actually avoided the New Dance Sensation, settling for a nonvocal spot, "Tea Time Tap."

It's interesting to read first-night reviews from this time, even those from the last years of the decade, for one sees not the slightest acknowledgment that, musically, the American theatre had launched an era. Reviewers would discuss a new Rodgers and Hart or Gershwin score in terms of what Rodgers and Hart or the Gershwins had already presented. But no critic saw the musical undergoing a decisive stage of development—as, for instance, Gilbert Seldes saw in American culture generally in his book *The Seven Lively Arts*, of our epochal year of 1924, when Paul Whiteman's Aeolian Hall night revealed the jazz culture.

Yet the information that something was tearing apart the Old and building up the New was everywhere available. One didn't have to go out, even. Sixty million dollars' worth of radios were sold in 1922, but that figure more than doubled in 1923 and more than doubled again in 1924, with a steady rise through the decade to nearly 850 millions' worth sold in 1929. And radio was jazz. Or: Jazz was radio. Jazz was Al Jolson and Al Capone. Jazz was what Europeans heard in the very word "America." Jazz was money. Jazz was black people. Jazz was crossword puzzles, F. Scott Fitzgerald, Lorelei Lee, "Peaches" and Daddy Browning, Charles Lindbergh. Jazz was sex. Jazz was even music. In fact, jazz was De Sylva, Brown, and Henderson.

The era's only major three-man songwriting unit, G. B. "Buddy" De Sylva, Lew Brown, and Ray Henderson were, as I've said, another essential piece of the decade that dissolved at decade's end. But then, how long could anyone keep up being the Voice of the Day? Porter managed it by subtly changing his style every few years, retaining some things (such as the list song), developing some things (such as the musical scene, which makes a few of his shows seem like operettas), and introducing some things (such as the Latin rhythm number, a feature of his music from the mid-1930s on). But De Sylva, Brown, and Henderson were very consistent collaborators. Their songs so reflect one another that virtually any given number could be fitted into any given show.

What most set them apart was, one, their absorption of the pop trends and catchphrases of the time, and, two, their use of the Broadway pit as a kind of nonstop jazz band that played everything in dance time. Not only operetta but much of musical comedy still counted on a certain rhythmic freedom and expressive hesitations. When Kern, Rodgers, or Gershwin wrote a love song, it was a love song. When De Sylva, Brown, and Henderson wrote a love song, it was a fox trot. Just their song titles alone constitute a retrospective of twenties gags, notions, and places: "Flaming Youth," "The Birth of the Blues," "Broadway," "Red Hot Chicago," "(Kiss me, dear) What D'ya Say?," "Baby! What?," "You're the Cream in My Coffee," even the self-descriptive "American Tune."

We last saw this trio presenting Broadway with what everyone agreed was the best revue score ever, in *The Scandals of 1926*, but thereafter they preferred book shows: *Good News!* (1927), the backstager *Manhattan Mary* (1927), the 1928 *Scandals, Hold Everything!* (1928), *Follow Thru* (1929), and *Flying High* (1930). All were hits—and note the emphasis on sport, which gave the shows the feeling of a series. *Good News!* was football, *Hold Everything!* boxing, *Follow Thru* golf, and *Flying High* aviation. (Okay, it's almost a sport.) To De Sylva, Brown, and Henderson, timing was all. Radio had whetted the public appetite for athletics in general, but *Hold Everything!* might have been conceived in direct response to the infamous "long count" boxing match between Jack Dempsey and Gene Tunney of the year before, and *Flying High* was virtually a Charles Lindbergh spoof, with Bert Lahr as a flyer so incompetent that he breaks records because he can't land the plane.

Like all of Broadway's major songwriters, the trio tried Hollywood in the first days of the film musical, and De Sylva liked it so much that he broke up the partnership to become a movie producer. Brown and Henderson returned to Broadway to do the 1931 *Scandals* by themselves, but there was still a strong feeling of __ _____, Brown, and Henderson about the score, a *twenties* feeling. This was a show heavy with stars (and Joseph Urban designed it), with Rudy Vallee, Ethel Merman, opera baritone Everett Marshall, Ray Bolger, Willie and Eugene Howard, and, in the chorus, Alice Faye. The authors gave them choice opportunities. Vallee had a made-to-order number in "This Is the Missus," a bouncy salute in which each phrase of the main strain gets a pushbeat kickoff, and he joined Merman on the heartfelt "My Song," though his throwaway style must have come off as bland next to Merman's Klaxon. She sang "Life Is Just a Bowl of Cherries"—a De Sylva title if there ever was one—and also got a copy of a Cole Porter list song in "(Ladies and gentlemen) That's Love." Like "Let's Do It" and "Where Would You Get Your Coat," "That's Love" looks to the animal world for romantic inspiration, as when a bull tells a cow, "Eventually? Why not now?"* Everett Marshall was saddled with the evening's outstanding curiosity, a blackface number called "That's Why Darkies Were Born" that made an operatic hymn out of the usual unfreed freedman's lament ("Someone had to pick the cotton . . ."). But were the authors exposing oppression, simply signing on to an established (and oppressive) genre, or knocking off "Ol' Man River"?

Let's consider the De Sylva, Brown, and Henderson style in *Good News!*, their most lasting title and also one that sheds light on modern practice in the reviving of twenties shows. *Good News!* was produced by Laurence Schwab and Frank Mandel, another very twenties concern, and another odd blend of jobs. Kalmar and Ruby wrote songs but also wrote books; Schwab and Mandel wrote books for *and* produced anything from the hippest musical comedies to the vainest operettas. Schwab, but not Mandel, wrote *Good News!*'s book, with De Sylva, and it's a sound one, keeping the love plot sensible while emphasizing comedy.

The college atmosphere was vividly presented. The ushers at the Forty-Sixth Street Theatre wore football jerseys, and George Olsen's band launched the overture with a college cheer: for Tait, pinning its hopes against rival Colton on team captain Tom Marlowe (John Price Jones). After the usual humdrum opening chorus ("Students are we of dear old Tait College," it begins) and coed Zelma O'Neal's apostrophe to the Big Man on Campus, "He's a Ladies Man," the students punch into one of the tightest expositions in Broadway history:

> WINDY: Say, Slats! Got a couple of extra tickets for the game?
> SLATS: Extra tickets for the big game of the season! The *coach* is
>   going to have trouble getting in.

* In the oil strikes of the very early 1920s, boom towns could grow from a population of 100 to a thousand times that within a year. One such was Louann, Arkansas, which celebrated its transient germination on a sign posted on a road leading into town: "Eventually? WHY NOT NOW? Louann—The Town of No Regrets!" The first four words became a twenties joke, another instance of how this team lapped up the very sounds of the day in its art. No wonder they split up in 1930.

Exactly three lines later, Babe O'Day (Inez Courtney) enters to provide a twist:

> BABE: Say, kids, have you heard the news?
> ALL: What news?
> BABE: Our dear teacher, Professor Charles Kenyon, has flunked
>   Tom Marlowe in Astronomy.

A flunked football hero is a benched football hero. But Tom's fiancée (Shirley Vernon) has a wallflower cousin (Mary Lawlor) who can coach Tom for his makeup exam. Tom and the wallflower fall in love. He passes the exam. (Actually, the supposedly mean-spirited Astronomy prof promotes Tom to a passing grade out of school spirit.) But now Tom has to marry his fiancée if he wins the game.

Never mind: it ends well. What matters is *Good News!*'s structure, the way it balances the elements of musical comedy. Operetta often had a problem with comedy; musical comedy often had a problem with romance. So many love plots are perfunctory, with an unmotivated "quarrel" for intermission suspense and an out-of-nowhere resolution. *Good News!*'s triangle is plausibly created, touchingly developed, and arrestingly concluded: the fiancée proves too smart to marry an unwilling man and releases him to the wallflower.

The comedy is top, though a lot of it comes in self-contained sketches, almost as if in a revue—lead comic Bobby (Gus Shy) buys car at eighteenth hand and stands by dithering as bully takes it apart piece by piece. ("My God, it runs!" he cries, as it careers offstage for his exit and the last big laugh.) Girl invades boy's dorm room, hides under beds and behind screen as various characters enter and exit. The same now naive-seeming girl is drawn into dice game and cleans the boys out. The energy level was high throughout: when Olsen and his boys were brought *into* the show as the college band; when the heroine's view of the big game through a knothole in a fence was opened up as a kind of "view through an enlarged knothole" drop came down to show us the winning touchdown, the actors running on a treadmill; when the first act ended without a full-scale finaletto, helping to pave the way for the retiring of this antiquated convention.

Still, what we remember is how the girl who has never had anything hits it off with a Universal Dream Man. This is what *Good News!* is about—not the collegiates dancing the "Varsity Drag" (the lyrics merely speak of "down on the heels, up on the toes," but the central gesture, popular at the time, was the banging of the two open palms against one knee), not the sorority sisters going into sentimental close harmony in

"The Girl of the Pi Beta Phi," not the boys cheering their own side of things in "Happy Days." Nor is *Good News!* about the comics' numbers, Babe's "(Aren't I just the type that needs a) Flaming Youth" or her duets with Bobby. "Baby!" he sings out. *"What?"* she answers. It's a cute idea, though their other duet, "In the Meantime," is the standard putdown challenge number typical of the secondary couple's second-act spot. No, *Good News!* is about Connie and Tom, wallflower and superhero, about her reverie over him, "Just Imagine," and their duets, "The Best Things in Life Are Free" and "Lucky in Love."

Maybe it was the persuasive idyll of a line such as "The moon belongs to everyone." Maybe the spell that operetta cast over the decade was trapping musical comedy. *Good News!'s* tremendous success spiraled outward. The London production did so-so business, but MGM filmed the show in 1930. The score was savaged, but the original Connie and Bobby and that "Varsity Drag" step gave it authenticity. Samuel French's Music Library picked the title up for stock and amateur use, and *Good News!* first tied with and then outperformed *The Gingham Girl* as the single most popular musical property among American high school drama clubs. Two generations were raised on it, keeping that imposing score—five hits, more than the Gershwins, Rodgers and Hart, or Cole Porter could manage then—fresh and festive.

MGM remade *Good News!* in 1947 as a Freed Unit special for Peter Lawford, June Allyson, and Joan McCracken. Again, much of the score was missing, but the big five songs were alive and well. Strangely, the show was never performed on stage professionally, at least not prominently. It was another of those famous titles, classic but not well known. At last, Harry Rigby and Terry Allen Kramer produced a revival in 1974, built around Alice Faye and John Payne, she as the re-engendered Astronomy professor and he as the coach. Abe Burrows wholly reconstructed the script, not well, and the score was cut back, losing all the comics' numbers to be flooded with De Sylva, Brown, and Henderson tunes from a variety of sources: "Button Up Your Overcoat" (from *Follow Thru*) and "Never Swat a Fly" (from the 1930 film *Just Imagine*) for the comics; the pop tune "Together" and "I Want To Be Bad" (also from *Follow Thru*) for Faye's solos; "You're the Cream in My Coffee" (from *Hold Everything!*) for Faye and Payne, as if they were back at Twentieth Century-Fox; "Sunny Side Up" (from the film of that title) for Stubby Kaye, as the team's trainer, and another intrusion for Faye, backed by the girls, "Life Is Just a Bowl of Cherries."

With so many interpolations, and with the book so finagled, this wasn't *Good News!* any more: so why revive it? A personable young cast of students and Hugh Martin's imaginative vocal arrangements gave the production some individuality—Martin's version of "The Best Things in Life Are Free," yet another spot for Faye and the girls, added new music and lyrics to the original and transformed it from the lovers' bonding piece to a veteran's "I'm Still Here" anthem. Yet the song never sounded better. But the critics, tired of revivals of old musicals with yesteryear headliners—*No, No, Nanette*'s Ruby Keeler, Patsy Kelly, and Busby Berkeley had arrived in 1971, and Debbie Reynolds and Kelly brought *Irene* back in 1973—tore this *Good News!* apart.

Truth to tell, it lacked *Nanette*'s spark. But it was much better than the overproduced, charmless *Irene*, a study in how to revive a show so unfaithfully that one isn't reviving but rather creating a new piece out of an old title, an old plot, and miscellaneous old songs. It was the worst sort of pastiche: decadent, pointless, its big numbers evil grins of cynical show-shop commercialism.

The revivals kept coming, often with hit-parade anthologies of the composer and lyricist rather than with integral scores. Goodspeed Opera House's 1980 staging of Kalmar and Ruby's *The 5 O'Clock Girl* reached Broadway the following year as something between a book show and a Kalmar and Ruby sing-off. Fewer than half the numbers performed belonged to the show, which swelled unnaturally with all-purpose hit tunes and lost the character and situation numbers that even a cheesy musical of 1927 would have striven for.

Granted, most twenties musicals were not rational. But they did have personality. *The 5 O'Clock Girl*'s character depended a great deal upon Mary Eaton's heavy singing duties—she was in nine numbers—and on the contributions of those vaudeville madcaps Al Shaw and Sam Lee. Goodspeed dropped the men's roles entirely and gentled the heroine down to today's idea of a "normal" singing lead for Lisby Larson: so it wasn't *The 5 O'Clock Girl* that we were seeing but a sensible, well-proportioned piece bearing *The 5 O'Clock Girl*'s title. Once again, why revive the show if you don't like it? Why turn a sweetly bizarre work into something unimportantly reasonable? Because then the entire show collapses—what's reasonable about a laundry clerk calling a society boy every afternoon at five?

Listen: twenties musicals weren't created to soothe a post-*Oklahoma!* public's worries about Fantastical Goings On in the musical. Twenties musicals are *supposed to be fantastical*. That was their charm. To be fair, this Goodspeed staging, directed by Sue Lawless and choreographed by Dan Siretta, was a pleasing package. As the laundry owner, Madame Irene, Goodspeed's Hildegarde was replaced on Broadway by Sheila

Smith, Larson played opposite *No, No, Nanette*'s Roger Rathburn, fifties ingenue Pat Stanley paired off with Ted Pugh (as Rathburn's valet) as the indispensable second couple, and Timothy Wallace enacted the heavy with a marvelous solo on the electric saw on one of the interpolations, "My Sunny Tennessee." "All Alone Monday" dropped in from *The Ramblers*, no less than two New Dance Sensations turned up, and yet another dance number slipped in from the Ruby Keeler bomb *Lucky*, "Dancing the Devil Away." Lawless's overall approach was sound: don't camp it, but enjoy the silliness. Fine—and why not enjoy the infinite silliness of the original show, while you're at it, instead of turning it into a piece of dislocated history? In any case, the show, so slim and pretty up at Goodspeed, failed to hold the stage in New York.

The 5 O'Clock Girl was a one-off, even an aberration. But *Good News!* is about to make a comeback, unfortunately in a version similar to that of the 1974 revival. There are minute textual differences: "Happy Days" is gone but that ghastly opening chorus is back; "On the Campus," dropped on the road in 1974, has been reinstated; "Just Imagine" has been moved to Act Two, turned from a "wish" number into a torch song; and, as if in trade, the "Varsity Drag" has been put back into its 1927 slot as an energizer two-thirds of the way through Act One rather than showing up as the finale, de rigueur after the MGM remake climaxes with the "Drag" as the Big Prom Number. Still, this is basically the 1974 revival: and that's not *Good News!*. Besides six of the 1974 interpolations, we get another *Follow Thru* number, "My Lucky Star," along with some new transitional music and lyrics. It's a confusion of sounds, an overkill of pop tunes that don't fit the story.

True, the two original duets for the comic couple aren't as hot as their replacements. But "Together," that lugubrious piece of fake nostalgia? "Life Is Just a Bowl of Cherries"? "Sunny Side Up"? "You're the Cream in My Coffee"? Is this the De Sylva, Brown, and Henderson radio hour? Why is it that the most successful by far of all these twenties revivals, *No, No, Nanette*, came into New York without a *single interpolation*?* Fiddling with the music isn't just historically fraudulent; it overtaxes the simple twenties stories with a Top Forty profile. The jazz gets murky, even fat, which it never was in the 1920s. Keep it gay, keep it *light*.

---

* *Nanette* opened in Boston with one new song, by Charles Gaynor, as an identifying number for Ruby Keeler and Hiram Sherman (replaced by Jack Gilford), "Only a Moment Ago." It was dropped just before the New York opening—so late in the day that it was recorded for Columbia's cast album (but deleted before release).

Let's Merge

THE NEW SOCIAL ATTITUDES

In 1920, Nora Bayes recorded a comic speciality, "The Argentines, the Portuguese and the Greeks," on the latest wave of immigrants to America. The verse fills in the historical background:

> Columbus discovered America in 1492.
> Then came the English and the Dutch,
> The Frenchman and the Jew.
> Then came the Swede and the Irishman,
> Who helped the country grow.
> Still they keep a-coming,
> And now everywhere you go . . .

As the chorus swings in, Bayes brings the listener up to date:

> There's the Argentines, and the Portuguese,
> The Armenians, and the Greeks.
> One sells you papers,
> One shines your shoes,
> Another shaves the whiskers off your cheeks . . .

Strangely, these menial jobs have given the newcomers great power as consumers. In stanza after stanza, Bayes reports on how these strangers are filling the best hotels, buying the hottest cars, and getting choice girlfriends. Bayes concludes on an ironic note:

And the funny thing, when we start to sing
"My Country 'Tis of Thee":
None of us knows the words but
The Argentines, and the Portuguese and the Greeks!

It was a comic spin on what, to some, was an urgent matter: an invasion of foreigners more "foreign" than those of the nineteenth century. It was common to speak of a "yellow peril," numerous pseudoscien-
tists agitated over theories of genetic superiority, and polyglot New York
City first earned its status as the place that Americans love to hate. Sentiment against continued immigration by certain less respected groups
became so popular that Congress repeatedly passed laws requiring that
immigrants pass a literacy test, apparently with the confidence that
Swedes would and Greeks wouldn't. Presidents Taft and Wilson both ve-
toed these laws, in 1913 and 1915, but by 1917 the legislative branch
was so determined that it overrode Wilson's second veto, and national
quotas for entry into the United States were established in 1921, 1924,
and 1927, to keep American culture "American."

By then, it was too late. The offspring of recent immigrants, adults
themselves by 1920, had already begun to influence American culture,
and nowhere more so than in the theatre. This opening up of the dramatis personae was possible partly because the threatregoing public was
changing its ethnic makeup and was hungry for self-affirmation, but also
because the theatre-making community was similarly changing and was
thus particularly sensitive on the matter of social tolerance. In the musical, the first two decades of the twentieth century were largely dominated by Jewish producers, and the two outstanding composers, Victor
Herbert and George M. Cohan, were Irish by birth or descent. Yet the
musical's characters were all *Little Johnny Jones, The Girl from Dixie,* or
Prince Danilo of Neverland.

By 1915, however, *mitteleuropäisch* Rudolf Friml and Sigmund
Romberg, Danish Otto Harbach, Jerome Kern, and Irving Berlin had begun their takeover. Adding in the newcomers of the 1920s—the Gershwins, Cole Porter, Rodgers and Hart, Oscar Hammerstein, Schwab and
Mandel, Aarons and Freedley, De Sylva, Brown, and Henderson, Vincent Youmans, and Kalmar and Ruby—the WASPs (Porter, Freedley, and
Henderson) are the minority group, and "their" people are slowly starting to be replaced by a more representative ethnic mix. For instance, it
must have occurred to Rodgers and Hart that writing about the doings
of people assumed to be WASPs in a setting so often New York was to
finagle reality. True, *Dearest Enemy* was set in *colonial* New York, where
virtually everyone *was* a WASP, or Dutch. But Rodgers and Hart's *Bet-*

sy (1926) was set wholly in the Jewish subculture of contemporary New York's Lower East Side.

This would happen more and more, making for example, the insistently WASP identity of *Zip! Goes a Million* seem almost militant, with its Montgomery Brewster of a hero, its "little sons of the rich" Archibald Vanderpool, Joseph MacCloud, Frank Bragdon, and Nopper Harrison, its Captain Perry and Miss Boynton and Margaret Gray and Janice Armstrong, and its tiny relaxation of the gene pool for Trixie Schmidt.* Such muscular Christianity only underlined the outdated air of this Princess show. Hints that there was more going on than a Sunny Peters here or a Blair Farquar there were widespread a few years later, so that even the resolutely Protestant *No, No, Nanette* included a mention of the imaginary private detective agency of Murphy and Isaacs. Giving the Irish and the Jews the sleazy business was a joke folding in on itself, for the truly sleazy business was American racial prejudice, and *No, No, Nanette's* authors knew it.

Truth to tell, the pop music industry had been striking this note, however opportunistically, since the turn of the century, most notably in the so-termed "coon song," not so much a genre as a collection of genres— the "Wish I Was in Dixie" number, the "Cakewalk" number, the "Courtship" (of Mandy, Liza, Miss Jackson of Mobile) number, the "Trouble with the Law" number, the "Mooching Relatives" number, and so on. These songs were ubiquitous; even Victor Herbert composed a few. Unfortunately, constant manipulation of clichés gave these pieces no contact with black culture. The odd bit of honest work would break through, as in the heartrending "Stay in Your Own Backyard," Lyn Udall and Karl Kennett's picture of a black woman trying to console her little boy, lonely because white kids won't play with him. Bert Williams's specialities, too, outwitted typing for the larger humanistic view, as in his signature tune, "Nobody," the lament of the man everyone takes advantage of, or simply ignores.

Even the worst of this file did at least remind the listener that the proper subject of American art was all of America. We see this especially in the first decade of Irving Berlin's career, when "Sweet Italian Love" shared honors with "When Johnson's Quartette Harmonize" (the sheet music cover made the four unmistakably black for anyone who missed the meaning of the code name "Johnson") and with "Cohen Owes Me Ninety-Seven Dollars," the tirade of a dying businessman. Berlin's use of cliché was basic—Italians are romantic, blacks are musical, Jews are

---

* Trixie Clayton in the *Brewster's Millions* script.

practical. But it is worth remarking that, as the 1920s gradually began to drop the clichés and treat minorities individualistically, Berlin himself stopped contributing to the catalogue. The reality proved more interesting than the cliché.

It was the performers, however, who most advanced the cause of integrating the musical. Yes, Ziegfeld fired off the first big gun when he brought Bert Williams into the *Follies* in 1910 and retained Williams for seven further editions, daring public censure. Black performers were not absolutely unknown to the musical, but appearances in white-based musicals would involve a specialty act brought on for a single scene. For a prominent manager like Ziegfeld to feature Williams in a prominent exhibit like the *Follies* was bold, all the more so when we consider that in 1919, when Williams made his last *Follies* appearance, headlined with Eddie Cantor, Marilyn Miller, Eddie Dowling, and Van and Schenk, mixed-race plays were routinely given by all-white casts with actors in blackface. Black characters were acceptable; black performers were not.

Ziegfeld also hired Jewish performers—Nora Bayes, Sophie Tucker,* Fanny Brice, Eddie Cantor, Al Shean, Ed Wynn, Belle Baker, Jack Pearl. It was as if Ziegfeld only wanted WASPs for his heroines and showgirls. They gave his shows sex; the comics gave them class. It was the performers, in fact, who kept reminding the public who they really were, sitting across the footlights, in Brice's patently Yiddish diction and true-to-life characters like Rose of Washington Square (who "Got no future, but oy! what a past!") or Second Hand Rose ("from Second Avenue"). Cantor habitually pumped Jewish gags into his scripts, and Al Jolson seemed to delight in getting off references so arcane that many Jewish people missed them.

One might wonder if all this was simply artistic freedom or the development of a political agenda. Given the stranglehold that both the big and the little sons of the rich had on American culture at the time, it all seems wonderfully subversive, like the casually shocking assaults on mainline morality that dilate all over today's television sitcom *The Simpsons*. Because the Jewish comics were in their early prime in the

---

* Now it can be told: Bayes was so alarmed at Tucker's rapport with the audience in the 1909 *Follies* that she made Ziegfeld demote Tucker to little more than a cameo. Twenty-nine years later, Tucker had Mary Martin's second-act coloratura showpiece cut out of the Cole Porter show *Leave It To Me*. A tearful Martin appealed to Tucker. Sophie said only that one day, Martin would understand. Martin understood so well that, twenty-five years after that, Martin had the promising Imelda de Martin's role in *Jennie* hashed to bits. Perhaps somewhere, somehow, Imelda de Martin is making life interesting for some nervy soubrette even as we speak.

late 1920s, they were eagerly absorbed by Hollywood in its talkie phase. Accent, inside jokes, and all, they went in. Yet what did America in general make of this? In an early sound short, vaudeville singer Harry Rose delivers "Frankfurter Sandwiches," a lively complaint about his courting of a woman with an insatiable appetite for hot dogs. "Even on Yom Kippur," Rose confides at last, "quietly I had to slip her," and he closes with "*frank*furter sandwiches, *frank*furter sandwiches, all night long!" Who knew what Yom Kippur was? Did audiences shrug it off? Ask a friend? Become worldly? Tolerant?

The integration of black performers came more slowly, for Jewish entertainers tended to establish themselves first and then open the Book of Revelation, as when Dora Goldberg played as Nora Bayes and Sonia Kalish as Sophie Tucker, both favoring the same sorts of song other singer favored and only gradually personalizing their acts. But black was black at first sight. At the turn of the century, there was a mild interest in all-black shows, such as *A Trip To Coontown* (1898) and the far more successful *In Dahomey* (1903), a sensation on its London tour. But *Mr. Lode of Koal* (1909) was Broadway's last musical of the cycle, and it got in only because of the popularity of its star, Bert Williams, in his first solo outing after the death of his partner, George Walker.

Ironically, the 1910s saw a tremendous upsurge in black migration from the south to the north, especially to major theatre capitals like New York and Chicago. There were many reasons for this—the revival of the Ku Klux Klan, the active recruiting of workers by northern industries, the usual social upheaval of wartime, the mid-decade drought and a boll weevil invasion the following year, and possibly even the cinema's disclosure, to southern blacks, of a relatively tolerant north. Certainly, by the 1920s Harlem in particular had become at once seething black ghetto and fastidious cultural center. It may have been one thing to the partying writer Carl Van Vechten, the bordello devotée Cole Porter, and the Cotton Club's all-white patrons and quite another thing to poets Countee Cullen and Langston Hughes, N.A.A.C.P. chief Walter White, and bandleader Fletcher Henderson. But the 1920s, the time of the so-called "Harlem Renaissance," was bound to have an impact on everyone, and most immediately on Broadway, where, suddenly, white playwrights tackled black subjects. Eugene O'Neill's *All God's Chillun Got Wings* (1924), an analysis of how a white woman's racism wrecks her marriage to a black man, was so brutally honest that the authorities made desperate but unsuccessful attempts to prevent its opening. They did at least destroy the beautiful symmetry of the play's frame, an opening scene of children of both races blissfully playing together paralleled by a devastating finale in which the insane wife regresses as her husband cries, "Honey, Honey, I'll play right up to the Gates of Heaven with you!" (The child actors were forbidden to appear, lest they be corrupted by O'Neill's poetry.)

Meanwhile, the black folk play was invented, most notably in Paul Green's *In Abraham's Bosom* (1926), DuBose and Dorothy Heyward's *Porgy* (1927), from Heyward's novel, and Marc Connelly's *The Green Pastures* (1930), a retelling of Bible stories through the eyes of black Sunday School children. The folk play used as raw material not just the tales but the language and folkways of its characters. Even a cynical sensationalist like David Belasco could get into the act, with his production of Edward Sheldon and Charles MacArthur's *Lulu Belle* (1925), on the life and death of a Harlem prostitute. The Green, Heyward, and Connelly plays were produced with black actors in the black roles (Connelly's cast was all-black), but Belasco used a black company headed by white leads in blackface. Still, Belasco had a long-standing reputation as one of the theatre's great realists, and he made up for his old-fashioned casting by building his staging around a spectacularly detailed Harlem street scene, complete with automobile.

The musical was bound to take up this trendy phenomenon, first by employing black specialty acts in otherwise white shows. An early Oscar Hammerstein title, *Queen O' Hearts* (1922), starred Nora Bayes as, to quote one of the characters, "the greatest matrimonial agent in the world." Somewhere in the plot was a black maid (Eva Taylor) and a black window cleaner, Alabama (Georgie Brown). The window man was good for a fast dance solo, with plenty of that swaggering quirkiness that audiences looked for in this territory. Remember, twenties musicals expected the choreographer to plot only the ensemble dancing: individual performers generally worked out their own routines. Thus, Brown's solo would have made a refreshing novelty, entirely in his personal style. In another part of the forest, the maid was good for the installation of social irony:

> GEORGIA: Ah don't know none o' dese new dances. I just learnt 'em from mah grandmother—and she danced like de ol' folks years ago over in Africa.
> ELIZABETH (BAYES): Why, Georgia, at the Ritz, at the Vanderbilt— all over New York—the biggest swells are dancing like your grandmother used to dance in Africa.

Later, just before Bayes's eleven o'clock spot, Brown and Taylor were given a duet, "My Highbrow Fling," which was really the reason they were in the show: not to give verisimilitude to servant roles but to make black music.

Black music—singing, dancing, and instrumental style—had become the vogue just the year before with the flash success of *Shuffle Along* (1921). A book show, this piece marked the union, really, of two very separate creative teams, the actors and writers Flournoy Miller and Aubrey Lyles on one hand and the songwriters Eubie Blake and Noble Sissle on the other. Miller and Lyles expanded their vaudeville sketch "The Mayor of Dixie" into a look at a mayoral campaign in Jimtown, a place of fantasy that nevertheless reflects the ways and wisdoms of black subcultural life. Two crooked pols vie for the top office, only to be defeated by honest Harry Walton—but the plot was no more than an excuse for an evening of black attitudes, jokes, and concerns. "I'm Just Wild About Harry," both a ballad and a campaign song, is the one title that became a standard (so much so that Jerome Kern had it quoted in the dance music of *Show Boat*'s final scene to help anchor that show's epic chronology). Still, such tunes as "Bandana Days," "The Baltimore Buzz," "I'm Craving For That Kind of Love," and "If You've Never Been Vamped by a Brownskin" gave whites a new taste in music, more of that jazz yet perhaps a purer jazz—right from the source, some would say. Then, too, the dancing was of that zesty new (to whites) style.

Shuffle Along ran for 504 performances, at that in the out-of-the-way Sixty-Third Street Music Hall just west of Central Park and in a slap-dash staging on an Irish-boiled-dinner budget. By choice or necessity, all four authors performed, Miller and Lyles as the two corrupt chiefs, Sissle in a supporting role, and Blake at the keyboard in the pit. (That was some pit; later choir master Hall Johnson played viola and classical composer William Grant Still blew oboe.)

Wednesday night midnight shows gave *Shuffle Along* extra cachet, because so many theatre people attended that the late Wednesdays became sellouts to a glamour-hungry bourgeoisie. It became The Thing to see *Shuffle Along*; but the rage didn't stop there. The next year, 1922, saw *Strut Miss Lizzie* and white producer Lew Leslie's *Plantation Revue*, both variety shows; and *Liza*, a second saga of life in Jimtown, this one by Maceo Pinkard and Irvin C. Miller. And 1923 brought *How Come?*, "a girly musical darkomedy," and *Runnin' Wild*, with Miller and Lyles back in Jimtown in their old roles, this time with a score by Cecil Mack and James P. Johnson. These two gave the public its money's worth in "Charleston," introduced by Elizabeth Welsh (later Welch) and probably the greatest New Dance Sensation in American history, king of the dance floor long after the Tickle-Toe, the Monkey Doodle-Doo, and even the Varsity Drag were retired.

One cliché about the all-black shows needs reinstructing—that they were mostly revues and therefore somehow not "equal to" book shows. First, this was after all an age passionately fond of revues; second, the black shows were *not* mostly revues. To 1923, we have had four book shows and two revues. Granted, some of the black book shows had, as Burns Mantle said of *Liza*, "just enough of a story to interrupt the specialities." Nonetheless, 1924 saw in Blake and Sissle's *The Chocolate Dandies* a book show and in Lew Leslie's *Dixie To Broadway* a revue (famed as the last New York appearance of Florence Mills, who died at the age of thirty-two); 1925 gave us *Lucky Sambo*, a book show; 1926 offered *My Magnolia*, a revue, and *Deep River*, a book show, this one written by whites, as we'll soon see; and 1927, just before the vogue climaxed, presented *Bottomland*, a book show, and two revues, *Africana* and *Rang Tang*.

So the score is about even between shows with scripts and shows that were a modern minstrelsy. Not that it matters, in the end, because it wasn't clear to black writers what form their stories would be allowed to take—that is, what the critics were expecting in a form that was, in effect, so new that nobody knew what the form *was* yet. Some critics complained when black book shows imitated white shows; other critics didn't get it when black shows forged a new path.

Another cliché tells us that all-black shows had to content themselves with unattractive bookings off the Broadway main line. But *Shuffle Along*'s success broke the color bar. The next year, *Liza* also had to pitch its tent in the West Sixties, but *Strut Miss Lizzie* played the Times Square Theatre, and the *Plantation Revue* played the Forty-Eighth Street Theatre, both worthy if not top-drawer houses. And note that *How Come?* opened at the Apollo, George White's favorite theatre, that *Dixie To Broadway* held the Broadhurst, *My Magnolia* the Mansfield (now the Brooks Atkinson), and *Deep River* the Imperial. Some shows had to make do with the Colonial, another north-of-Columbus-Circle house (most recently named the Harkness, where Robert Morse pulled the geographical meaning of the term "Broadway" about ten blocks north for *So Long, 174th Street* [1976]). And poor *Bottomland* could find no better booking than the Princess, by then a disused little nowhere of a place that was about to become a movie house. But, in all, *Shuffle Along*'s commercial success led theatre owners to value the potential of the all-black show.

How Harlem felt about these productions is not well documented. Some of the "talented tenth" (culturally speaking, the upper 10 percent of Harlem residents) may have resented the stereotypical humor—the "ghost scares a darkey" scene as old as the minstrel show, the characteristic twosome of slick con man and brainless dupe that, for instance, Miller and Lyles played from show to show as Steve Jenkins and Sam Peck. But outsiders saw beyond the temporal. Interviewing the avant-garde Austrian director Max Reinhardt, academic Alain Locke and sociologist Charles Spurgeon Johnson were horrified when Reinhardt praised *Shuffle Along* and *Runnin' Wild*. All *they* saw was incorrect messages about the Race. What *Reinhardt* saw was a new theatre form coming into being, talents of a new kind being discovered—the evolution that keeps theatre vital.

Had Reinhardt been in New York just a little later, he might have seen *Deep River*, "a native opera with jazz" and probably the most inventive of all the black musicals. As I've said, whites wrote and produced it, but it could not have been conceived without the black shows' having first created the very notion of black shows. Even so, *Deep River* marked a complete break with the style that *Shuffle Along* and its successors had popularized. A play with music, *Deep River* showed a disdain for the joyous song and dance that had stamped the black musical from the start. Here was a serious show, steeped in history and folklore. Its producer, Arthur Hopkins, was not only one of Broadway's most prestigious managers but entirely associated with nonmusical productions and thus not conversant with trendy styles. Why need he be, when the show was a tragedy of gallantry and race relations set among the Creole aristocracy of old New Orleans? And let us note that the company was wholly integrated, whites playing whites and (mostly) blacks playing blacks—unheard of for a musical of 1926.

With book and lyrics by the straight-play author Laurence Stallings (coauthor with Maxwell Anderson of *What Price Glory?*) and music by Frank Harling (later known as W. Franke Harling) and a physical production by Robert Edmond Jones, *Deep River* was, if nothing else, ambitious. And it *was* something else: a melodrama so constantly broken into by music that it might have been an operetta. But the music was more for atmosphere than for plot or character. Soloists and chorus would, as it were, harmonize "under" the action, letting the play unfold almost on its own, like a Greek tragedy in which the chorus does most of the singing, with a very occasional solo or duet for leading characters.

Stallings worked in a heavy dialect. The first spoken line reads thus:

OCTAVIE: Dat young M'sieu Tourney will be de one for you to catch, Sara, tonight at dis quadroon ball.

The action, set in 1835, centers on the ball, where the evil old Brusard will take control of lovely young Mugette. But Brusard shoots a white man, the Kentucky colonel Streatfield, in a duel. Before dying, Streatfield extracts an oath from his handsome and very young brother, Hazzard, to avenge Streatfield's any-minute-now death by stealing Mugette from Brusard "before all N'yawleans." Streatfield weakens. "Then . . . kill . . . the bastard . . . For he's killed me." Streatfield falls dead. Curtain.

The amazing second act is entirely concerned with a voodoo ceremony that had audiences chattering through the intermission like wind-up toys. The third act goes back to the revenge plot. Hazzard loves Mugette but, of course, cannot even dream of marrying a black woman. He eradicates the awful Brusard in a duel, then leaves Mugette to unite with the poor young black man who truly loves her. Violence, chivalry, folkways, history, spiritual, opera: here's another of our lost twenties classics, not least because of the unique nature of the score. No other musical of the decade sounds like this one, Stallings's simple lyrics striving for the poetry of folk songs and Harling's music using simple melodies but dramatically tense harmony. Hazzard's "Serenade Creole" has the rich tango flavor of a piano solo by Louis Moreau Gottschalk, and his two duets with Mugette, "Love Lasts a Day" and "Two Little Stars (peep through your eyes)," both build from the basic to the soaring with a power that at once suggests yet overwhelms the tenor-soprano duets of costume operetta. All the odder that Harling never composed another show, though he did write two musicals for Paramount, giving Jeanette Mac-Donald "Beyond the Blue Horizon."

Reading *Deep River*'s script today is a strange experience, because Stallings went into arresting detail in his stage directions, almost as if *Deep River* were an excuse for his autobiography. About the great difference in age between Streatfield and his younger brother, Stallings wrote this into *Deep River*'s text:

As every woman of the South at that time died at the age of thirty-five at the birth of the tenth child (half of the brood died in infancy) it is quite commonplace that [Hazzard] should be the half brother of a man twenty years his senior. I know that my Grandfather had three stalwart sons killed in the Civil War, when my father was one year old.

The critics loved *Deep River* for the most part, but, as sometimes happened then, they were ahead of their readers, who thought this dire Creole love song a doubtful prospect in a season that offered *Criss Cross, Oh, Kay!, The Desert Song, Hit the Deck!, Peggy-Ann, Rio Rita, Queen High* (now forgotten, along with its once ubiquitous hit tune, "Cross Your Heart," but a smash in its day), Kálmán's *Countess Maritza, The Ramblers, Honeymoon Lane* (another George M. Cohan run-off by coauthor and star Eddie Dowling), along with annuals from Ziegfeld (not the *Follies*, nominally: a row with Abe Erlanger, the original producer of the first *Follies*, left Ziegfeld legally enjoined from using his title for the time being; he called this edition *Ziegfeld's American Revue*), George White, and Earl Carroll, not to mention the holdover hits *Sunny, The Vagabond King, No, No Nanette, Dearest Enemy*, "*Tip-Toes*," and *The "Cocoanuts"*.

So *Deep River* didn't run. As early as in New Haven during the tryout, producer Arthur Hopkins could see that the show was In Trouble. The worst of it was that the baritone Jules Bledsoe—soon to sing "Ol' Man River" in *Show Boat*—was far more a singer than an actor and could not seem to accommodate theatre technique. On Tuesday Bledsoe would enter stage right; on Wednesday he'd enter stage left; on Thursday he'd crash through a wall. He also had a fear of acting and would deliver all his numbers straight front, avoiding his colleagues' eyes. Through every performance, Hopkins would grunt, curse, and groan. One night, a woman in front of Hopkins suggested that he give his neighbors some peace and go to the box office and get his money back.

"Madame," cried Hopkins, "if only I *could!*"

Two years after *Deep River* came the high point of the black musical cycle (for this, too, was a distinctly twenties thing, tapering off into nothing in the early 1930s), Lew Leslie's *Blackbirds of 1928*. Here, for once, was a white-made black revue, one steeped, all the same, in the black style. The white-made *Deep River* was bizarre from the start, but *Blackbirds* fell right into the line pioneered by *Shuffle Along* and *Runnin' Wild*: Jimtown throws a party. The white Leslie's earlier black shows had been black-authored affairs, but for *Blackbirds* Leslie hired a youngish white songwriting team that had been contributing to Cotton Club shows, composer Jimmy McHugh and lyricist Dorothy Fields (daughter of Lew and sister of Herbert and Joseph and the François Villon, remember?, of Rodgers and Hart's school-show *Vagabond King*). Leslie also hired the brilliant Kiviette for the costumes, though the deliberately plain scenery, little more than backing curtains, was hired off the rack. Who wrote the sketches and choreographed the show is unknown: Leslie gave no such credits in the program. (He himself directed.)

It was as if Leslie wanted to boil the whole concept of a black musical down to its essentials: the music and the performers (a full hundred of them, or so Leslie claimed). Leslie had made the discovery and presentation of black talent his career since his *Plantation Revue* in 1922— another odd case of the minorities advancing each other's cause, for Leslie was Jewish. He had first mounted a *Blackbirds* in London, in 1926. (The year 1927 saw a Leslie *Whitebirds*.) All the while, Leslie was assembling a black cast to top all such—singer and dancer Florence Mills, singer and dancer Bill Robinson, singer Adelaide Hall, and comic Tim Moore. With Mills's unexpected death, Leslie promoted Aida Ward and opened his first of several Broadway *Blackbirds* shows to mixed reviews but immediate public interest.

One aid was, again, the midnight show; another was the high quality of the *Blackbirds* score, an apotheosis of the black revue song types— the hot jive number ("Diga Diga Do"), the dance numbers ("Shuffle Your Feet and Just Roll Along" and "Bandanna Babies"), the folk-ceremonial number ("Magnolia's Wedding Day"), the ballad of a repeating vocal melody over a chromatically descending bass line* ("I Must Have That Man"), the New *Black* Dance Sensation ("Doin' the New Low Down"). To wrap it all up, McHugh and Fields created the single most popular title of the cycle, "I Can't Give You Anything But Love (baby)."

Clearly, the music made the show, for the comedy, however expertly played, was the same old stuff. The usual graveyard sketch, called "Picking a Plot," found Tim Moore bedeviled by A Departed Brother and Another Departed Brother. There was a boxing sketch, a cheating-at-poker sketch. There was also Leslie's version of *Porgy* ("with apologies," read the program, "to the Theatre Guild and Dorothy and DuBois [*sic*] Heyward"; that's Du*Bose*), which ushered in Aida Ward as Bess, singing "Porgy" in a hymn to the new life his love has given her, backed by the Hall Johnson Choir.

Surely George Gershwin heard Ward's "Porgy." Surely, in fact, George was taking in the black musical as a genre, for he could not have conceived of *Porgy and Bess* without some exposure to this explosion of musical gifts, of the possibilities it opened in theatre. The range of emotions that *Porgy and Bess* so avidly explores was not remotely anticipated in the twenties black musical, except for *Deep River*. But the variety of the talent, the relentless virtuosity of the instrumentalists, and the stunning freedom of the jazz vocalists—saxophones with a human face— must have caught Gershwin's ear.

---

* For which the classic example is George and Ira Gershwin's "The Man I Love."

Here's another improvisation of history that brings us close to the source. In 1932, Ziegfeld decided to remount *Show Boat,* and Jack Kapp, Brunswick Records' Artists and Recordings man, decided to do a *Show Boat* album. There had never been a full-scale reading of an American musical production before. The English had been at it for so long that recording pioneer Emile Berliner had caught the original cast of *Florodora* in 1900. But American shows got at most singles, occasionally "creator" discs (as when Edith Day laid down two numbers from *Irene*—but Day and her London colleagues made a whole *Irene* album), more often medleys and dance-band singles by studio regulars.

Kapp's *Show Boat* made no attempt to simulate the theatregoer's experience. He was simply making the music available, on eight twelve-inch 78-RPM sides. Framed by an invented overture and finale, the album sang only the six *Show Boat* standards, three by Helen Morgan and Paul Robeson of the 1932 company, the rest by Brunswick contractees James Melton, Frank Munn, and lavish, mysterious Countess Albani.

Kapp was virtually to invent the Broadway original-cast album ten years later in his renderings of *This Is the Army* and *Oklahoma!,* and he was already moving in that direction when he decided to follow *Show Boat* with a *Blackbirds* album. Kapp had recorded seven sides of the show when it was new. Now he proposed to give it the star treatment, using Adelaide Hall and Bill Robinson of the original cast, Ethel Waters and the Cecil Mack Choir of Lew Leslie's *Rhapsody in Black* (1931), and various Brunswick artists, including the Mills Brothers, Cab Calloway, and Duke Ellington's Orchestra. The result, on twelve ten-inch sides, preserved eight of *Blackbirds'* twelve numbers, plus one cut number, "Baby!," cover versions of two numbers, and the Wake Scene from *Rhapsody in Black,* built around W. C. Handy's "St. Louis Blues."

We have no idea to what extent Kapp's artists are respecting the true *Blackbirds* style. Are these newly arranged studio versions? Surely we can't assume that Ellington is at any point playing what the *Blackbirds* pit played. Nevertheless, the Brunswick *Blackbirds* swings us back to a time and place in American culture when black music was "separate but equal," its own thing, highly regarded by some and not much understood by anyone except by musicians. These twelve *Blackbirds* sides are astonishing, separate but unequaled, one of the great show albums of all time.

The two-sided medley, by Ellington's band, is mostly annunciatory, though the emphasis on the syncopated main strain of "*I Can't Give You Anything* but Love" is a warning, and "Diga Diga Do" is *very* free, almost an improvisation. Side three brings us Ethel Waters's spin on "I

Can't Give You Anything But Love," relatively straight till she turns bass in the second chorus, then reaches for a climax repeating "dit" on a rising line that sounds like The Joy of Sex—taken directly from Louis Armstrong's 1929 Okeh cut of the same number. She actually sounds like a trumpet.

Cab Calloway slides in on "Doin the New Low Down," and this is total jazz singing, with the Mills Brothers as straight men. The instrumental breaks sound so vocal and the vocals so instrumental that all it's all one molecule, like a pane of glass.

Sides five and six belong to Adelaide Hall, scatting the second chorus of "I Must Have That Man" so eloquently that we hear Goethe's *Ewig-Weibliche* in her very timbre; her "Baby!" irresistibly begins with Hall herself singing the vamp, in nonsense syllables. Now the Mills Brothers and Ellington take on "Diga Diga Do," first with the words, then in pure scat. Still, they make their best impression with a couplet. "Let those funny people smile," puts in one of the Millses. "How can there be a virgin isle with Diga Diga Do?" Another of those coded messages coming in from the social frontier.

The Millses also encore "I Can't Give You Anything But Love," in gentle part-singing to a lone guitar. Then Bill Robinson tackles "Doin' the New Low Down" complete with taps. Three sides later, Waters returns for "Porgy," three years—at the time of this recording—before Gershwin's *Porgy and Bess*. It's fascinating to consider what might have happened if not Gershwin but the authors of *Shuffle Along* or *Blackbirds* had written *Porgy: the Musical*. The "St. Louis Blues" closes the set in a mini-opera, opening with a dialogue between the mourning chorus and the mortician, then leading on to Waters's refrain, again in a preview of *Porgy and Bess* (the "My Man's Gone Now" wake scene). In all, we have heard a style unveiled in its spontaneity and ingenuity, a unique yet very typical twenties item. Waters, Hall, Robinson, Ellington, and the Millses are not only telling us who else was there: they're making themselves prominent and influential.

The ethnic emergence in the 1920s takes in the English as well, though no one thinks of them as having an ethnicity. From the start, America and its institutions were anglophile, the theatre especially so. English works and traditions and talent *created* American theatre. But the English style had far more impact on the spoken than on the sung drama, though it was the English style in musical comedy that helped launch the Second Age of the musical theatre in such extremely popular works as *Florodora* (1900) and *A Chinese Honeymoon* (1902). But by the 1920s the American musical had thrown off all foreign influence, and it is notable that just a few revues and only *one* book musical, *Bitter Sweet*, came to broadway from London's West End from 1920 to 1929. Yet how many American musicals went to London? A total of twenty-five: *Sally*, *The Music Box Revue*, *The Blue Kitten*, *Wildflower*, *The Student Prince*, *Lady, Be Good!*, *Rose-Marie*, *No, No, Nanette*, *The Vagabond King*, *Sunny*, *"Tip-Toes"*, *Castles in the Air*, *Oh, Kay!*, *The Desert Song*, *Peggy-Ann*, *Rio Rita*, *Hit the Deck!*, *Good News!*, *A Connecticut Yankee*, *Funny Face*, *Show Boat*, *Hold Everything!*, *Heads Up!*, *The Three Musketeers*, and *The New Moon*.

We've already encountered the earliest of these English revues in André Charlot's exhibits in 1924 and 1925; we should note as well *By the Way* (1925), the New York debut of the married English favorites Jack Hulbert and Cicely Courtneidge. But the English revue style was most decisively represented here in Charles Cochran's production *This Year of Grace* (1928), entirely written—music, lyrics, and sketches—by Noël Coward. Moreover, while Cochran presented the show in London earlier that year with Jessie Matthews and Sonnie Hale heading the cast, the New York version starred Beatrice Lillie and Coward himself. Such versatility rivaled the great George M., albeit in a far less anodyne style.

Coward wrote *This Year of Grace* with a burst of melody, a pride of clever lyrics, and an oblique approach that made some of his numbers maybe profound and some of them maybe impenetrable. "Mary Make Believe" (possibly a reference to Eleanor Abbott's 1916 novel *Molly Make Believe*, about an aggressive Pollyanna), on a young woman given to dreamy introspection, is something of a dreamy introspection itself, enlivened only by a bouncy middle section. "Lorelei" seems pointless till a late line, "What could be more obscene than vamping a submarine?" The wistfully aching "World Weary" is straightforward, the lament of an office boy—but Coward gave it to Beatrice Lillie to sing in drag, perched on a high stool and munching an apple, turning a simple revue spot into a high point of saucy camp.

In all, New York had never heard such elegance in pop music, just as there never was a performer as elegant as Coward himself, foremost of the "Don't ask, don't tell" entertainers of the age of codes and cautions. New York had already seen four of Coward's straight plays, including one, *The Vortex*, complete with Coward. But hearing Coward's music wedded to Coward's thoughts enlarged him. Who was he? A hard-working and prolific thespian or a Beardsley study in a dressing gown uttering graveyard whimseys and thinking up scandals to get into? Like the performers in the black shows, Coward clearly seemed to know a few things about the world that the audience didn't, which gave him not only novelty but gravity.

He had surprising strengths. For one thing, he truly understood jazz as a medium of liberalization. Anything the authorities tried to close down had to be good for the individual. *This Year of Grace*'s big dance number, "Teach Me To Dance Like Grandma (used to dance)," is a put-on, an alibi, like most of Coward. He claims to despise the Black Bottom and the Charleston in music that only pretends not to ape them. What Coward was against was not the license of the 1920s but its democracy: everyone's getting in on the secrets, getting asked and telling.

Coward may have "hated" jazz, but he needed it. It was the "now" music, and Coward was the "now" celebrity, sub-branch English Haughty. When the black shows tied jazz to sensuality, so that, say, a torch-singing Ethel Waters or Adelaide Hall could turn the "I lost my boy friend" genre into "I lost a good lay" by the hot vocal doodads they'd flip into the vocal line, Coward tied jazz to fashion. It was the ethos of the day, the cause of wonderful and even necessary corruptions of all kinds. In the black shows, jazz was sex; in Coward's shows, jazz was history.

From the very opening of *This Year of Grace*'s overture, Coward was ringing in the age. A drum pounded, the winds and brasses churned out incoherent syncopations on rising phrases, and Coward was already out-jazzing America. Eventually, all this settled into the urbane cacaphony of "Dance, Little Lady," on the notion of music as a drug that blurs all time, all trouble. but then came the lighter Coward of "Try To Learn To Love," with piano obligation decorating the seesawing tune. By the time the insistently offbeat "Mad About You" crashed into hearing, the audience at the Selwyn Theatre knew it was in for something different: its own sound style deconstructed for the purposes of analysis. It was Coward's own private Aeolian Hall.

True, Coward could do plain revue as well: in the typical "love for two" number, "A Room with a View" (but note that brightly allusive Coward, this time borrowing his title from E. M. Forster, and the naughty wit of the dominant seventh augmented fifth chord in the second measure), or in the usual spoof of the theatrical season, a staple of revue from that first *Passing Show* in 1894. This was a sketch called "The Theatre Guide," which skewered its prey so efficiently that, in the London version, Frederick Lonsdale was impaled on a single line: "Kiss me as passionately as you did last Wednesday in the Royal Enclosure at

Ascot!" For New York, Coward switched to a takeoff on "Any Civic Repertory* Play": a black-clad woman groaning, "Oh the *pain* of it!"

In the end, Cochran and Coward came up with a piece unlike any other, sparely but imaginatively designed, over the top when it had to be (and with Beatrice Lillie in the cast it had to be), and "artistically" stylized. It was especially so in the "jazz" number, "Dance, Little Lady," sung by Coward and then danced by Florence Desmond, surrounded by a gang of emotionlessly crazed partygoers in grisly masks designed by Oliver Messel. "The high tone of moral indignation in the lyric impressed a number of people," Coward later recalled, "including . . . Aimee Semple Macpherson."

Cochran also gave London Coward's operetta *Bitter Sweet* (1929), and it, too, reached New York within the year of its premiere, with Ziegfeld and Arch Selwyn reproducing the original staging, supervised by Coward in designs by Gladys Calthrop and Ernst Stern. Legend tells that everyone, from the start, had Evelyn Laye in mind as the heroine. But Laye was still fretting over *This Year of Grace*, in which her husband, Sonnie Hale, met Jessie Matthews and quickly became Mr. Matthews in a notorious divorce. Peggy Wood took the part, opposite George Metaxa. But Laye played New York's *Bitter Sweet*, opposite Metaxa's understudy, Gerald Nodin, and even spelled Wood back in London.

Now for the legend of the show itself: Coward hears a 78 orchestral medley of tunes from *Die Fledermaus* and suddenly realizes that Romance has died and that it's up to Coward to revive it. Vienna, uniforms, a drinking chorus, a café waitress, young love denied. (Apparently, no one had told Coward about *The Student Prince*.) But he gave Cochran one of the West End's biggest operetta hits ever and managed to combine the unthought-of and the conventional in his uniquely Cowardesque way.

Bitter Sweet has too much of the conventional, be it said, what with servants' choruses, bright-young-thing choruses, officers' choruses, and the Coward verbal tics in which partygoers are eternally "tight" and anything even remotely energetic can lead to "wear and tear." In fact, *Bitter Sweet*'s lyrics bear more clichés than the worst Broadway musical of the same era; *The Gingham Girl* sounds fresh by comparison. Worst of all are the out-of-the-action ensemble set pieces (long characteristic of the English musical), two quartets and a sextet. Gilbert and Sullivan,

---

* Eva Le Gallienne's high-minded troupe, devoted to Shakespeare, Molière, Ibsen, Chekhof.

two generations earlier, would never have countenanced such lack of integrity.

Still, this is Noël Coward, so *something's* got to take a little spin. The story does, first of all: in a flashback frame, from the present to the 1870s, a young Englishwoman (Laye) elopes to Vienna with her Austrian singing teacher (Nodin), sees him killed, and returns to England and the nobility, only to urge a younger version of herself to do what *she* did—run off with her singing teacher. The death of the hero was a bold touch, especially in the second act of a three-act work, as it killed off the emotional suspense with which virtually every operetta up till this point had kept its audience engaged. Then, too, the flashback let Coward open the show with 1929 jazz, a shocking twist in a score that was intended to revive Romance with the waltzes and marches of the Romberg-Friml style. Commentators have tried to link *Bitter Sweet* to Edwardian operetta, even to Lehár, but its sound is that of twenties *Broadway* operetta with British lyrics. What is "I'll See You Again" but Friml, what "Tokay" but Romberg? Coward's own, however, are "Zigeuner," "What Is Love?" (though its first phrases presage "He's in Love," from *Kismet* or, if you prefer, echo the Polovyetski Dances from Borodin's *Prince Igor*), "The Call of Life," and "(We'll have a) Dear Little Café." Yet it must be said that Coward was the most American-influenced of all English songwriters of his time. You'd never mistake him for Berlin, no. But Coward believes that there cannot be such a thing as "English jazz." When he goes into his jazz mode he's writing American.

True, in the end *Bitter Sweet* is vastly operetta in style, with little of the modern. But it does have a cabaret number still in use today as precisely that, a cabaret number: "If Love Were All." Aficionados point it out as the essential Coward number for its sorrowful self-portrait of one who has nothing more to offer than the famous "talent to amuse." Is this indeed Coward himself, Mary Make Believe, like so many artists fearful that his perspective and intelligence have cut him off from the life force? One is reminded of Thomas Mann's category of the "folk who fall down in the dance," clumsy and stupid but vital, appetitive. Living comes naturally to them; Coward poses. But his coy honesty can be slashing. One of *Bitter Sweet*'s quartets, "Green Carnations," set before Broadway four men in tails, smoking cigarettes and singing avidly about the gay life. They even called it so by name. It was like certain numbers in the black shows, or Cab Calloway's records in the early 1930s, when euphemisms were but barely euphemistic. "Kicking the Gong Around," one learned, from Calloway's rendition of that song, meant "doing coke"; "Triggeration" was sex.

Would Max Reinhardt have found as much vitality in *Bitter Sweet* as he found in the black shows? Ha. Yet Coward's work, no less than *Shuffle Along* and *Blackbirds*, thrust open the door of truth, getting *information* into the musical. "A DECOROUS ENTERTAINMENT" ran the headline over Brooks Atkinson's review of *Bitter Sweet*. (He loved it.) This is hardly what the *Times* would have said of a black show. Decorous? Their joy was their very lack—better, ignorance—of decorum. Yet all the forces of social change were, in their separate ways, in a kind of alignment to renegotiate the musical's democratic content. The musical had not truly been politicized—that would come in the 1930s. But the musical had begun to move beyond its generic racial and national structures. It was no longer recommending a narrow world; it was describing a wide one.

The first work in all this *must* be a redefinition of the heroine, another of the very few elements that had been dominant since the musical's inception. Twenties style had scarcely touched the star comic, we know. Whether in reactionary shows like Fred Stone's or more contemporary ones like Eddie Cantor's, the comic was still unfettered, even licensed for chaos. But the Cinderella heroine was no longer suitable. The "flapper," or the "young modern," or the "flaming [female] youth" of the cigarettes and the no-no reading matter and the sansculotte fashions was in fact as conformist as any party-liner always must be. But to outsiders, and especially to F. Scott Fitzgerald, she was onto something: the New Woman. Now, who was that, exactly? Social worker Jane Addams? Birth control pioneer and pariah Margaret Sanger? Hollywood star and mogul Mary Pickford?

Or perhaps Mae West? She is not recalled as a singer, least of all as a member of the shall-we-say musical comedy community. Yet she had her moments—remember, she sang Friml, in *Some Time*. By the 1920s, West had abandoned the musical for straight plays, always challenging the authorities on the then unsettled question of what First Amendment protection the theatre could demand. West got ten days in the workhouse and a $500 fine, supposedly for writing, coproducing, and appearing in *Sex* (1926), but she was more likely punished for daring to publicize the ultimate three-letter word in Broadway neon. *The Drag* (1927) was actually shut down before it could open—note, again, the provocative title. Still, West made her truest history in Hollywood, in the 1930s, and is thus beyond our survey.

I think the more catalytic influence in the shift from the passive to the aggressive heroine in the musical was Sophie Tucker. Now, Sophie was vaudeville, not Broadway. In a sixty-year career, she made only seven appearances in American stage musicals (plus two in England) and in the 1920s proper hit Broadway but twice, only in revue. But then, it was hard to cast Sophie Tucker in a story show. A buxom and ebullient singer, she treated the genres of the day, from crazy novelties to Dixie numbers. (She'd worked a blackface act, early on). Yet she quickly found that playing herself was stunningly effective. She would sing as Sophie, commissioning or snapping up specialty material that contributed to her imaginary biography as the first of the liberated women and the last of the red hot mamas—"Papa, Better Watch Your Step," "I Ain't Takin' Orders from No One," Aren't Women Wonderful," "You've Got To See Mama Every Night," "I Know That My Baby Is Cheatin' on Me (But maybe my baby don't know that I'm cheatin', too)," and, after her first talkie, "Hollywood Will Never Be the Same." She'll urge her sisters to "Meet 'em, greet 'em, fret 'em, and cheat 'em" in one song, rave about "My Extraordinary Man" in another, then turn the torch song on its head in her signature tune, "Some of These Days." Let Ruth Etting and Libby Holman pine for lost love; let Helen Morgan intone "Mean To Me" as if she loved it. Sophie carries the torch for no man. It's *his* life that's the poorer for their breakup. On the best of her many recordings of the number, in 1926 with Ted Lewis, Tucker builds her defiance into a kind of jazz bel canto over Lewis's quasi-klezmorim players, and we are caught by the fact that "Some of These Days" was the work of Shelton Brooks, a black man.

So this is more of that ecumenical American art, more of the idea that women and men of good faith are working together to pull off an ethnic emergence. Tucker is the most forward of all in her robust allusions to her Jewish background. In "There's Something Spanish in My Eyes," Tucker tolerates the risible pseudotango arrangement on the condition that she can spoof all ethnicity, all the pseudo in the culture: "My mother is Jewish, my father is Irish, which means that I'm Spanish and I love you."

Yet this is not Fanny Brice's Jewish, not ghetto-accented or characterized like Second Hand Rose. Brice is of the ghetto. Tucker has never seen one, and she's never some "Rose," always Sophie, free, unparked, a woman without debts. She doesn't even owe her listeners a voice, and sometimes talks her way through a song till a climactic high note.

"You've Got To See Mama Every Night" is a tipoff. This is early 1920s, a year before *Lady, Be Good!*, yet the musical structure of the arrangement is pure 1905, even 1895: the orchestra—a garage band, from the sound of it—gives us a taste of the refrain, then hits the vamp, an anticipation of the verse. Tucker comes in like a wolf in wolf's clothing, confident and total as if bustling onto a vaudeville stage to the crowd's cheers. It's sheer old fashion, so antecedent to the newer, younger singers of 1923 that no one knows exactly when this style began. Nor was this style suitable for the microphone, introduced in 1925 and favoring the easy delivery of the crooner, the torch *diseuse*. It is no accident that the course of American singing shifted from Jolson to Crosby very shortly after this time, in the early 1930s: from pushy to smooth.

There was nothing smooth about Tucker—but wasn't that her strength? She was a new-wave personality cloaked in old-time delivery. That protected her air of challenge and, I think, helped instill on a national level the New Woman whom Tucker was proposing, the non-WASP who is neither frail nor docile: independent. She doesn't need your conventions, your morals, even your God. She has her Own, and even He's got to see Mama every night. Sophie's ever ready and under no one.

How did she influence the musical if she was scarcely in any? Remember, Tucker's vaudeville was, in the 1910s and after—like television today—one of the few things that virtually all Americans experience. Recordings, too, had an impact on a broad scale by the early 1920s, and Tucker was a prolific recorder. Remember as well that the musical in the early 1920s was almost monotonously filled with Cinderellas, masquerading heiresses, and bullied princesses. Something had to give, and both the musical's writers and audience were waiting for someone to embody the new heroine.

It could not be Tucker. This was still the time of Marilyn Miller and her imitators, anything but the voluptuous mama whom Tucker portrayed. Behind the scenes, it turned out, Miller was as red-hot as any, loving life, love, and heavy-shouldered chorus boys, to Ziegfeld's despair. Somehow, he kept hoping that his favorites would be chaste dollies impervious to all admiration but that of the Master. But Ziegfeld's art was itself a sensuality, inveigling as a carnival midway show. Ziegfeld flooded Broadway with sex; what did he think was going to happen? The swelling of convents and monasteries?

Still, Ziegfeld's Miller, as Sally, went directly from poster girl of the season to icon of the age; then she quarreled with Ziegfeld and signed with Charles Dillingham, who thought this absolute twenties heroine would be a wow as the hero of the previous age—Peter Pan—in a musical version of the Barrie play. Barrie said, *"What?"* All right, all right, we'll just do the play. But Miller was too womanly to enact the ephebe, and Dillingham's *Peter Pan* bombed. *Sunny* followed, and, as we know, Miller's reign as queen of musical comedy was secured. Then, for reasons that have died with the communicants, she returned to Ziegfeld and *Rosalie* (1928), this one organized very quickly around two recent headlines, the American visit of Queen Marie and Princess Ileana of Rumania and Charles Lindbergh's solo flight across the Atlantic.

In the Ziegfeld version, Princess Rosalie of Romanza visits America to win aviator hero Richard Fay despite the tyrannical queen's attempt to force her into an arranged marriage with a Romanzan prince, and Rosalie and Fay are at length united when he flies the Atlantic to be with her. Meanwhile, her ineffectual king of a father has abdicated, depriving the queen of all her power and Rosalie of her title. For her last entry, that smug Romanzan prince announces her as "Her Royal Highness, the Princess!" But the king counters with, "Nothing of the sort. It's simply . . . Rosalie!"

Miller was never simply anything, especially in a Ziegfeld show. Speaking of entrances, a famous quotation should now be consulted, one so frequently used to summon up the character of the twenties musical that to omit it would be irresponsible. Here is Alexander Wollcott, critic of the *New York World*:

> Down in the orchestra pit the violins chitter with excitement and brasses blare. The spotlight turns white with expectation. Fifty beautiful girls in simple peasant costumes of satin and chiffon rush pell-mell onto the stage, all squealing simple peasant outcries of "Here she comes!" Fifty hussars in fatigue uniforms of ivory white and tomato bisque march on in columns of fours and kneel to express an emotion too powerful for words. The lights focus on the flowered gateway upstage, the house holds its breath, and on walks Marilyn Miller.

What sort of heroine is Miller playing, in the end? As Sally, she was spunky, an orphan aspiring to the *Follies* and a marriage into society. As Sunny, she was spunky, too, though less aspiring. As Rosalie, she was . . . spunky. But then, the authors of books for Marilyn Miller shows didn't need to create an individual because they already had one in Miller as she was. They had only to provide her with opportunities—at least one spot each for her tap, ballet, and novelty dancing, as well as sensational costumes, which in *Rosalie* take in not only Romanzan festival dress but West Point cadet drag when Rosalie disguises herself as drummer boy Gerald Kickelbush.

Perhaps it's best to see Miller as a Cinderella gamine, with variations. Sally's an orphan and Rosalie's a princess, but Miller is at all times a gifted sock-it-to-'em American talent whose charm was that she'd come out of nowhere to become the Ziegfeld Girl *assolutissima*. Perhaps that was why she left the likable Dillingham for the importuning, treacherous Ziegfeld: there was no such thing, in American fame, as a Dillingham Girl.

Even while Miller was in her prime, however, the role of the heroine was undergoing reevaluation. We may analyze this in a trio of *Girl* shows of the second half of the era: *The 5 O'Clock Girl* (1927), *Treasure Girl* (1928), and *Girl Crazy* (1930). We've already met the 5 O'Clock Girl, Patricia Brown, who telephones playboy Gerald Brooks every afternoon. But we haven't met Mary Eaton, who played Patricia and was Ziegfeld's intended replacement for Marilyn Miller. Eaton, in fact, went on for Miller in *Sally* and was the nearest approximation of Miller that Ziegfeld could find—the fair coloring, the hoofing and ballet, the soprano voice. But Eaton was too approximate. She lacked beauty, danced clumsily, and fielded a harsh singing tone. And, despite Ziegfeld's expectations, Eaton had no allure whatsoever as a Broadway heroine. Any number of women below the top rank of stardom owned a far greater helping of public favor—Louise Groody, Janet Velie, Elizabeth Hines, Helen Ford, Eleanor Painter, Queenie Smith. Eaton wasn't even the *star* of *The 5 O'Clock Girl*, merely costarred with the appealing but hardly major Oscar Shaw. Ziegfeld had dropped Eaton after three editions of the *Follies* and *Kid Boots* in 1923, and all the stage work that Eaton had after that was *Lucky* (1927), a Dillingham disaster about Ceylonese pearl divers, *The 5 O'Clock Girl*, and one London show before she gave it up, not yet thirty.

Interestingly, of all Eaton's roles in story shows, only the unfortunate and long-forgotten *Lucky* might have been a Miller role, with big-star buildup before the first entrance, lots of dancing, and acting lost and friendless, a typical Miller condition. Given Dillingham's lavish staging, *Lucky* might have been a hit with Miller; Eaton couldn't carry it. *The 5 O'Clock Girl* was more her speed, a Philip Goodman production on his characteristic tight budget, almost a dainty show, befitting its dainty heroine. *Lucky* was a spectacle; *The 5 O'Clock Girl* was a block party leading up to a nice little wedding. It was not unlike all those Cinderella shows of the early 1920s.

So the old-style heroine was very much alive; Marilyn Miller cast a long shadow. But *Treasure Girl* gives us a far more active heroine in an Aarons-Freedley show with a Gershwin score, all for Gertrude Lawrence in her first solo starring vehicle. Having enchanted New York in two revues for André Charlot and in *Oh, Kay!*, Lawrence was clearly being readied as the next major musical comedy star. She had an advantage over Mary Eaton: she wasn't a second-rate version of anyone. Lawrence even had an advantage over Marilyn Miller: a reign that counted two kingdoms, London and New York. Broadway saw her in her two greatest roles, in *Lady in the Dark* (1941) and *The King and I* (1951), but the West End saw her in her unique one, as the vagabond schoolgirl in search of the perfect lay in *Nymph Errant* (1933), a Charles Cochran superproduction with a Cole Porter score.

Lawrence was a looker, and she split the difference between airy and earthy. If her singing was uneven (but lovely) and her dancing derivative, she had spontaneity. She could put over her part of a comic duet, such as *Treasure Girl*'s "I Don't Think I'll Fall in Love Today," as if she had just thought of the lines a moment before uttering them; and so rend the heart in a ballad, for instance *Treasure Girl*'s "Where's the Boy? Here's the Girl!," that the audience, at each performance, though it must be getting her most impassioned delivery of the show's entire run.

She was quicksilver, unpredictable, even unprofessional: that spontaneity was real. One night she's launch "I Don't Think I'll Fall in Love Today" upstage right, another night downstage center, yet a third night reclining on a bench, throwing off her vis-à-vis, Paul Frawley. But that was *his* problem. To Lawrence's public, the looks of surprise from her colleagues were part of the fun, what you expect when you greet someone with a joy buzzer. You couldn't count on Lawrence to perform a dance the same way twice, to show up in last night's costume. And why should she? In the twenties view of things, a play wasn't written or rehearsed—a play was *performed*. Besides, last night was last night. Lawrence's motto might have been "Born Today." It was as if she weren't acting: she was living, but in the theatre.

She was not as versatile as Miller, for she couldn't handle ballet, but then ballet, by 1928, was something the chorus did, especially the Albertina Rasch girls, prancing on to cover a set change. Ballet was a relic; Lawrence was modern, jazzy, tough. After all, Kay was a bootlegger. Could Marilyn Miller have played a bootlegger?

So *Treasure Girl*'s Ann Wainwright marked something of a breakaway for Broadway's singing heroine: hard-edged, man-abusing, and out to nab $20,000 on a treasure hunt. Her ex-beau, Neil Forrester (Frawley), is on hand for her to snarl at and—but you know this already—fall back in love with. Unlike the usual Aarons-Freedley romp, *Treasure Girl* was not stuffed with supplementary screwballs and bizarre plot turns. All centered upon Lawrence, her boy friend, and the treasure hunt, with some mild assistance from comic Walter Catlett and secondary couple Clifton Webb and Mary Hay. This really was Lawrence's show: soloing or duetting in the five top numbers (the two already mentioned, plus

"What Are We Here For?," "Feeling I'm Falling," and "Oh, So Nice," so oddly accented that it sounds like a waltz in $\frac{4}{4}$ time), duking it out with everyone, and playing some sharp comedy with that wonderful English tact that seemed so welcome on Broadway after a generation of waiting for the American "hook 'em in the gills" style to die out. For instance, to avoid process server Catlett, Lawrence pretends to be her own twin sister. Ann herself is dead, alas—drowned in a river. Suddenly, Webb blunders in, fudging the story. *He* says she was drowned at sea.

> CATLETT: (*suspicious*) She fell in the ocean and was drowned in
> the river?
> LAWRENCE: (*delicately*) Such an unusual death.

The other players helped Lawrence keep the tempo up. Webb and Hay had three fine duets, "K-ra-zy For You," "What Causes That?" (both of which were heard in the latter-day Gershwin pastiche *Crazy for You* [1992]), and "I've Got a Crush on You," which went unnoticed at the time. Vic Arden and Phil Ohman once again made the two-keyboard piano sound in the pit. Still, the shebang rode on Lawrence and she, increasingly throughout the evening, rode on Frawley, badgering and scorning. In the second act, stranded on an island, they find their mysteriously vexed relationship exploding with a ferocity unknown to bickering musical comedy lovers. Ann's stage directions tell us what was going on—"Blazes, triumphantly savage," "sneers," "shrilly," "softly hisses." Finally, goading him "in a frenzy," she shouts:

> Come on, Mr. Cave Man . . . You're going to break me in two,
> are you? *I don't believe you!* You couldn't break anything! You're
> beaten! I've beaten you! I've—

He grabs her and gives her the shaking she has been provoking all evening, but the damage, among critics, was considerable. Brooks Atkinson thought the heroine "a malicious liar and a spoiled child" and called the book "an evil thing." Some found *Treasure Girl* dull in general, but most had unkind words for Lawrence in particular. She had simply worn the role too well, and *Treasure Girl* was a flop.

Whether the critics were simply unhappy with a flawed character (Ann) or reacting against a new form of woman (Lawrence) is not clear. After all, they had adored her as Kay, and she was to remain a lifelong critics' pet. Interestingly, it was Aarons and Freedley who unveiled the next New Woman, one even Newer than Lawrence, though no one realized it at the time. This brings us to probably the most fabled debut in the musical's history: an utterly unencountered Ethel Merman pads onstage late in Act One of *Girl Crazy,* sings "I Got Rhythm," Stops the Show Cold, and goes on to the longest star career Broadway ever knew, forty years on top.

Like many fables, this one is too trim to be true. Merman was unknown, but she didn't pop up in *Girl Crazy* out of nowhere just to sing, and the song wasn't "I Got Rhythm." Merman had a *role* in *Girl Crazy,* that of Kate Fothergill, married to the good-for-nothing Slick (the slightly built, baby-voiced, mustachioed William Kent). "Gee, look at Diamond Lil!" cries one character upon Merman's entrance, about twenty-five minutes into Act One. The allusion to one of Mae West's roles tells us how book writers Guy Bolton and John McGowan saw Merman: glitzy, sensual, beyond the reach of prevailing moral standards. From the first, she's playing sarcastic comedy:

> KATE: Is this the famous Churchill dude ranch?
> JAKE: Yes, but haven't you made a mistake?
> KATE: Have I? Wait till you see him. (*Calls offstage*) Slick!

For the rest of Act One, Merman continued in this vein. No one in the audience had any reason to suspect that she had been discovered (by Freedley) singing at the Brooklyn Paramount between movie shows and had been rushed into *Girl Crazy* as, indeed, a vocalist. But Slick has become the manager of a saloon, so, by musical comedy logic, his wife shall entertain the customers with song. In the last scene of Act One, in the bar, Merman came out in a light-colored, loosely draped silk top and dark skirt, flicked away her cigarette, and, to the canoodling onstage piano, sang out, "Delilah . . . was a *floozy,*" and the public went on red alert. She *sings,* too? Merman flooded the Alvin Theatre with "Sam and Delilah," a cautionary saga in the style of "Frankie and Johnny," and immediately followed it with "I Got Rhythm," charging up to that famous moment when she held one note for the entire first A of the refrain while the orchestra played the melody, held the same note for the entire *second* A yet again, and stood calmly taking it in while the house went mad.

She was a kid from Astoria, Queens, a twenty-one-year-old stenographer named Ethel Zimmerman, but nothing impressed her, not even her own uniqueness. She was oddly pretty for someone whom the expert Aarons and Freedley had typed as a comic, and her too-slim figure would round out delightfully in the early 1930s. Yet something was "wrong" about her, at least compared with the established twenties heroines. They had a playful innocence; Merman had a been-there reality. The very power of her voice told of a womanliness less limpid than that of the "Tea For Two" heroine, and not just the power but the placement. It was Merman who popularized the so-called "belt" style. Technically, this means singing everything in the lower "chest" register and never using the soprano's higher, lighter "head" register. Culturally, this means infusing heroine music with a dark, strong, loud, and invulnerable sound. This in itself marked a challenge to the sweeter noise that the Cinderella heroine made, but the Cinderella age was over, and Merman was one reason why.

Granted, she was not *Girl Crazy*'s heroine: Ginger Rogers was. But it's worth remarking that Rogers, too, was no soprano, and no Cinderella. *Girl Crazy* cast her as the postmistress of Custerville, Arizona, and while she was romantically paired with a society hot shot from the east, her Molly Gray hadn't the slightest desire to star in the *Follies*, marry rich, or run a cookie business. Ambitionless, she was content and trendy, full of the wisecracks that the early 1920s heroine seldom resorted to.

Typically, on Rogers's Broadway debut in Kalmar and Ruby's *Top Speed* (1929), she sang the "down, boy" number "Keep Your Undershirt On," and her simultaneous movie debut (shooting by day at Paramount's Astoria studios during *Top Speed*'s run) found her running through *Young Man of Manhattan* as Puff Randolph to introduce a national catchphrase, "Cigarette me, big boy!"

The late 1920s, clearly, were the transitional time between *Sally* and *Forty-Second Street*, wherein Rogers appears as Anytime Annie. It's ironic that the Banton raids on Broadway during the 1920s always targeted the obvious subversions of the dominant sociocultural controls—O'Neill and his mixed-race couple or Mae West and her revelations of the erotic. Had Banton known anything about culture, he should have raided Ethel Merman.

I'd like to follow the *Girl* shows with a few *Boy* shows, but there weren't any, because the musical never really produced male stars, except comics and Irish singer Chauncey Olcott. True, there was George M. Cohan, always exceptional. But, like Al Jolson, Cohan as performer functioned essentially as a comic. He also sang and danced, but so did virtually every comic save W. C. Fields. Not till Alfred Drake and Robert Preston, way off in the late 1940s and the 1950s, did the musical realize a male star who was not a comedian, dancer, or singer but a personality, like Miller, Merman, Mary Martin, Carol Channing, and such. This is partly because the musical is a fantastical medium whose icons must be fantastical—i.e., freaks. Americans don't mind freak women in show business, but freak men are threatening, and not just to Joab Banton. So the men stars were generally comics, freakish by nature and therefore forgivable.

There were a few near-miss men stars. Eddie Buzzell, whom some took as a combination of the worst parts of Cohan and Jolson, worked nonstop through the 1920s, from *The Gingham Girl* and an obscure Kalmar-Ruby show, *No Other Girl* (1924), and through *Sweetheart Time* (1926) and *The Desert Song* to the hero of *Good Boy* (1928) and the comic villain of *Lady Fingers* (1929), which he coauthored. Still, it's not likely that Buzzell's name on a marquee would have stimulated much business. He was simply another of the many assistant experts of the day, and, after Hollywood called, for Buzzell to play (in effect) the young Cohan in First National's talkie adaptation of *Little Johnny Jones* in 1929 he soon gave up performing for movie directing.

Of course, Buzzell's stage work emphasized an old-fashioned archetype, the bumpkin-turned-slicker doing hat tricks in loud checked suits, a convention of the 1890s and a cliché before Marilyn Miller took her first ballet class. More innovative was Jack Donahue. Tall and blessed with a good "stage face"—big features, readable in the last row of the New Amsterdam—Donahue was an all-arounder, especially known for his rubber-limbed dancing and his easy, even friendly sarcasm. He specialized in sidekick parts, but so prominently that, in two Marilyn Miller vehicles, *Sunny* and *Rosalie*, Miller had more duets with Donahue than with her romantic interest. Of *Sunny*, Gilbert Gabriel said in the *New York Sun* that "the chief ingredient is, of course, Jack Donahue"—not unlike saying that the chief ingredient in the original *Funny Girl* was Danny Meehan.

Clearly, Donahue had something. He was graduated to stardom in *Sons o' Guns* (1929), a World War I show, in which playboy private Donahue serves under his former valet, Sergeant William Frawley (the eventual Fred Mertz on *I Love Lucy*, and not to be confused with twenties juvenile lead Paul Frawley). The *Sons o' Guns* score, by Arthur Swanstrom, Benny Davis, and J. Fred Coots, was pure pop tune, but *Sons o' Guns* was a Grade-A production, with Joseph Urban sets and two song hits, "Why (is there a rainbow in my sky)?" and "Cross Your Fingers." It was one of the year's biggest hits. What Donahue's career might have led to is an intriguing speculation, for his gifts (he was a librettist as well as a performer) and the critics' enthusiasm suggest something special—a twenties male star who was not a freak. Tragically, Donahue died in 1930.

Then there is the case of Dennis King, our Jim (in *Rose-Marie*) and François Villon (in *The Vagabond King*). Here was a strange case, an

Englishman who started off in the speaking theatre in everything from
light comedy to Shakespeare who suddenly became the leading hero of
American operetta. (Stranger yet, one of King's first jobs was in the premiere of Andre Messager's specially-for-London operetta *Monsieur
Beaucaire* [1919], in which King played Townbrake, a nonsinging part.)
King was Broadway's only operetta honcho. Guy Robertson and J.
Harold Murray did solid service, Robertson in *Wildflower,* on tour in
King's role in *Rose-Marie,* in Kálmán and Romberg, as Chopin *and* Johann Strauss in life-and-work shows; and Murray in a fifteen-year-
career that consisted entirely of dreck and *Rio Rita.* Still, twenties
audiences had the impression that it was King who controlled the field,
that he liked hamming it up, that he'd sooner say Zounds! than Swell!

He wasn't a giving colleague. He upstaged, moved on other actors'
lines, would fluff a cue and then glare at someone as if to blame *him*
for the gaffe. But in his mannered way he was a fine actor and a smash-
ing singer, a baritone with a fierce, bright upper range. Like many an
English-trained performer, he knew how to change his appearance to
suit the role. Look at photographs of Guy Robertson in any two parts
and you see only cute, smiling Guy Robertson. Look at King as Jim and
as François Villon and you see two different people.

King's star potential in the musical was hurt when operetta crashed
apart in the 1930s. He never stopped working, mainly in straight theatre, though he did play Goethe in Lehár's *Friederike* in 1937 (no doubt
dwarfing Guy Robertson's Johann Strauss: what's waltz king against
philosopher-king?) and even presented the next generation with a little
King, his son John Michael, the first Freddy in *My Fair Lady.*

Operetta was only one of many pre-1920s and of-the-twenties things
that vanished when the Third Age found its new styles and people and
properties and began to develop them. Above all, two energies identify
this decade: artistic experimentation and a liberal social agenda. Even
as, say, Oscar Hammerstein starts trying to build a unique musical out
of a unique story instead of pasting contentless story elements onto star
personalities, or as Laurence Stallings sees in the black theatre style a
chance to energize the folk play, the musical is welding together two revolutions. One is purely about the possibilities of form; one is about the
possibilities of character.

The result, in the long run, will see the musical through its golden
age, into the 1960s. In the short run, it will produce the greatest of all
musicals shortly before the end of the 1920s. First, let us catch up on
the fortunes of what are now virtually the only two forms available in
the book show: operetta and musical comedy.

In Love with Love

OPERETTA REINVENTED

One notable difference between operetta in the early half of the 1920s and operetta in the later half lies in the eventual accession of Sigmund Romberg and Rudolf Friml as the genre's champions, even monopolists (and, finally, seventy years after, as the names that absolutely evoke this form in this time). This was so even in the season of 1926–27, when Emmerich Kálmán, after Strauss and Lehár the third of Middle Europe's Big Three in operetta, was represented on Broadway by two of his major titles and a new show composed expressly for New York.

This is all the odder in that both Romberg and Friml lost their hold on the national ear at this time, Romberg sporadically but Friml almost consistently. After *The Vagabond King* in 1925, Friml suffered two failures, had a success with a score that left no memory, and, after two more failures in the 1930s, retired. The more prolific Romberg, too, suffered failures. But he had hits as well, including two of the most popular operetta scores of the decade. Moreover, though Romberg worked only at intervals thereafter, he managed to weather operetta's eclipse by accommodating changing tastes and lasting into the 1950s, when his final title, produced posthumously, was an out-and-out musical comedy, *The Girl in Pink Tights* (1954).

True, Romberg chose better collaborators than Friml—even if Harbach and Hammerstein could come through beautifully for Friml on

161

Rose-Marie or for Romberg on *The Desert Song* but suddenly run on empty in Firml's *The Wild Rose* (1926). For instance, consider this proposition offered to Romberg: Mr. J. J. Shubert will produce an adaptation of *The Prisoner of Zenda,* Anthony Hope's tale of the commoner and the Prince of Ruritania who are physical doubles, involving the commoner in court intrigue and romance with the prince's intended, Princess Flavia. This has all the appeal of the Neverland gallantry that Romberg loved, along with a pleasingly doomed interclass love affair of *The Student Prince*'s kind. Mr. J. J. promises a physical production to defy Ziegfeld, with the ravishing Evelyn Herbert and—specially imported from England—the dauntless Harry Welchman. Book and lyrics will be the work of Harry B. Smith, new to Romberg but an old pro— in fact, the greatest old pro the American musical ever produced, in terms of longevity and success. And how can we miss with the built-in device of the male lead's playing both prince and commoner, a delight of audiences since E. H. Sothern originated the stage version in 1895?

Yet *Princess Flavia* (1925) missed. Its run of nearly five months sounds good for the time, but not at half-sold houses. Romberg blamed Smith, Smith blamed Welchman, Welchman blamed Mr. J. J. But what drove *Princess Flavia* down was the feeble score. How many more helpings was operetta to serve of "Comrades" (the all-male Loyalty Chorus), "I Love Them All" (the Lothario's anthem), "Only One" (the heroine-and-courtiers' Flirtation Scene), "Yes or No," "Convent Bells Are Ringing," and the conversational musical scene, "I Dare Not Love You," which starts out with a dashing waltz but ends in a tawdry $\frac{4}{4}$ refrain that must be the weakest Love Duet in the entire Romberg output.

Came then Romberg's *The Desert Song,* which I'm saving for later. But came also Romberg's now forgotten *Cherry Blossoms* (1927), sort of *Madama Butterfly* mixed with *Maytime; My Maryland* (1927) and *My Princess* (1927), both with *The Student Prince*'s librettist, Dorothy Donnelly; and *The Love Call* (1927), a rangers-versus-Indians western, again with Harry B. Smith. All were burdened with generic scores, generic characters, generic thinking. At least generic musical comedy was propulsive and salty. Generic operetta was Mr. and Mrs. Potato Head going into a Valse Duette.

Oddly, one of this Romberg group, besides *The Desert Song,* was a hit. A smash, even. *My Maryland* was an adaptation of *Barbara Frietchie,* Clyde Fitch's 1899 version of John Greenleaf Whittier's Civil War folk heroine who dares to fly the Stars and Stripes before Stonewall Jackson and the Confederate Army. Quoth Whittier:

"Shoot, if you must, this old grey head,
But spare your country's flag," she said.

Fitch, who arranged his plays for charismatic young women as a cater-
er programs a banquet, turned the octagenarian Frietchie into a young
beauty, and Romberg turned her into Evelyn Herbert. Smart move. *My
Maryland* caught on so big so early that the Shuberts canceled the New
York opening to allow the Philadelphia tryout to find its natural limits
in an open run, which lasted an unheard-of forty weeks. The New York
stand ran up 300 performances, and at least five touring companies
were roaming the nation at one point in the late 1920s.

So why has this show vanished? Its "Stouthearted Men" piece, "Your
Land and My Land," remained in the patriotic canon and survived into
the 1950s in MGM's Romberg bio, *Deep in My Heart*, with Howard Keel
leading a chorus of Boys in Blue. *My Maryland*'s more hummable numbers, "Silver Moon," "Mother," "Boys in Grey," and "Won't You Marry
Me?," could be heard on the radio through the 1940s, and the show
was staged as recently as 1976, in Indiana for the Bicentennial. Still,
My Maryland is a dead item—not a conjuring title that we never actually hear, like *Blossom Time*; not an aficionado's collectible, like *Apple
Blossoms*; not even a title that survives on disc alone, like *Sitting Pretty*. For all its success in 1927, *My Maryland* is now as departed as such
ungainly flops of that year as *Polly of Hollywood*; *The Seventh Heart*, a
creepy vanity production produced, written, and composed by one Sarah
Ellis Hyman; and *Oh, Ernest!*, Robin Hood Bowers and Francis DeWill's
version of Oscar Wilde.

The music is the reason. In an age that loved operetta, *My Maryland*'s
score was correct, appropriate, what one expected. That's the problem:
we have heard all these songs before. Not these melodies, but these reasons for singing. As with *Princess Flavia*, the all-too-congested arena of
twenties operetta gave its authors very little creative room. There had to
be the martial number, the courtship waltz, the merrymaking chorus,
the heroine's ambition anthem, and so on. It took really first-rate tunes
to enliven these tired notions. Rodgers and Hart or De Sylva, Brown, and
Henderson could animate a musical comedy at a power level (from one
to ten) of six or seven. But the more cumbersome operetta format needed Romberg at full ten.

That he was in *The Desert Song*, to my mind the best of the classic
twenties operettas,* boasting a score as strong as those of *The Student*

---

* No, I haven't overlooked *Show Boat*, because *Show Boat* isn't an operetta. See
Chapter 9.

Prince and *Rose-Marie* with a much stronger story. In fact, a unique one. For once in operetta, the authors—book men Harbach, Hammerstein, and Frank Mandel and lyricists Harbach and Hammerstein—actually make an inquiry into the nature of this "romance" that other operettas take for granted. To whom does romance apply and for what reasons? Is it based entirely upon physical attraction, power—or are trust and security at least as important?

To understand why *The Desert Song* works so well, we must consider the format of late-twenties Romberg-Friml, the most constricted and conventional program in the musical's history. Early-twenties operettas were more variously derived, transitional works leading away from the "comic opera" of Victor Herbert's day toward something more up-to-date and less European in sound. *Wildflower,* with its fox trots and nimble comedy turns, is typical; if it were revived today, audiences would be startled at how much sheer Broadway moxie was slipped in with the romance. But after *The Student Prince* and *Rose-Marie,* Romberg and Friml concentrated their view of operetta's content and structure, creating a rigid blueprint. Their collaborators were obviously of similar mind, and even other writers fell into step, so that Gershwin and Stothart's *Song of the Flame* observes the matrix (if only because of *Flame's* librettists, Harbach and Hammerstein). Even Vincent Youmans, trying operetta in the Gold Rush epic *Rainbow* (1928), to a book by the adventurous Laurence Stallings, seemed to want to adhere to formula, albeit in a highly unusual story. But then, Hammerstein was *Rainbow's* lyricist and, unbilled, revised Stallings' script.

This Romberg-Friml plan calls for *one,* a historical setting (e.g., the Paris of Louis XI; old California) or an imaginary or picturesque one (Ruritania, Borovina, Japan). *Two,* the central couple must be separated by class differences (Prince Karl Franz and his waitress, *The Wild Rose's* American Monty Travers and Princess Elise of Borovina) or by such impediments as his being accused of murder (*Rose-Marie, Rainbow*) or her leading the Russian Revolution (*Song of the Flame*).

Three, there should be a military background (Mounties getting their man, a rebel faction usurping the Borovinian throne), which necessitates isolating the men's chorus for at least part of the evening (as Heidelberg students, Confederate soldiers, gold prospectors) to thrill the audience with high-powered part-singing (whether in *The Student Prince's* melting "Serenade" or *The Vagabond King's* lusty "Drinking Song.").

Four, as for characterization, he'll be on the sardonic side, she of fiery personality (in Hammerstein's books, especially), somewhat anticipating

the meet-cute-bicker-interminably-but-secretly-love-each-other model
that MGM created for Jeanette MacDonald and Nelson Eddy. *Five,*
there should be a temptress or a rival woman figure, generally a mezzo-
soprano (*Rose-Marie*'s Wanda, who sings "Totem Tom-Tom," vamps men,
murders one, and eventually exculpates the hero; *The Vagabond King*'s
Huguette, who loves Villon but must die to clear the way for the soprano; *Rainbow*'s Lotta, who counters the heroine's grandeur with
cabaret torch and seen-it-all expressions*). *Six,* there should be a baritone villain (*Rose-Marie* offers two, the heroine's brother and her un-
wanted fiancé, and it's three if one counts Sergeant Malone, who must
arrest the hero for the crime he didn't commit; *My Maryland* offers
something similar, with a father instead of a brother, and the *heroine's*
crime isn't murder but treason).

As for comedy, *seven,* this was still limited to one or two characters,
who may or may not be singers (*The Vagabond King* is the most ab-
stemious, using only Villon's servant; *Rainbow* made the most of Charles
Ruggles as the muleteer "Nasty" Howell; *Rose-Marie* allots a sizable
chunk of both book and score to Hard-Boiled Herman and Lady Jane;
and *The Wild Rose* used three comic players, Gus Shy and Inez Courtney as what we might call a "zany couple," along with Courtney's exasperated father, William Collier, a last-minute replacement for the ailing
Lew Fields).

There were a few variables in this layout. Dance might consist of ethnic specialists, where available, or simply an Albertina Rasch ballet. Gus
Shy and Inez Courtney danced through *The Wild Rose* as if in a musical comedy, their usual rendezvous, but operetta's serious characters
never danced at all. Still, in general this was a highly controlled aes-
thetic, a dictatorship by the waltz, so to say. If *The Desert Song* is truly
worthy, surely it will smash the mold in an individual way.

But there were no individual operettas in this group; the form was
too newly conceived to need regeneration yet. Besides, *The Desert Song*'s
strength derives precisely *from* the structural limitations. As Wordsworth
tells us while defending the sonnet's tight form, "Nuns fret not at their
convent's narrow room." *The Desert Song* has, *one,* the exotic setting of

---

* This was, in fact, the great cabaret star Libby Holman. Because of operetta's
need for legitimate singers, its casts in the 1920s were drawn as if from a stock company, with the same names constantly turning up in lead roles—Howard Marsh, Desire Ellinger, Allan Prior, Walter Woolf, Tessa Kosta, Greek Evans, Robert Chisholm,
among others. These were not famous players, but operetta would have been incon-
ceivable without them. All the odder, then, to encounter Holman, the last person
one would have expected to find singing the second woman lead in an operetta.

North Africa, with plenty of atmospheric scene-painting from Romberg, with the Berber drums, the bugles of the occupying French, and highly erotic strains fit for a Valentino movie. (Valentino died just three months before *The Desert Song*'s premiere.) The show's opening music, a *Maestoso* tutti dominated by rhapsodic strings, is typical, especially in its dramatic alternation of major and minor chords, sun-drenched, lurid, glorious. One can hear the relief in Romberg's voice at being free of that piffling farce of a *Louie the 14th* the year before. This time, Romberg has something to sing about.

Especially because the central couple, *two*, is separated not by class but by his double life. At the Foreign Legion fort, Pierre is a risible no-account, a general's son yet a sissy. Heroine Margot wants more from a man. "I must know that he can master me," she sings—a man, in short, like that dashing Captain Fontaine. But Pierre, *en masque*, is the intrepid Red Shadow, leader of the anti-colonial Riffs who have sworn, *three*, to drive the French from Morocco. In fact, the Riffs had been fighting the French in North Africa for much of the decade, and that, along with the national memory of Valentino as the desert sheik who is a terror to men and an elation to women made *The Desert Song* seem highly contemporary. Like *Rosalie,* this was Headline Operetta.

In Robert Halliday and Vivienne Segal, *The Desert Song* had front-runners of the new school, he less wooden than many a hero and she one of the few twenties operetta stars who continued to play leads on Broadway long after the Romberg-Friml vogue had ended. And yes, *four,* he had fun at her expense (as the Red Shadow, of course; as Pierre he was pitiful), and she was the challenge of his military career.

The reason for this is that, unlike most of these operettas, *The Desert Song* tells *her* story, not his. Margot is the protagonist, and her dreams, not his politics, propel the action. If she must know that he can master her, why does she so fear the Red Shadow's power? His numbers—"The Riff Song" (the "Stouthearted Men" chorale) and the title love song, however appealing, are the generic pieces. It is Margot's numbers that tell us what is happening—the wondering "Romance," the conversational duet "Then You Will Know," the flirty "I Want a Kiss" (in which Margot breaks the leads-don't-dance rule and executes a fox trot with Captain Fontaine), and the soaring "Sabre Song," in which the Red Shadow's sword becomes symbolic of what she both loves and fears in him, his ruthless masculine self-belief.

The temptress rival, *five*, is Azuri, a Berber who skulks around more or less everywhere, like la Gioconda; does a torrid vamping job on Captain Fontaine; and sets the whole show into motion at the end of scene one, when, alone on stage, as the set of the Red Shadow's hideout is changing to that of the Foreign Legion fort, she cries out, "Oh, Allah who sees all things, help me to make her suffer! *Margot Bonvalet!*" In New York, Azuri was Pearl Regay, *Rose-Marie*'s Wanda. But, in the first of three Warner Brothers *Desert Song* movies, she was Myrna Loy, in perhaps the most striking of the many Eastern bombshell roles she played in early talkies.

The baritone villain, *six,* is the Berber chieftain Ali Ben Ali, though he is not the Red Shadow's enemy but rather the enemy of Pierre's ideal of romance. "Let Love Go" is Ali's advice, in a scene dubbed "Eastern and Western Love." "One woman you have once caressed," Ali reasons, "soon strikes you very like the rest." But Pierre's succeeding solo is "One Alone (to be my own)." In its dotted-note melody and harmonic structure, it is the one Romberg tune that sounds as if Victor Herbert had written it. (Friml thought that everything Romberg wrote sounded as if Rudolf Friml had written it.)

Some might call Captain Fontaine the villain of the piece; he's certainly rude to Paul and no good for Margot. But the role is composed for a light baritone with higher tenor options, a lyric version of Pierre, while the traditional Romberg-Friml villain is virtually a bass, with the black sound that can hold down the bottom line in ensembles. Remember, by this time Romberg and Friml were reveling in their economic power; operetta supplied less than 20 percent of the annual musical output, yet more than 50 percent of the decade's biggest hits were operettas. So the composers had every right to stuff their scores with singing to outdo the Met. Thus, before "One Alone," as Romberg reaches the dominant seventh chord that will resolve in the tonic on a reprise of "Let Love Go," he directs that a tenor soloist rise to a high C as some of the chorus basses sink to the lowest possible C, an astonishing effect over the choral harmonic chord of C^7. For all Romberg's and Friml's and Hammerstein's musings in interviews on how operetta is about "a good story" or "charm" or "the old things," operetta was pulling ever further from musical comedy to reveal just what it was that operetta was about: good music very well sung.

True, operetta still had to figure out what to do with, *seven,* those comic characters, and here *The Desert Song* comes through as well, with Bernie, a reporter, his girl friend, Susan, and Clementina, another temptress, with whom Bennie enjoys a mock-seduction duet, "One Good Boy Gone Wrong." Bennie was Eddie Buzzell, very strong casting for what is basically a comic-relief throwaway part of no importance to the action. Yet both Hammerstein and Romberg knew that comedy was an essential element in the musical. Friml seemed to feel that operetta didn't need it—maybe shouldn't have it. He habitually ignored the comic figures, forcing his producers to commission interpolations to supply the comedians with a musical identity. (These pieces were not printed in the scores and disappeared without a trace when the shows closed.)

What Friml was thinking, in the theatre, while these intrusions were being imposed upon his music is unknown to record. But, clearly, Romberg's idea was, "In a Romberg show, better an intrusion by Romberg." So, when Hammerstein got the idea of punching up the Bennie-Susan subplot with a number in which he gives her bad marks for low sex appeal (capped by a reprise in which he upgrades her after their first kiss), the authors came up with "It," after novelist and Hollywood know-it-all Elinor Glyn's term for charisma, a dancy two-step of the kind that Romberg used to churn out for Shubert revues in the 1910s. This was why Romberg held an active place on Broadway till his death, while Friml had to bow out for nearly forty years of retirement.

Ironically, *The Desert Song*'s producers, writers (except Harbach), choreographer (Bobby Connolly), and even leading man Halliday suffered an out-of-town closing on a show not only as beautifully scored *The Desert Song* but almost as fondly remembered and even occasionally revived—*The New Moon* (1928). However, the Philadelphia shutdown marked not a misfire but rather a show with a lot of potential whose authors were unable to perfect it. In the fecund 1920s, the musical's honchos were so busy that they sometimes found themselves writing one title, in rehearsal for a second title, and in Atlantic City trying out a third title, all at the same time. When *The New Moon* opened at Philadelphia's Chestnut Street Opera House in late December 1927, Romberg was frantically seeing *Rosalie* through its last revisions and Hammerstein was exhausted by having brought *Show Boat* into New York the preceding night. Rather than shove *The New Moon* before New York's critics at less than full power, producers Schwab and Mandel closed it, overseeing a complete rewrite. Two lead actors and nine songs were dropped, and the result won great acclaim, running just over the 500-performance mark. It was, in fact, the last of the great twenties operettas.

It's a somewhat political tale, set among the American French in the late eighteenth century, of how evil people like to get into power so that they can persecute well-intentioned people. As its hero is a freedom fighter and its heroine an aristocrat and as their romantic resolution occurs simultaneously with the outbreak of the French Revolution, we

note the continuing trend toward liberal views of humanity's social condition, along with something like eight firmly established song titles in
operetta's golden catalogue: "Marianne," "The Girl on the Prow," "Try
Her Out at Dances," and the "Stouthearted Men" number, "Stouthearted Men" itself, along with the undisputed ballad hits "One Kiss
(one man to save it for)," "Lover, Come Back To Me," "Softly as in a
Morning Sunrise," and "Wanting You." What a score! All this and Rosi-
ta and Roman for a dance speciality, too!

The great thing about *The New Moon* is how confidently Romberg
folds all the appropriate but also *various* operetta sounds into his music. Like Friml, he knows the value of a taste of tango in the ballad in
the heroine's honor (in "Marianne," mirroring Friml's "Rose Marie" and
"Ma Belle"). Unlike Friml, Romberg is sharp at comic and rhythm numbers—"Try Her Out at Dances," another of those jazz-age numbers
equating sound sex technique with expertise on the dance floor, is one
of the most irresistible of the decade's fox trots. Friml would have
thought it beneath him; fox trots were why God made Herbert Stothart.
And what a pleasure to see how fluently Romberg stuffs his numbers
with subsidiary and connecting tunes that are as appealing as his thou-
sand-dollar melodies are inspiring. In sheer volume, this may be the
biggest score in twenties operetta.

What Romberg has, especially in *The New Moon*, is balance. Hero-
ism, spoof, lyricism, gaucherie, solos, duets, ensembles—the whole
thing is in synch with itself. This is a Romberg hallmark. Other operetta
scores too often throw everything into the love music and the military
stuff, all else a makeweight. In Romberg, every note matters. From the
verismo-like high B flats and C of the supporting tenor's "Softly, As in
a Morning Sunrise" through the huge first-act finaletto (which leaves
the heroine smoldering unhappily in the villain's arms as the hero is led
away in chains thinking she has betrayed him) to the finale, a reprise of
"Stouthearted Men" that the heroine begins alone, joined bit by bit by
the rest of the cast . . . from beginning to end, this show gleams with
musicianly imagination.

Unfortunately, present-day revivals reveal how absurdly zealous the
characters are, how fraught their circumstances. The Romberg-Friml
school did not treat everyday naturalism, we know, but *The New Moon*
must be the most absurdly stylized of the set. As so often, the hero's servant (along with *his* two rival girlfriends) provides nearly all the comedy. In the do-or-die romantic leads, Robert Halliday and his real-life
wife, Evelyn Herbert, apparently knew how to play (and, especially, sing)
this sort of art. But a modern audience would titter through a *New*

Moon that did not lighten the direr aspects of the book and whittle down the monumental score.

In 1928, of course, operetta made its own rules. The critics were ecstatic to a man, except for George Jean Nathan, who as always delighted in detecting the most glancing resemblance between a new song and (usually) some unknown old melody and building this into an act of high piracy. "Lover, Come Back To Me," Nathan wrote, "owes at least a share of its royalties to Gershwin's 'The Man I Love.'" Nathan, you're deaf. Far more receptive to the great silly wonder that was Romberg-Friml operetta was *Life*'s Robert Benchley:

> We haven't seen such refayned acting since the days when the Mysterious Stranger with the white plume turned out to be Prince Boris in disguise. And *then* what merry-making at the inn there was! A toast, a toast to Prince Boris!

After all that, it's comedown to treat Rudolf Friml, even when he was in good form, as in the adaptation of Edwin Milton Royle's 1905 potboiler, *The Squaw Man*, as *The White Eagle* (1927). Here was the *Vagabond King* crowd again—producer Russell Janney, librettists Brian Hooker and W. H. Post, designer James Reynolds—and the same results, albeit without success: a fine score but a dreary book based on an outdated pseudodialect melodrama by another playwright with three names. In this story about an English noble who quits a corrupt society to live more purely in the American west, Friml found plenty to sing of, with the expected "Regimental Song," the "art" number, "Gather the Rose," and even an "Indian Love Call" solo for the tragic Silver Wing (Marion Keeler), "Alone," with the drum beats, feverish high lines, and chromatic harmony we heard in *Rose-Marie*. Friml did achieve one hit, "Give Me One Hour." But after a generation of use by opera singers going pop on radio, it faded away to nothing.

This was a grim time for Friml, who but two years before was on an even footing with Romberg because of *Rose-Marie* and *The Vagabond King*. Then Florenz Ziegfeld proposed a salvational intervention in an adaptation of Alexandre Dumas's *The Three Musketeers*, with Clifford Grey and P. G. Wodehouse doing the lyrics, the usual Joseph Urban and Albertina Rasch, and Dennis King as D'Artagnan. This one, surely, could not fail, right?

There was one problem: the book was to be the work of Ziegfeld's house hack, William Anthony McGuire, alcoholic and undependable, a man who thought nothing of handing out last-minute script revisions on opening night. Tales of his pranks and dodges on this show especially

have passed into Broadway legend, as when he made an amorous invasion of the office of Ziegfeld's assistant, Goldie Clough, who warded him
off with a letter knife. McGuire gallantly kissed her hand, D'Artagnan-
style, and, with a giggle, Goldie dropped the knife. "Jesus Christ, there's
the bedroom scene!" cried McGuire, grabbing pencil and paper to write
this bit into the show, in the confrontation between D'Artagnan and the
vile Milady de Winter in her bedchamber. Another time, late in rehearsals, with the second act not ready, Ziegfeld gave McGuire a deadline—two full scenes by the next afternoon *or else*. Came the afternoon,
the McGuire announced that he had arranged a screening of Douglas
Fairbanks's 1921 *Three Musketeers* film for the entire cast, to purify
their seventeenth-century plastique. While everyone watched the movie,
McGuire scuttled off to a bar and turned out the required pages.

Is any of this true? *The Three Musketeers* script doesn't read like a
hasty patchwork. On the contrary, it's rather carefully derived from the
novel (actually only the first third of it, on D'Artagnan's arrival in Paris,
his meeting with Athos, Porthos, and Aramis, his romance with Constance, and the episode of the twelve diamond studs,* two of which the
hero and his friends must recover to save the Queen of France from hu-
miliation). Most remarkable about McGuire's script is its extreme
length. This is hardly the work of a man beating a deadline.

More interesting to me is P. G. Wodehouse's credit as lyricist. The
Britisher had first strayed into Ziegfeld's compass less than six months
earlier, on *Rosalie*; now here's the spry Princess poet working on a land's
end of operetta, the very opposite of everything the Princess style was
celebrated for. We expect history to be made, genre criticism, a wicked
commentary from within. After all, in his youth with Kern and Bolton
but ten years before, Wodehouse couldn't be serious in musical comedy. Imagine what he'll do with operetta. But not a single lyric of *The
Three Musketeers* betrays anything more than the plodding, good-
natured talent of Clifford Grey. (There was nothing special in the lyrics
credited to Wodehouse on *Rosalie*, either.) Historians have occasionally
hinted that Wodehouse's *Musketeers* byline was more a matter of Ziegfeldian prestige than of actual involvement. For me, the fatal witness is the
Three Musketeers vocal score, published in England only. Grey is the
sole lyricist credited.

Add to this a gigantic feud between Dennis King and his Constance,

* These were changed to a large diamond heart in the show, simply because it
would be easier to see from the middle and back rows of the Lyric Theatre. Diamond
studs are for camera closeups.

Vivienne Segal, an evening stuffed with 'Twas, 'Twould, and 'Tis, and Friml at his *most*, so deeply into his schmalz that virtually every number is a High Operetta Number: "March of the Musketeers," "My Sword and I," "Queen of My Heart," "My Dreams," "Your Eyes," "Welcome To the Queen," not to mention the by now relentless Albertina Rasch damosels (starring Harriet Hoctor, billed in the program as "Premiere Danseuse of the Court," as if Louis XIII had a resident toe dancer doing entrechats during diplomatic lulls). Nothing's real. Nothing's, even, a fox trot. Was this the Jazz Age?

True, Friml, slipped that savor of tango into the release of "Ma Belle," and the comic, D'Artagnan's servant, Planchet, sang "The Colonel and the Major," a Hard-Boiled Herman type of coward-defies-the-bullies joke, and "Court Gossip," both added by unknown hands as Friml shrugged. He did unbend enough to offer one uptempo, contemporary number, late in the evening, for Constance and Planchet, "Ev'ry Little While." It's a little as though somebody had started singing "The Night They Invented Champagne" at a funeral. Where'd *that* come from?

The Three Musketeers sounds like a disaster. However, while it failed to run the full year expected of hit operettas and didn't produce a Friml standard after "Ma Belle" had enjoyed its season of play, the show did succeed. Credit the lavish production, the two stars, and Dumas's great story. Credit even Harriet Hoctor. But this was Friml's farewell in every real sense, and the last of the Romberg-Friml operettas to show a profit. One problem with the form was the production expense. When the relatively modest *Apple Blossoms* and *Blossom Time* were succeeded by more sumptuous productions with casts of a hundred, spectacle became one of operetta's conventions. This was a problem from 1929 on, when the Depression shaved audiences by a considerable margin.

Another problem was the outmoding of the very sound of operetta in a Broadway being reoutfitted by Gershwin, Rodgers, and Porter, not to mention the form's deadly earnest nature at a time when such zesty younger writers as B. G. De Sylva and Herbert Fields were infusing musical comedy with satiric power.

It wasn't only Romberg and Friml whose business was threatened. Consider Arthur Hammerstein, operetta's most faithful producer. It was Hammerstein who cultivated Friml in the 1910s, Hammerstein who produced that key work in operetta's renaissance, *Wildflower*, Hammerstein who first thought that French Canada would provision a great musical. Now it was Arthur Hammerstein who was opening his own theatre, a would-be temple of operetta, on the west side of Broadway between Fifty-Third and Fifty-Fourth streets: the Hammerstein, named for his awesome father, Oscar I. Doors this proud must open upon something regally festive, and that, Arthur decreed, shall be *Golden Dawn* (1927), which some see as an overproduced blandishment, others as a racial embarrassment because of the many principal and chorus roles played by whites in blackface (though some of the cast members were biologically black), and still others see as an aberrant detour in Emmerich Kálmán's earthly voyage. (You'll never guess whom Hammerstein hired to spell Kálmán as cocomposer.)

I see *Golden Dawn* as *Rose-Marie* set in German East Africa. The authors are again Otto Harbach and Oscar Hammerstein, and their heroine is again racially exotic: as Rose-Marie is part Indian and part French among the Canadian English, Dawn is a white girl living in a black tribe. Both love a disgraced hero (respectively, Jim and Steve), who is then turned against his law-enforcement buddy (Sergeant Malone; Captain Eric). The villain (Hawley; sadistic native overseer Shep Keyes) lusts after the heroine, and a dialect comic (Jewish Hard-Boiled Herman; Mr. Pigeon, in Cockney) adds saucy fun. Both shows claimed to be too intermittently musical to list a program, simply citing a few outstanding titles. Both scores feature the hero's love song titled after and in praise of the heroine, "Rose-Marie" and "Dawn," and her establishing song ("Lak Jeem" and "My Bwana") is *her* praise of *him*. Both shows' plots are resolved when the Dark Lady (Wanda; Dawn's demented mother, Mooda) reveals a Secret. Both shows capitalized on vivid, previously unexploited locales, emphasized spectacle, and employed huge casts—seventy-two in *Rose-Marie*, one hundred eleven in *Golden Dawn*. Finally, both shows totally adhered to the Romberg-Friml structure.

How this all came about was, simply, that Emmerich Kálmán was in New York for a staging of his Viennese show *The Circus Princess* early in 1927, and Hammerstein seized the day. His cast lacked the charisma of *Rose-Marie*'s Mary Ellis and Dennis King, for if hero Paul Gregory and villain Robert Chisholm were dependable singer-actors, Louise Hunter was a minor Met soprano who never really got anywhere. But there was a stirring chorus and a marvelous turn by voodoo dancer Jacques Cartier, and trivia buffs love to point out the presence of Cary Grant (then named Archie Leach) in a small role.

Of course it was Herbert Stothart who spelled Kálmán in the comic ditties, and the title song had been composed and published in Germany two years earlier by Robert Stolz as "Komm in Den Park von Sanssouci!" (Stothart got equal billing on the new sheet music merely for lengthening the original's clumsy, abrupt ending with three extra notes.) Hammerstein billed *Golden Dawn* as "a new musical comedy," but Kálmán's extraordinary power makes it one of the utmost of the operettas. "A stately opera," the *Herald Tribune*'s Percy Hammond called it. "The music," wrote E. W. Osborn, of the *World,* "was of real grand opera type." In fact, almost all the critics singled out the score as a glory, while regretting the lack of comedy and the show's dull pacing in general. "Near midnight," John Anderson of the *Post* remarked, "some restless first-nighters seemed to fear that the title might be altogether too literal." Walter Winchell dubbed it *"The Golden Yawn."* Then, too, its seldom seen but notorious 1930 film adaptation, which foolishly retained the casting concept of whites in blackface, has made *Golden Dawn* the campiest of titles. What, a whole African tribe thinks this white woman is one of them? But most late-twenties operettas had ridiculous story lines. *Golden Dawn*'s real problem was an ill-advised makeup plan.

Though its glorious music never caught on even marginally, *Golden Dawn* actually made money. Operettas could run, even flawed ones, like *Castles in the Air* (1926). To the music of Percy Wenrich and the book and lyrics of Raymond W. Peck, this one slipped out of the Romberg-Friml stranglehold as a modern-dress show whose first and third acts were set in Westchester. Act Two, however, takes us to yet another fableland, Latavia, where college-boy cutup John Brown is passing himself off as the local prince to impress American heiress Evelyn Devine. This "American Operatic Comedy" also troubled to inflect the entire evening with humor; what other operetta had a hero who could be called a cutup? Still, the score mostly assumed the usual positions. "I Would Like To Fondle You" is jazzy, and "Baby" (accented on the second syllable, just to fit the melody), the authors assure us, is a "foxtrot lullaby." But "Hail To the Prince" is the usual hero-mustering-the-populace item, "The Rainbow of Your Smile" the usual drippy waltz, and "My Lips, My Love" the usual duet. "Lantern of Love" at least brings out the musician in Wenrich in a descending, syncopated two-note hook used in both the A and B strains. A good second-rank number, it sounds like something that Stothart might have sneaked into a Friml score. With J. Harold Murray and Vivienne Segal heading the cast, *Castles in the Air* ran 160 performances, a good showing for a work without distinction.

But operettas were also *not* running, even operettas that should have run—*Rainbow,* for instance. As we've seen, this was Vincent Youmans's take on the Romberg-Friml program, and historians regularly call it one of the most lamentable casualties of all time. We are told of a bold and brilliant show that used operetta's conventions in highly unconventional ways. For instance, though the love plot was very strongly felt, there were no love duets. The lovers' sole number together was a comic song, the ironic "I Like You As You Are." Rushed into town by the producer Philip Goodman when still in need of trimming and technical rehearsals, *Rainbow* suffered a disastrous first night. This is usually cited as the reason that it ran less than a month. There was also the problem of the out-of-the-way theatre, the Gallo, only a year old then and located on Fifty-Fourth Street just east of Eighth Avenue.

First-night disasters notwithstanding, however, *Rainbow*'s reviews were unanimously enthusiastic. Granted, most critics noted the show's problems, and a few lashed Goodman for poor showmanship. But even George Jean Nathan liked it; he liked not only the score but the book! Why didn't the public respond? Why did they also fail to support *A Wonderful Night* (1929), a version of Johann Strauss's *Die Fledermaus* copied (by Mr. J. J. Shubert) from Max Reinhardt's celebrated 1928 staging at Berlin's Deutsches Theater. Reinhardt was the talk of Berlin for his free interpretation of the classic, with filchings from the Strauss catalogue to alter the score, a pantomime during the overture, and a gala revolving stage, novel in Berlin and unheard of in New York. "Take notes!" Mr. J. J. warned his house designer, Watson Barratt. "Steal everything but the ushers!"

The Shuberts had produced an earlier *Fledermaus* as *The Merry Countess* (1912), with José Collins and the Dolly Sisters; this new one had Cary Grant (still named Archie Leach) as Eisenstein. Many a book tells us that Grant lip-synched his music while standing in front of a male chorus. Nonsense. Only in the second act and the third-act finale is Eisenstein in the company of a chorus; Reinhardt hadn't changed Strauss *that* much. Besides, as we know from the film *Suzy*, Grant could sing. Not as well as Dennis King, no, but better than more than a few actors who played leads in musicals.

The main thing is that, even with Reinhardt's superb production (for the purloining of which the Shuberts had to see him in court; the Widow Strauss sued, too), *A Wonderful Night* limped along for a few stubborn months to empty houses. And the notices had been terrific, too. Noël Coward's *Bitter Sweet* also did disappointing business, though back home it was the longest-running English musical of the decade.

Even sadder was the quick collapse of Vincent Youmans's *Great Day* (1929), a tale of the old south that went through perhaps the most extensive tryout revision in the annals of musical theatre. Convinced that producer Goodman had sabotaged *Rainbow* with bad business decisions, Youmans determined to mount his own shows. But he hired mediocrities and leased a black cat of a house way up on Columbus Circle that hadn't had a hit since *The Wizard of Oz*, twenty-six years before—the same house where Ziegfeld saw *Louie the 14th* fail to draw. At the first sign of trouble, Youmans started firing, and he didn't stop till he had replaced everything but the little metal brads that bound the script pages. It was his tragedy to be at his most inspired just when his shows were bombing almost as a rule, and, while *Great Day* left behind "More Than You Know," "Without a Song," "Happy Because I'm in Love," and the title number, a rouser in the revivalist tent-show style that Youmans commanded without equal, the show itself crashed to pieces. Like *A Wonderful Night* and *Bitter Sweet*, *Great Day* opened within hours of the Wall Street Crash. But so did *The Street Singer, Sons o' Guns,* and *Fifty Million Frenchmen,* and they were hits.

The Crash didn't kill operetta; musical comedy did. Or, rather, musical comedy's vitality made operetta's hauteur look absurd. American art is always centered upon energy, not upon elegance. In fact, even this early in its development, Third-Age operetta had been redesigning itself to suit the national taste.

Rio Rita (1927), for example, tempered operetta's cult of romance with musical comedy's anything-for-a-laugh, in effect setting up two separate shows that alternated throughout the evening without ever really connecting. One show was quasi-Romberg-Friml, about the love of a Texas Ranger (J. Harold Murray) for a tempestuous Mexican beauty (Ethelind Terry), with the complication that he's hunting a bandit known as the Kinkajou, who may be her brother. The second show was a comedy vehicle for the brand-new team of Wheeler and Woolsey, cherubic Bert Wheeler playing the perennial dupe and thin, nervous, cigar-smoking Robert Woolsey playing the perennial shyster.

Both shows were written by Guy Bolton and Fred Thompson with a score by Harry Tierney and Joseph McCarthy, all four of them specialists in musical comedy rather than operetta. Oddly, the score was far stronger in the love music than in the fun stuff, especially the New Dance Sensation, "The Kinkajou," which sounds like the clunky solos that beginning piano students play. The obligatory martial air, "The Rangers' Song," sports lyrics that make "Stouthearted Men" ring like Shakespeare, and it's amusing to find Tierney and McCarthy turning the first big love duet spot into a fox trot with a pseudo-western clopping bass, "Rio Rita (life is sweeta, Rita, when you are near)." This is not the brand of music that Dennis King sang to Vivienne Segal.

But that must have been the *Rio Rita* that Ziegfeld wanted. He had planned the show to be the initiating event at his own theatre, and like the building itself—designed, like all Ziegfeld productions, by Joseph Urban, who was in fact an architect as well as an artist—the primary attraction must be above all a Thing of Beauty. No doubt *Show Boat* would have been a more impressively inaugural work. But *Show Boat* was still under construction; Kern and Hammerstein had signed their contract with Ziegfeld in November 1926, and the Ziegfeld Theatre opened on February 2, 1927. (As it was, *Rio Rita* was still running when *Show Boat* pulled into town at the end of the year, and Ziegfeld moved *Rita* elsewhere to make way for the Mother of All Musicals.)

It may be that Ziegfeld couldn't use anything substantial to open his house, for he wanted attention focused on his new baby. For a generation, Ziegfeld had used the New Amsterdam Theatre as his house of choice, so constantly that the theatregoing public assumed that Ziegfeld owned it. No: brutal Abe Erlanger was in charge on Forty-Second Street, and Ziegfeld had long wanted his own place. As it happened, William Randolph Hearst had just built the Warwick Hotel, on Sixth Avenue at Fifty-Third Street, and Hearst hoped that further construction would jazz up the property values on dank Sixth Avenue. As always, Hearst decided to make the history himself, and it was he who bankrolled the Ziegfeld, which rose directly across the avenue from the Warwick, about as far from the New Amsterdam as one could get and still be, more or less, in the theatre district.

So *Rio Rita* was that rare thing in musicals, a vehicle not for the star but for the theatre. All night, between *Rita*'s ravings and the Wheeler-Woolsey high jinks, there were opportunities for glorious visuals and a ton of dancing (as in a "Moonlight Ballet," a "Spanish Shawl" number, a "Black and White Ballet"). In keeping with *Rio Rita*'s half-and-half genre, Sammy Lee choreographed the musical comedy numbers and the inescapable Albertina Rasch ruled the ballerinas. The show *looked* great, but the theatre, with its egg-shaped auditorium and fabulous Urban mural overhead, looked greater. *Rita* was the perfect tenant for the Ziegfeld Theatre. Brooks Atkinson's appreciative *Times* review mentioned the producer's name eight times and Urban's three times but never named the show's authors.

Another Ziegfeld "operetta" teaches us how eager this form was to marry musical comedy. We must return to *Rosalie*, Ziegfeld's version of Marilyn Miller as the princess of Romanza but also as Charles Lindbergh's girl friend, a notably contemporary princess indeed. The imaginary European country, the exotic costumes and folkish dances, and the name of Sigmund Romberg on the poster alerts us to an operetta atmosphere. But Romberg composed only half the score; the other half was by the Gershwin brothers. Apparently, Ziegfeld was in a hurry, and everyone was busy—Romberg on the first version of *The New Moon*, which was just about to go to Philadelphia for tryouts, and Gershwin on *Funny Face*, which was already on its tryout and undergoing savage reconstruction. Why the two composers didn't simply say no to Ziegfeld is a question no historian has yet asked. Perhaps one simply didn't say no to the master showman: who could know when you would need him desperately to produce your masterpiece?

Anyway, Gershwin and Romberg said yes and divided up the score. Alexander Woollcott wondered if "we shall soon have a novel written by Harold Bell Wright and Ernest Hemingway." But perhaps Ziegfeld had more in mind than buying music off the rack. Maybe he liked this hybrid format in which the Gershwin's "Oh Gee! Oh Joy!" showed off Miller's exuberance while the Romberg-Wodehouse "Kingdom of Dreams" savored her wistfulness, in which Romberg and Wodehouse could go Romanza in the "Hussar March" while the Gershwins could sell us on that "New York Serenade."

According to the legend, the Gershwins had three weeks to come up with their half of the score, which explains why so much of it was that staple of twenties musical composition, trunk material. The perennial dropout "The Man I Love" was dusted off, to no avail. From *Primrose*, "Wait a Bit Susie" got new lyrics as "Beautiful Gypsy," a duet for hero and heroine. "Show Me the Town," dropped from *Oh, Kay!*, and "How Long Has This Been Going On?," dropped more or less that very second from *Funny Face*, provisioned the comic soubrette, Mary (Bobbe Arnst), who got another *Funny Face* number, "Dance Alone with You," with new lyrics as "Everybody Knows I Love Somebody" for her duet with Jack Donahue, her love interest.

It sounds as though Romberg scored the romantic and marital numbers and Gershwin the jazzy ones. But it was Gershwin who wrote the martial "Follow the Drum" and Romberg who wrote a comic number, "The King Can Do No Wrong." So what *was* this *Rosalie*, in the end? It's too up-to-date for an operetta yet too Romanzan for a musical comedy, for the princess has not only a fiancé drawn from the nobility but a King father and a Queen mother. However, unlike most of operetta's kings and queens, these two provide much of the laughter in the Guy Bolton-William Anthony McGuire book, as the dithering King (Frank Morgan) is crushed and crushed again by the venemous Queen (Margaret Dale). Perhaps *Rosalie* is not even part operetta, just a musical comedy with a Royal Family.

The most ingenious attempt to blend operetta's High Maestro lyricism with musical comedy's blunt pizzazz was Kern and Hammerstein's period piece *Sweet Adeline* (1929), one of the glories of the age. Abundantly musical yet extremely funny in an at times low-down way, broad of scope yet finished in its details, this show shows us how far the musical had developed from *Sally, Irene,* and *Mary.* But then, *Sweet Adeline* especially illustrates how far operetta itself could move from *The Student Prince* and *Rose-Marie.* With *Show Boat* already under their belts, Kern and Hammerstein had no trouble creating a revisionist form. Their very instincts had become revolutionary; hit or flop, they never wrote anything ordinary again. But *Sweet Adeline* is particularly notable as the last of the decade's Great American Operettas because it so consistently flouted operetta's conventions.

First, *Sweet Adeline* has no central love plot. *What?* An operetta with no Karl Franz and Kathie? No Rose-Marie and Jim? Who's going to sing "Indian Love Call"? Who's going to bash that fancypants Dennis King in the tummy just as he goes for a high note, as Vivienne Segal, irked at King's rush-hour technique, reportedly did one night in *The Three Musketeers?* But *Sweet Adeline* is more about its heroine's rise in show business than about the Man She Loves. There are three of them, in fact, for she loses the first (a callow cutie) to her sister, then trades in the second (a stalwart bore) for the third (artistic, like her).

Second, while Addie and her boys are all serious people, the show is otherwise loaded with comics—dizzy Ruppert Day (Charles Butterworth), brother of boy friend number two; piccolo player Dot (Violet Carlson), Ruppert's vis-à-vis; Dan Ward (Robert Emmett Keane), a press agent; and his wife, a "hokum queen" of burlesque,* who was played by an authentic vaudeville star of the old school, Irene Franklin, in a rare Broadway appearance.

Franklin typifies *Sweet Adeline's* odd generic tone. What other operetta's second woman lead (and it's a huge part) was a vaudeville headliner? Try to imagine a vaudeville diva strutting through *The Student Prince,* or even *Rosalie.* But then Hammerstein was always keen on furnishing his backstagers with atmosphere. Ziegfeld's Sally may leap from dishwasher to *Follies* star, but Addie's rise is more gradual—from waitress-singer at her German father's beer garden in Hoboken through burlesque to Broadway. The episodes involving burlesque are especially fetching—luring unsuspecting backers, auditioning the New Find (it's Addie, singing "Why Was I Born?"), and the dress rehearsal, as an Ori-

---

* It is important for the reader to keep in mind that the burlesque I speak of, at the time of *Sweet Adeline's* turn-of-the-century setting, was a thoroughly respectable but downmarket theatre art, one that especially favored the versatile woman—singer, comic, and actress in one. She was known in those days as a "serio-comic."

ental Number is overwhelmed in a frenzy of hammering, shouting, blundering, sets flying up and down, and things falling over. This is in fact the first-act finale, capped as Franklin erupted onstage in harem dress screaming, "Where the hell are my finger cymbals? *Props!,*" as the curtain dropped to the floor.

Note the character's colloquial approach; this is no "zounds" operetta. It covers a full social scale, bringing together Knickerbocker aristos (Addie's supporters), the middle class (Addie's family), and the proletariat (the thespians) in a very Hammersteinian concept: theatre harmonizes class distinctions, because theatregoing itself is a democratic concept. One art fits all.

Still, the back-alley patois informs much of the show's personality, especially in Franklin's scenes. Demonstrating a song called "Naughty Boy" to Ruppert, Lulu invites him to take part in the staging, in effect recreating one of the old-time musical's favorite trope, the girls-flirting-with-a-man number:

> LULU: You sit in this chair, and you play the part of the tenor.
> RUPPERT: What does he do?
> LULU: He don't do nothin'—he's a tenor.

There's a lot of traditional humor in the book:

> DAN: I met a gal last week who'd never been kissed.
> NELLIE: I didn't know there was any gals like that no more.
> DAN: (after two beats) She ain't like that no more.

But Hammerstein can surprise you, as when Dan and Lulu are discussing a woman Lulu doesn't approve of:

> DAN: She had twins last month, didn't she?
> LULU: There's a story goes with that—one of those twins ain't his!

Actually, the casting of Franklin symbolizes another of *Sweet Adeline*'s breaks with the Romberg-Friml format. Twenties operetta took off with *Apple Blossoms*'s ultracontemporary and realistic Manhattan but quickly turned make-believe and Ruritanian. *Sweet Adeline*'s Manhattan was antique and therefore exotic, true, but the show made a point of not just borrowing the colorful setting but recreating it. It was old but *familiar* old, not fantasy old. Right at the top of the evening, customers were greeted not by the usual medley of the tunes but by "Fin de Siècle," Kern's own arrangement of "melodies of the period," as the program put it: a twee fanfare, then on to such classics as "A Bicycle Built For Two," "The Band Played On," and the utterly evocative vamp to the

Florodora Sextet, which would bring old-timers straight back to the day when a line of Young Ladies bearing parasols and dancing on stage right while a line of Young Men danced on stage left was the height of showmanship. A two-seater bicycle was in fact one of the show's props, and the redolent set designs included one that recreated the bar of the Hoffman House in Madison Square, a famous vaudevillians' hangout where, in Act Two, that great old vaudevillian Jim Thornton appeared, portrayed by . . . Jim Thornton.

Of course, this was no more than a touching cameo. It was Irene Franklin who really pulled *Sweet Adeline* into the reality of America's show biz past, for she owned a substantial part of it. Playful and pretty, she wrote her own material, songs and sketches that isolated "types"—the crone who drives everybody crazy with endless questions at a ticket window as the line behind her grows and grows; the crazy waitress; the streetcar passenger who wants to get to Watt Street (Conductor: What street? Irene: That's right. Conductor: No, *what* street?), a forerunner of Abbott and Costello's "Who's on First?." Franklin tended to marry her accompanists. She fell in love with Burt Green while working with him at Tony Pastor's, though Green was married—and *Sweet Adeline* mirrors this when Franklin refers to her husband's ex-wife as "the woman he was married to when I first met him." *Sweet Adeline* even got a song out of it, and Hammerstein let the fecund Franklin write her own lyrics, to Kern's music, in "My Husband's First Wife," a complaint about the Eternal Paragon, ever healthy, ever home, ever giving birth. The children were perfectly tended, clean, trim, their "shoes always hooked." "They were born in the morning," the song concludes, "but dinner was cooked."

For her second number, Franklin again wrote the lyrics, this time to music by her second husband (and accompanist), Jerry Jarnagin. It may seem strange that Kern and Hammerstein relinquished their authors' rights, but, remember, this was a time of collaborative bylines. Ziegfeld had commissioned two separate teams for *Rosalie*'s score, interpolations were still common (though less so than even five years before), and Kern in particular loved adulterating his scores with true-life ambiance—a glee club performing a medley of actual college songs in the college musical *Leave It to Jane*, for instance. How better to reassert the Franklin style—to revisit, by synechdoche, the world of the serio-comic—than by having Franklin repossess it herself?

But Irene Franklin was not *Sweet Adeline*'s star. Helen Morgan was, as a reward for the eminence that she had gained as *Show Boat*'s tragic Julie. Here was another of *Sweet Adeline*'s breakways, for operettas were never star vehicles. Sure, Dennis King told historian Stanley Green that Ziegfeld phoned King, offered to star him, asked what he would like to do; King says *The Three Musketeers*; Ziegfeld says Done. It sounds unlikely; King wasn't that big. Anyway, Ziegfeld vehicles were built exclusively around heroines and comics—Marilyn Miller, Eddie Cantor, Mary Eaton, Leon Errol.

So here was an operetta with a musical comedy star surrounded mostly by musical comedy types in an atmosphere almost realistic in its recreation of 1898. Maybe "musical comedy star" doesn't do justice to Helen Morgan's rich identity. Though a genuine (if very light) soprano, she was far more a cabaret than a theatre singer, and her nonstop pathos made her unique in the line of twenties heroines. (At *Sweet Adeline*'s first night, Morgan's colleague Helen Ford, who had exhilarated *The Gingham Girl* and *Dearest Enemy* with let-'er-rip energy, turned to her producer-husband, George Ford, and whispered, "Doesn't that dame ever stop weeping?") Kern and Hammerstein made the most of Morgan's natural style, setting the tender Addie among the brash theatre folk, military men, and socialites like a Snow White in the forest so that Morgan's songs varied from the overtly sentimental to the plangent. No "Come, Boys, Let's All Be Gay, Boys" or "French Military Marching Song" for this heroine. "Don't Ever Leave Me" is typical—wistful and clinging. "Here Am I" is even more so, its refrain a poem that Addie has written to the first of her three beloveds, which she sings in reprise, heartbreakingly, when the man sends the same poem as a pledge of love to Addie's sister.

It's the music, of course, that really makes *Sweet Adeline*—and that pursues the show's break with operetta cliché. First, there is very little three-quarter time, that lingua franca of traditional romance. Addie's "waltz ballad" with the third of her men, "The Sun About To Rise," is quickly rescanned into a two-step, and all the other romantic numbers are in $\frac{4}{4}$. The only soldiers' song, a "march ballad" called "Out of the Blue," has a strange mixture of pep and beauty that no "Rangers' Song" ever knew. True, the verse does sound a martial note, but the refrain is indeed a ballad, its subject the pleasures of mail delivered to the front lines, not the camaraderie of warriors or here come the mounties.

Ironically, *Sweet Adeline*'s outstanding song is not the hit "Why Was I Born?" or the recurring time-setter, the German-folkish "'Twas Not So Long Ago" (sung at one point in German as "Es war schon damals so"). No, the big number is "Some Girl Is on Your Mind," a huge male choral scene involving all three of Addie's men (and Addie's voice, from offstage) that has stopped the show in every revival, not only because it's so powerful as sheer lyrical expression but because the audience is stunned to discover unknown music of such high calibre. It's *Sweet Adeline*'s "Ol' Man River," a tune that builds to such formidable self-expression that one realizes that the American musical has indeed discovered its own voice at last, that this Third Age of jazz and broads and stories is going to see the musical through its era as an art complete, no one's little brother but a thing-in-itself. It is just becoming protean and unpredictable, capable of taking any form it needs to, tackling any subject.

That was great news to Arthur Hammerstein, no doubt, but his central concern was that, after offering *Show Boat* to Ziegfeld, nephew Oscar and Jerry Kern took *Sweet Adeline* to Arthur, and it looked like a sure thing. It opened, in Hammerstein's theatre, in very early autumn of 1929 to a sizable advance sale, glowing reviews, and sell-out business. But the Crash cut down ticket sales so sharply that though the piece lasted 234 performances, it failed to pay off. Thus shelved, *Sweet Adeline* never entered the canon of twenties operettas, but then it never was an operetta in the first place.

Sweet Adeline was, as the program billed it, a "musical play." Smarter than operetta yet more intense than musical comedy, this form would prove to be the essential one in musical comedy history, from *Show Boat* and *Carousel* to *West Side Story* and *Follies*. Before we consider the first of these musical plays, let us see what musical comedy has been up to.

Add a Little Wiggle

MUSICAL COMEDY REINVENTED

Here's another difference between musical comedy and operetta. In the latter, the songs constantly surge up out of the action, even overwhelm it. In musical comedy, the songs generally interrupt the action.

At least, they did so in late-twenties musical comedy, because shows' content most often lay in stars and scores, not in story. However, as operetta had known for decades, in art, story contains everything: character, theme, attitude. Without story, one has nothing but miscellaneous fun.

But then, some of the most successful late-twenties musical comedies were just that. The Aarons-Freedley show reveled in its lack of content, in its abundance of fun. I've already discussed how ultra-twenties their *Funny Face* (1927) was, with its Astaires and Victor Moore and Gershwin score. *Smarty*, they called it out of town, because the show looked great and sounded great and moved great and, by the taste of the day, was great. Unique storytelling wasn't an issue in the late 1920s any more than it had been earlier in the decade. Again and again, unique performers were the issue.

The De Sylva, Brown, and Henderson shows seem to have adopted the Aarons-Freedley approach; the authors even wrote for Aarons and Freedley—but not yet. *Good News!* (1927), the trio's first book show after the *Scandals*, had no stars, an affront to the Aarons and Freedley

First Rule of Musical Comedy Showmanship: start with the Astaires or Gertrude Lawrence or at least Queenie Smith. *Manhattan Mary* (1927) was an Ed Wynn vehicle, but George White produced it and, during an especially dispiriting rehearsal period, considered junking the script and turning it into *George White's Scandals of 1927*. It wasn't a good show. White's version of *Sally*, with Elizabeth Hines as the heroine and Wynn in Leon Errol's role of the waiter who aids the Cinderella's backstage rise, *Manhattan Mary* ended as *Sally* did, with Mary starring in the *Scandals* just as Sally had crashed the *Follies*. The score was terrible, without a single hit, though by now a number like "Broadway (the heart of the world)" should have brought out the beat in the team. What they came up with was a syncopated funeral. And whose idea was the aimlessly busy New Dance Sensation, "The Five-Step"? The songwriters wrote the script, with William K. Wells and George White, who played himself onstage—well, that's one thing Ziegfeld hadn't thought of. White even let Wynn, as Crickets, manipulate a *Scandals* audition in Hines's favor. Wynn favors the "egg-wiped" approach.

> WHITE: I never heard of that.
> CRICKETS: *(exasperated)* I'm telling you what it is. Egg-wiped! Egg-wiped! They spell it "E-G-Y-P-T."
> WHITE: Oh, *Egypt*.
> CRICKETS: That's what I mean. That's theatrical history. It goes back to 250 B.C. when the Egyptians used to pick chorus girls for understudies for their musical comedies.
> WHITE: Why, there weren't any musical comedies then.
> CRICKETS: Yes, there were. What are you talking about? I still use some of the jokes. What was the name of the Egyptian king at the time? I read his name recently. Not Pyorrhea. I have it. Tootie Ankerman. It's an historical fact that in 250 B.C. Tootie Ankerman put on a musical comedy, but the leading lady became suddenly ill. That's the same predicament that you're in. . . . They just lined up the girls and . . . counted seven from his left and he took that girl.

That girl, after further fudging and dodging by Wynn, turns out to be Hines, and a star is born.

Manhattan Mary sorted out its problems before the New York premiere, though it lost Hines on the first night of the tryout, to be replaced by Ona Munson. The show scored a hit, as did the next De Sylva, Brown, and Henderson title, *Hold Everything!* (1928). Here was another dead score, with one hit stranded in the middle of it, "You're the Cream in my Coffee." In the age of Jack Dempsey and Gene Tun-

ney, a boxing musical was inevitable, but how about one with an ingra-
tiating welterweight as the romantic hero, a demented clown as a boxer wannabe, and an impedient manager sabotaging the few moves the
wannabe manages to get right? Producers Aarons and Freedley saw Jack
Whiting as the hero, Victor Moore as the manager, and, as crazy Gink
Schiner, they offered a discovery, Bert Lahr.

Lahr's amazing career exceeds the parameters of this book, chrono-
logically (he was still on Broadway in the 1960s), generically (opposite
E. G. Marshall, he played lead in Broadway's first taste of absurdism, in
Waiting for Godot in 1956, and he played in more spoken drama from
Feydeau to Perelman), and professionally (his Great Role was in the
movies, as the Cowardly Lion in MGM's *The Wizard of Oz*). Yet in *Hold
Everything!* Lahr was already There, his persona as fully inflected as the
veteran Ed Wynn's. Lahr was a Dutch comic, sort of, but a very physical one. Some clown: he could jump from mock-lover to mock-bully to
genuine victim in a line. He liked to. Something in Lahr's comic instinct
led him to blend many parts of legitimate characters into one perfectly
implausible character. Thus, he could create a boxer who was as much
tyrant as coward, even as much passerby as champion.

This was new in comic identities, and no one saw that more clearly
than Victor Moore, playing Lahr's manager. As John Lahr, Bert's son, recounts it in *Notes on a Cowardly Lion*, Moore tells Lahr, "You've got the
part in the piece. There's nothing I can do about it. Now, I'll help you
all I can. . . . But don't you do anything not to help me."

Lahr, always a considerate colleague, didn't need the coaching. But it
fixes a point in history in which Mr. Potato Head came up against the
Wild One. In fact, Moore's great days as William Gaxton's partner (in
six shows) were yet ahead of him. Whiting, too, had plenty of run left
before he bowed out as the oily mayor of the future in *The Golden Apple* (1954). But Lahr, newer than either, walked off with the show. "It's
the humor of complete, almost manic lack of restraint," said the *Post*.
"One of the quaintest drolls I have ever seen," said no less than St. John
Ervine, in the *World*. The *American* summed it up in its headline: NEW
COMEDY KING CROWNED IN MUSICAL PLAY.

From them on, Lahr did indeed reign, like all great jesters his own
stereotype, at once universal and inimitable. Lahr's *gnong-gnong* alarm
noise, his rubber face, his tough-timid antics were rich enough for a career. But there was more, for Lahr added an absorbing conflict, that between the proletarian kid and an imagined all-American princeling. No
one spoofed WASP ice better than Lahr; no one else so intensely in-
habited the fraudulent calm of the insecure celebrity or so exposed the

concentration of the loser who thinks he's winning, as when Moore found Lahr shadow-boxing in his dressing room minutes before his climactic fight:

MOORE: Look out, you'll foul yourself.
LAHR: Leave me alone, I'm winnin'.

Lahr was as new as the 1920s could get, another of the burgeoning minority class that was going to remake the rules for ethnic humor. Unlike Fanny Brice, Al Jolson, and Eddie Cantor, Lahr never played Jewish humor. His predecessors inherited certain perceptions about who they were allowed to be, whom they could play. Lahr invented himself from top to toe.

It must have been something watching Lahr face off with old-timer Moore. But in a way Lahr was facing off far more, for just across the street from *Hold Everything!*, at Erlanger's Theatre (today the St. James), was the last George M. Cohan musical, *Billie* (1928), an adaptation of Cohan's 1912 hit *Broadway Jones*. The year before, Cohan had made his last appearance in a Cohan musical, *The Merry Malones*, which had opened the Erlanger. Cohan's absolutely unevolved art was an ironic choice with which to inaugurate a new house, but then Erlanger was a generation older even than Cohan. As always in Cohan's twenties musicals, both shows were filled with dancing. And the Old Man hadn't lost his touch, as in *The Merry Malones*'s famous subway-car scene, in which a horde of chorus people sat boy-girl, the boys in light suits with checked tam o' shanters and checked vests and the girls in white cloche hats and white skirts with checked jackets. *Damn*, but that guy had it!

Yet he lost it in the overall, for he was still doing the Cinderella, and the Irish, and the sentimental, as if *Lady, Be Good!* had never happened. *Billie*'s score is shockingly *usé* for 1928, perhaps defiantly so, with "I'm a One Girl Man," "Personality," "The Two of Us," "Ev'ry Boy in Town's My Sweetheart," and "Go Home Ev'ry Once in a While" sounding the preacher's note. Was Cohan reproaching the Jazz Age for overturning his idols of God, Country, Family? Never had his compositional skills seemed so rudimentary, as in the idiotic tonic-dominant pulse of "Happy" or the atrociously dreary "Where Were You—Where Was I." *Billie*'s title song, a pretty waltz, was another of those girl's-name anthems (last line: "My parents expected a boy"). *The Merry Malones* did okay business, *Billie* failed, and that was the last time that "Book, music, and lyrics by George M. Cohan" was seen on a theatre marquee for a new show.

There were other superannuated holdovers—a tuneless adaptation of

Ethel Barrymore's 1901 vehicle *Captain Jinks of the Horse Marines* as *Captain Jinks* (1925), with its would-be hit, "I Could Be Fond of You (if you could be fond of me-ee)," which sounds like one of the many inspirations for *The Boy Friend*'s score but was in fact so unsung that it's doubtful that Sandy Wilson ever heard it. That same year, *Mercenary Mary* blithely reasserted the legacy-with-a-catch plot, though it did have a lively, quite up-to-date score. Another of the old-school Dutch comics, Sam Bernard, made a last stand in *Piggy* (1927), a new musical setting for his most famous part, the title role in *The Rich Mr. Hoggenheimer* (1906), itself a musical, though, by 1927, as gone a one as D. W. Griffith's Biographs were when Warner Brothers made *The Public Enemy* with James Cagney.

A lot can happen in twenty years. Even Fred Stone finally lost it in *Three Cheers* (1928), an extravaganza updated enough to set its second act in Hollywood, with the usual team of producer Charles Dillingham, authors R. H. Burnside and Anne Caldwell, heroine Dorothy Stone, villain Oscar Ragland, and so on. But the Raymond Hubbell-Caldwell score needed De Sylva, Brown, and Henderson interpolations, and an ailing Stone had to cancel, to be replaced by his good friend Will Rogers, utterly out of his element. Rogers's charisma saved the production, but Stone's career in musicals was all but over, and he took extravaganza with him.*

Dependable genres held their place in exhibits both ordinary and influential. The "New York City" show, for instance, made a bit of history in *Good Boy* (1928), an Arthur Hammerstein production—so you already know who composed half the score. Right. Working with Herbert Stothart were Kalmar and Ruby. Harbach and Oscar Hammerstein (and Henry Myers) wrote the book, about two Arkansas brothers (Eddie Buzzell and Charles Butterworth) tackling the big town. Buzzell was, as always, the fast talker and Butterworth the gentle stooge, but the main thing here was the staging (by a team of technicians), a dazzling blueprint for treadmills, backcloths, and bit pieces flown in and out to keep the action almost cinematic. (Hammerstein would return to this plan nineteen years later in *Allegro*.) Each of the two acts had sixteen scenes, the first act reaching its finale as a hotel suite broke apart to bring Buzzell and Barbara Newberry onto a balcony overlooking, it seemed, the entire metropolis. The score was substandard, peaking in the rather

---

* There was one last one, *Simple Simon* (1930), a Ziegfeld show starring Ed Wynn with a Rodgers and Hart score. Given that spectacle and a star comic were extravaganza's chief assets, and that a tuneful score never hurt, this sounds like a smash. It bombed. The form had outlived its audience.

mere "I Wanna Be Loved By You," sung by the Betty Boopish Helen Kane, and a wild and crazy tryout despoiled the second act of almost all its music. Still, the unusual production put *Good Boy* over and also paved the way for technical experiments in the 1930s. As with the revolving stage of *A Wonderful Night,* a very science of theatre production was being discovered, one that would affect theatre writing in the way that the action could now span a wide and swift geography.

The Cinderella backstager held up in *The Street Singer* (1929), one of the decade's most forgotten hits. But then Niclas Kempner, Sam Timberg, Graham John, and Edgar Smith were uncelebrated then and even unfootnoted now, and the musical's history structures itself around Names, not titles. Queenie Smith and Guy Robertson led the cast; "From Now On" was the fox trot, "Jumping Jimminy" the New Dance Sensation, and "You Might Have Known I Loved You" the hesitation waltz, still popular in this age of jazz; and the Parisian setting led Smith to the heights of stardom not at the *Follies* or *Scandals* but at the Folies Bergère.

One of the most enduring genres, by now about thirty years old, was the innocent-in-alien-land trope, a staple of turn-of-the-century Broadway. Ziegfeld and Eddie Cantor took it over in *Whoopee* (1928), from Owen Davis's 1923 comedy, *The Nervous Wreck,* and here was one of the hits of the age. Cantor played his usual manipulative victim, the alien land being the American west of bullying cowboys and grudge-bearing Indians and Cantor's hypochondria furnishing a substantial fraction of the evening's jokes. As so often in a star comic vehicle, he was, however essential to the entertainment, incidental to the plot itself, which concerned a Romeo-Juliet romance between a white girl (Frances Upton) in love with an Indian (Paul Gregory)—actually only part-Indian and thoroughly assimilated into white culture. But she has been promised to mean Sheriff Bob (John Rutherford). Cantor's inadvertent flight with Upton, with the sheriff and his posse in evil-eyed pursuit, provided that little plot *Whoopee* had.

For, make no mistake, this was a Ziegfeld show in the fullest sense of the term—not a story-tight piece like *Show Boat* or *The Three Musketeers* but a variety show with a plot that promises never to hobble the fun. This was high 1920s, a time in which the major authors were tightening and refining the musical's very structure—but *Whoopee* had no major authors. The procrastinating William Anthony McGuire was so late with the book that, on the first day of rehearsal, only the first scene was on paper. The score was assigned to Walter Donaldson and Gus Kahn, dependable Alley men who lacked Broadway experience.

None of this mattered to Ziegfeld or his audience. Cantor is perfectly cast, so there will be plenty of comedy, not least because, except for the villain and the two lovers, virtually everyone else in the show will play comedy as well. Designers Joseph Urban and John Harkrider will provide the sumptuous Ziegfeldian look. Donaldson and Kahn may not know anything about extended, operettaesque first-act finales (in fact, *Whoopee*'s was played entirely in dialogue), but they'll be tuneful and, in the end, will come up with two hits, "Makin' Whoopee!" and "Love Me or Leave Me." Comedy, spectacle, music . . . and of course those glorified girls.

That was the great thing about a Ziegfeld show—it was so roomy you could put anything into it. A heifer on a lead for Cantor's entrance, a gypsy ballet let by Tamara Geva, a Car Scene (with two of them, head to head on a mountain road), George Olsen's band (and even his wife, Ethel Shutta, as Cantor's amorous nurse), a Modernistic Ballet in Black (for class and also to give Geva something to do in the second act), a party scene with Olsen's boys on a platform, and cowgirls, Indian maids, some bridesmaids to dress the stage while Cantor puts over "Makin' Whoopee!," girls tapping, girls toe-dancing, and, best of all, the Big Indian Showgirl Parade, performed on a set representing a rocky gorge through which shirtless muscleboys led horses bedecked with Ziegfeldian beauties, each one nude except for headdresses that grew more colossal with each entrance.

With such a brilliant melange of entertainments, all for one ticket (at a hefty $6.60 top), no one complained that *Whoopee*'s story was silly or its score largely irrelevant. Of the seventeen vocal numbers, only five fit the plot. For instance, *Whoopee* includes a character named Leslie Daw, who pops up at various times to sing without the slightest motivation. Why? Because she can; also because she's Ruth Etting, and who wouldn't want Ruth Etting to sing in a musical? Just before the arranged wedding that never occurs, the father of the bride asks Etting if she, too, has a man. Well, she *did*. "He danced his way into my life," she explains, as Olsen's men park their chewing gum behind their ears and drop their papers, "and danced right out again." That gives us "Gypsy Joe." Later, a film company is shooting in Etting's vicinity. What are they shooting? A gypsy scene. We've already had "Gypsy Joe," so now Etting presents "The Gypsy Song (Where the Sunset Meets the Sea)," which also provisions Geva's first-act spot. The height of non sequitur song placings, however, is "Love Me or Leave Me," which Etting delivers all alone in a lush Urban poppy field. The lyrics are not addressed to any character in particular, nor has Leslie Daw any reason to wish to be

loved or left. Not a line of dialogue even pretends to introduce this novelty. The lights come up on the poppies, and Etting digs in. Why? Because, behind the backdrop, stagehands are striking the Indian gorge set
and setting up the Indian village set.

While we laugh at these entertaining yet obtrusive song spots, we
have to remember that their most important function was to bring a lis-
tenable voice into the vocal texture. It was only operetta that counted
on solid singing tone; musical comedy frequently made do with more
functional voices, the kind you forgive because the performer does
everything else so nicely. Rodgers and Hart had to give the big love song
of *Spring Is Here* (1929) not to the hero (Glenn Hunter) but to his
rival (John Hundley), because Hunter was a charm performer who
couldn't sing. Fine. But it unbalanced the show somewhat when the audience instinctively sided with the man so fervently singing "With a
Song in My Heart" when they were supposed to prefer Hunter.

One odd advantage of the operetta revival is that it attracted to Broadway many gifted singers, some of whom would then take jobs in *any*
show between bouts of Romberg and Friml. Thus, a perfectly ordinary
musical hit called *Take the Air* (1927), another aviation-themed evening,
offered as its leads Dorothy Dilley, Will Mahoney, and the ridiculous
Spanish dancer Trini. Not much singing insurance there—so up popped
operetta regular Greek Evans (the original Dr. Engel in *The Student
Prince*) to soothe the wounded ear.

One can imagine, then, the public's collective sigh of pleasure when
the lights brought up *Whoopee*'s poppy field to the orchestra's promising intro. At last: music! In fact, *Whoopee* counted two other solid voices in Paul Gregory and Met baritone Chief Caupolican. Still, Etting's
very appearance was a signal, a way of flattering the public by producing a favorite while assuming that they all know why she's there. "Love
Me or Leave Me" may be excrescent to *Whoopee*'s story but it isn't excrescent to *Whoopee* itself, to the very concept of a Ziegfeld show.

Speaking of concepts, Cantor played *Whoopee* as if he were an alien
twice over: as a timid soul among gun-toting he-men but also as a Jewish city boy among outdoor Christian and Indian cultures. Cantor made
the most of it, perhaps inspired by the explicit racism of the western
setting, perhaps spurred on by comic possibilities. The Indian lad, com-
plaining of how whites treat him as an outsider, reminds Cantor that "I
was educated in your schools." Cantor, punning the meaning of "your,"
replies, "An Indian in a Hebrew school? Tell me, how did you get along?"
What do you mean *we*, white man? Even more telling is Cantor's response when Sheriff Bob throws a cordon around the ranch house

where Cantor is hiding. They're going to flush him out, and the sheriff tells the posse, "Don't let a white man get by you." So Cantor strolls out in his blackface makeup. What do you mean *white man?* Cantor not only moves freely among the races; he changes race at will. Some may call this a comic's opportunism. I call it cultural satire on a well-nigh Voltairean level. And note that Cantor is an equal-opportunity racist-baiter: he does not only Jewish and black but "Indian," too, during the second-act reservation sequence.

Do we sense an explosive attitude, a progressive agenda that is becoming exasperated, angry? Cantor delivers a virtual sermon on tolerance at *Whoopee*'s close, when the Indian chief reveals that our Romeo is all white, a foundling raised by the tribe. Sheriff Bob, still hot for the heroine, accuses the chief of lying. But Cantor cuts right to the point of it all: so what if the hero *is* Indian? "Look at Senator [Charles] Curtis, our newly elected Vice-President," says Cantor in his oddly subdued "reasoning" tone, so useful when disarming bullies. "He's part Indian. And what's wrong with my friend Will Rogers [who was famously of Cherokee blood]?" It sounds mild, but this was but four years after white Alice Brady's kissing of black Paul Robeson's fingers was feared to promise riots in the auditorium.

Whoopee was a smash, still playing at capacity when Ziegfeld, bankrupted by the Crash, sold the film rights to Samuel Goldwyn. It was Goldwyn's plan to film a cut-down version of the show with the stage cast, and one of the contract's clauses demanded the immediate closing of the show, at 407 performances. And away they all went to Hollywood. (Except for Ruth Etting, whose highly extracurricular role would have seemed odd in the more realistic film medium than it had on stage.) With the talkie then in major development, the musical stood high in moguls' programs. (As Jack Warner once said, "Who the hell wants to hear actors *talk?*") Many Broadway musicals were being bought, many talents enticed to California. In all this, the film *Whoopee!* (Goldwyn, obsessed with imitating yet outdoing Ziegfeld, added the self-advertising exclamation mark) remains the first actual sighting for us moderns of what a twenties musical was like. Granted, the score is ravaged and partly replaced, the choreographer (Busby Berkeley) is not from the stage production and takes the numbers at least partly into kinetic development not possible on stage, and there is an occasional new jam in the stage script, as when the original silly-romantic ending for Cantor and Shutta becomes a gender war, as the beleaguered Cantor begs to "bury the hatchet" and the assaulting Shutta, axe in hand, cries, "That's what I'm trying to do!" No matter; Goldwyn's film is, in effect, a document of the Ziegfeld style in musical comedy, even unto the Showgirl Parade, though Goldwyn, slightly, dressed the models.

Obviously, the comic's vehicle was in good health. Joe Cook of the four Hywoyans and the elaborate inventions turned up in the hit *Rain or Shine* (1928) as the manager of a circus troupe in a bright band-master's coat with matching plumed hat, a famous sight of the day even to those who hadn't attended the show. The four Hywoyans were tem-porarily on hold, but the invention was the Fuller Construction Com-pany Recording Orchestra. Like every Cook gizmo, it filled the stage with concentrated nothing. As historian Stanley Green recounts it, "Joe pulled a lever which started a whirling buzzsaw which goosed a man holding a soda-water siphon which squirted a man whose gyrations turned a Ferris Wheel whose five passengers took turns bopping Dave Chasen on the head with their violins. Each time he was hit, Chasen reacted with a look of childlike wonder as he tapped a triangle with a hammer, thus producing the teeniest tinkle to accompany Joe's trumpet playing of 'Three O'Clock in the Morning.'"

A new gang, Clayton, Jackson, and Durante, got into a Ziegfeld back-stager with a Gershwin score featuring* Ruby Keeler, *Show Girl* (1929). Jimmy Durante, one of America's most enduring comics, gave the act its energy, with his exaggerated New York accent ("tee-ay-ter"), his blend of testy ego and elated showmanship, his malapropisms and coinings ("So I ups to him," recounting his response to an insult; and the mispronunciation "Ziegfield" that prevails to this day). Lou Clayton and Eddie Jackson were little more than along for the ride, and Du-rante was a single by the early 1930s (though he loyally kept his part-ners on the payroll and even, implausibly, reconstituted the act in the 1940s).

Show Girl, based on J. P. McEvoy's novel of that title, tells of Dixie Dugan's rise to stardom in a narrative structure that uses only letters, telegrams, and such. It's an aggressive rise—Dixie's another heroine halfway from Marilyn Miller to Ethel Merman—and it leads to Ziegfel-dian apotheosis on the very stage of the theatre, Ziegfeld's own, that the show was playing in. This is Pirandellian, especially when, in a twice-told tale, Keeler gets opening-night nerves during her big number,

---

* Not starring, as is sometimes said. Ziegfeld starred *stars,* at that sparingly. Anna Held, Marilyn Miller, Leon Errol, Eddie Cantor, the Astaires, and Evelyn Laye were among the exclusive crew whose names joined Ziegfeld's above a show's title. And, throughout the history of the *Follies* in Ziegfeld's lifetime, *no one* was ever starred. Ziegfeld liked PR, but he also liked clean poster credits: producer, title, theatre. If it's hot stuff, they'll come.

"Liza," and husband Al Jolson rises from his aisle seat to sing the refrain, hearten Keeler, and thrill the town.*

Actually, it was Durante who thrilled, basically playing his vaudeville act with his partners. Even Brooks Atkinson, not thrilled, had to hail Durante's "sizzling energy." Durante's best number, his own composition, was "(Everyone knows I can do without Broadway, but) Can Broadway Do Without Me?," a one-of-a-kind entry, love it or hate it. It's less a song than a series of spoken riffs, traded with his two partners, on such events as trying to one-up "Ziegfeld" and going on for Jolson, on one knee. (Backstage, Mr. J. J. Shubert tells Durante, "Jimmy, put in both knees. . . ." "And?" his partners cue. "And *Jolson goes!*")

Meanwhile, the Marx Brothers enjoyed their last Broadway musical in 1928, *Animal Crackers*, during which they filmed a abridged version of *The "Cocoanuts"* (by day, on Paramount's Astoria lot). Thus began their movie career. Like *The "Cocoanuts"*, *Animals Crackers* had a book by George S. Kaufman and Morrie Ryskind (though this time Ryskind had name billing). The plot—no more than a premise—takes us to the Long Island house party of Mrs. Rittenhouse (the usual Margaret Dumont), attended by Emmanuel Ravelli (Chico), the Professor (Harpo), Horatio Jamison (Zeppo), who is secretary to Captain Spalding (Groucho), the well-known big-game hunter, Mrs. Whitehead (Margaret Irving), Mrs. Rittenhouse's scheming social rival, Roscoe W. Chandler (Louis Sorin), the celebrated financier and art expert, and Wally Winston (Bert Mathews) of the *Evening Traffic*, a mild spoof of the *New York Graphic*'s Walter Winchell. There's some undercurrent about Dumont's daughter loving a penniless artist and the purloining of a sculpture, but this is trivia. *The "Cocoanuts"* suffered from an excess of plot; *Animal Crackers* is absolutely Marxist, the ultimate comedy musical.

Perhaps Kaufman and Ryskind had learned from seeing how the brothers extemporized upon the *"Cocoanuts"* script, as if it were Diabelli and they Beethoven. *Animal Crackers* was written not just around the Marxes but entirely in the center of them. There is a Kalmar-Ruby score

---

* First, it wasn't her number. It was Nick Lucas's number; Keeler was only dancing the postvocal chorus. And nervous? She'd already played three leads on Broadway by then. *Could it be* that Jolson rose up *during a dress rehearsal* out of *jealousy* that the *house* was *focused* on *his wife* and *not on himself*? And that Ziegfeld, knowing that *Show Girl* was a two-ton turkey, asked Jolson to repeat his impetuous solo on opening night so that the critics could write of it and give the piece a needed PR boost? (Not that it helped, though Jolson kept it up for a week.) Decades later, an interviewer asked Keeler about the incident, and in her lovably blunt way she said, "I wasn't nervous. Al just stood up and started singing."

somewhere in there, but even it is absorbed by the Doings, for example in an opening chorus (of Mrs. Rittenhouse's servants) so perfunctory—because how can an opening chorus be funny?—that it's over in about forty seconds. In this show, everything runs to the laugh.

Some of the laughs are simply typical, others new. Typical: Groucho's entrance is a loony musical scene, "Hooray for Captain Spalding," in which he arrives pith-helmeted in a sedan chair carried by four Africans. The orchestra halts as Groucho haggles with his bearers:

> SPALDING: Well, how much do I owe you? (The reply is unintelligible.) What, from Africa to here, $1.35? It's an outrage. I told you not to bring me through Australia. That it was all torn up. You should have come right up Eighth Avenue. Where do you come with that stuff? . . . I don't think you fellows are on the square.
> MRS. RITTENHOUSE: (*radiant with formality*) Captain Spalding—
> SPALDING: I'll attend to you later.

Groucho now goes into a bit of vocal nonsense, "Hello, I Must Be Going," which leads into the rest of the "Captain Spalding" chorus. At its close, Groucho starts an effusive speech, which the chorus breaks into with a short reprise. Again Groucho launches his address; again the chorus. Finally, Groucho begins his speech only to leap into the chorus himself, explaining, "Well, somebody's got to do it."

Mrs. Rittenhouse, that florid and pretentious old dame that only Margaret Dumont could make adorable, wants to praise Groucho as no VIP has been praised before—and the 1920s was the decade that reveled in celebrity journalism:

> MRS. RITTENHOUSE: Fearlessly you have blazed new trails, scornful of the lion's roar and the cannibal's tom-tom. Never once in all those weary months did your footsteps falter. Cowardice is unknown to you. Fear is not in you.
> (*Chandler takes something from Spalding's coat.*)
> CHANDLER: Pardon me, a caterpillar.
> (*Spalding faints.*)

A bit later, Signor Emmanuel Ravelli is announced, and Chico parades in with "Where's the dining room?"

So the boys are, as always, here to offend and create havoc. There were Harpo's and Chico's harp and piano specialties, of course, and a few self-contained sketches, as when the latter two take on Mrs. Rittenhouse and Mrs. Whitehead in an absurd bridge game, or when a thin second act is filled out with a dream sequence in which Groucho is King

Louis XV. Mrs. Rittenhouse is the Queen, Mrs. Whitehead is DuBarry, and the other brothers are musketeers, leading to a number for the comics, "We're Four of the Three Musketeers."

The new touches included a taste of topical Broadway satire such as the revues loved, when Groucho several times interrupted a scene with Mrs. Rittenhouse and Mrs. Whitehead by going into a *Strange Interlude* interior monologue. (The O'Neill play had opened the previous season but was still a town topic.)

There was also a very unusual scene for Chico and Harpo in which they unmask Roscoe Chandler as the former fish peddler Abe Kabibble, from Czechoslovakia. Ever since the 1960s, the Marxes have been the younger generation's official "cool" movie comics, because they humiliate the pompous. In fact, the Marxes humiliate virtually everybody, but it is true that Chandler is pompous, so one is not all that sorry to see his privacy invaded:

> CHANDLER: All right, boys, I confess. I was Abie the fish peddler.
> But don't tell anyone, please don't tell anyone.
> RAVELLI: How did you get to be Roscoe W. Chandler?
> CHANDLER: Say, how did you get to be an Italian?
> RAVELLI: Never mind that. Whose confession is this, anyhow?
> . . . Of course, we wouldn't tell anyone if it was worth our while.

Chandler offers five hundred dollars in hush money, but Chico and Harpo reject this, Chico shouting, "He's Abie the fish man! He's Abie the fish man!" as Harpo whistles and races around.

> CHANDLER: Please, please, boys, just a minute. Wait. I happen to have a check with me, which I received this morning, for five thousand dollars. Here, I will give it to you.
> RAVELLI: Is it good?
> CHANDLER: Of course it is good. Who would give me a bad check?
> RAVELLI: I would.

The brothers reject the check and again run around denouncing "Abie the fish man." Harpo is in especially good form; besides the blackmail, he manages to steal Chandler's tie, handkerchief, and teeth. "Ganefs!" (Yiddish for "thieves") is Chandler's *mot d'agonie* as he storms off.

It's an odd moment, typically Marxian in its crazy logic but another example of that ethnic emergence that must have bewildered at least some of the audience. Abie the fish man? Czechoslovakia? Who but the enlightened few would correctly construe this as the Marxes' highly invasive cultural outing of poor Chandler, whose only sin is a mildly pretentious bearing? But then, the one thing comedy has no respect for is privacy.

Like The "Cocoanuts", Animal Crackers was filmed at Astoria. The movie is a treasurable memento, for while the earlier show's score was gutted in filming (other numbers were cut before release), Animal Crackers almost wasn't a musical in the first place, even if it did trouble to give the young lovers ballads and the chorus a New Dance Sensation, "The Long Island Low-Down." Only one number really counted in this show, Groucho's entrance, because it bent the genius of musical comedy to meet the genius of Groucho. But for the chorus's deadpan Gilbert and Sullivan tooting and Dumont's pseudo-operatic wheezes, the whole scene might have been extemporized.

Indeed, the Animal Crackers film preserves "Hooray for Captain Spalding" and all the major comic scenes. The show's big love song, "Who's Been Listening to My Heart," was replaced (by Kalmar and Ruby) with "Why Am I So Romantic," the excrescent French dream was dropped, and the Captain's name respelled as "Spaulding," apparently to avoid confusion with a real-life Captain Spalding. The crazy core of the show survives; as with the Whoopee film, we are, seventy years on, in the presence of the real thing—those people and that style.

If the Marxes (and Eddie Cantor) mark a culmination of the twenties idea of a comic musical, Rodgers and Hart are the exponents of musical comedy. Their colleagues either stepped over into operetta now and again or simply could not compete in terms of sheer output. De Sylva, Brown, and Henderson wrote five musical comedies; Rodgers and Hart wrote fourteen (through 1930). Moreover, while De Sylva's gang stuck to formula, Rodgers and Hart sometimes invented new kinds of shows.

Peggy-Ann (1926) typifies the musical's unending quest for new forms. Here was another Rodgers-Hart-Fields title, based on the 1910 musical Tillie's Nightmare, in which a boardinghouse matron's daughter (Marie Dressler) dreams of glorious adventures. Fields's updated script drew on trendy expressionism to create absurdist versions of those adventures, as his heroine (Helen Ford) dreams herself out of Glens Falls, New York, onto Fifth Avenue, into a department store her small-town boyfriend (Lester Cole) suddenly owns, onto the sea in a yacht, and off to Havana before she wakes up back in Glens Falls. There was no plot. Peggy-Ann quarrels with her boyfriend and then makes up with her boyfriend. The fun lay in the odd look of her dream—policemen with pink moustaches, a talking fish, family members taking control by wearing giant hats—and in the score, one of the team's liveliest. As always when Fields wrote the book, critics complained of the salty nature of it all. One song, "Give This Little Girl a Hand," applauded prostitution, and "A Little Birdie Told Me So" offended the prurient. Grow up, whiners. This was a first-class show and a first-class hit, lasting 333 performances, albeit at the Vanderbilt theatre, little more than twice the size of the Princess.

Over the years, *Peggy-Ann* developed a reputation as being the first "daring" musical, with no opening chorus and a very quiet finale, a dance in the dark. (The show ends on the evening of the day on which it began.) Now, its fantasy action is certainly unusual. But plenty of musicals before this one had begun without a chorus. What was unknown was a musical's starting without music of any kind, something that, to my knowledge, was not attempted till *Lady in the Dark* (1941), which lacks even an overture. As for *Peggy-Ann*'s dance-in-the-dark finale, it wasn't the finale. After it, the company trooped on stage to reprise "A Tree in the Park."

That company took in a chorus of nine girls and five boys, a complement fit for the Vanderbilt. But note the extra women. Broadway choruses were not cast on an even boy-to-girl ratio because the musical was to an extent still playing out a history that began with the Girls as a major element in production. The boys were hired to do time steps; the *girls* were the thing. To choose one big show as an example, *Golden Dawn* balanced a chorus of thirty-five men against fifty-four women. That was the musical in the 1920s.

One exception was Rodgers and Hart's *A Connecticut Yankee* (1927), another huge hit at the little Vanderbilt and, because Mark Twain's novel put such emphasis on round-table knights, a rare show with twelve chorus women and *sixteen* chorus men (and mostly male principals on top of that). Here was another Fields book, this one as dull as *Peggy-Ann*'s is surprising, founded on a voyage back to Camelot by a modern-day American (William Gaxton) whose termagant fiancée (Nana Bryant) beans him with a champagne bottle. Like Peggy-Ann, he dreams the whole thing. And, as in *Peggy-Ann*, all the contemporary characters reappear in the imaginary adventure, along with some newcomers. At length, Gaxton awakes, now aware that he loves The Other Girl (Constance Carpenter).

The score is fine, counting two standards, "My Heart Stood Still" and "Thou Swell," and two also-rans, "I'd Feel at Home with You" and "On a Desert Island with Thee." Oddly, the one genuine comic song, Carpenter's solo, "I Blush," was cut out of town, though its references to Tristan and Isolde (very *d'après* Wagner, and not only in the spelling of the names—one line runs, "Oh dear, how they yodeled of love and death") richly denote Hart's erudite side. All the great Third-Age lyricists were well read, but Hart had given himself an outstanding education and was one of the smartest men in New York.

Tryout adjustments also played heck with Nana Bryant's role, giving one of her songs to June Cochrane and cutting the other. This left Morgan Le Fay without a single line of music, even in the first-act finaletto, surely a mistake for a musical's second woman lead. It's especially ironic considering that, sixteen years later, Rodgers produced a revival of *A Connecticut Yankee* with six new songs, and *this* show was virtually built around the Morgan, Vivienne Segal, the only star in the cast. Of the six added numbers, three were for Segal, and one of these, "To Keep My Love Alive," has joined "My Heart Stood Still" and "Thou Swell" as the show's three survivors.

This 1943 revival was not a success, and it's hard to know why the original was, for Fields's book reduces Twain to the one-joke culture shock of anachronism:

> LE FAY: Merlin, act thy age. Methinks thou art in thy second childhood.
> MERLIN: Aye, and methinks I do enjoy the second better than the first.
> LE FAY: Merlin forgets that I, too, am no mean sorceress.
> MERLIN: Sauceress . . . Ah, thou art the whole set of dishes!

The team grew adventurous in *Chee-Chee* (1928), after *Rose-Marie* and *Golden Dawn* our third twenties musical to claim too densely integrated a score to list more than a handful of song titles in the program. In truth, this show did toy with the use of fleeting ditties in the manner of *The Beggar's Opera:* script pauses, ditty is sung, script continues. While *Peggy-Ann* demonstrates the musical's delight in innovation and *A Connecticut Yankee* its sense of commercial self-preservation in convention and shtick, *Chee-Chee* reveals the musical's salacious side, the erotic component in Offenbach's *gai primitif*. It was based on Charles Petit's novel *The Son of the Grand Eunuch* and told of the succession of this noble position of old China, from father to son. Problem: Number One Son doesn't want to.

The myth of *Chee-Chee*, which lasted a month and then vanished, is that the critics recoiled from its subject matter and fell on it like the fold on the wolf. In fact, it got five pans, two half-and-halfs, and six raves. The *Daily Mirror* called it "a revolutionary musical show," the *Evening World* saw "a rousing tale of stage adventure with a finale that was greeted by rousing cheers," and the *Sun* found "quality, novelty, a merrily made score, and an utterly charming mounting." But the book, almost all felt, was slow going, and, indeed, the subject gave more than a few viewers the feeling that the musical had become not so much liberal as pointlessly smutty.

Rodgers and Hart retrenched in their next offering, *Spring Is Here* (1929). For one thing, Herbert Fields was busy elsewhere—Owen Davis adapted his own quite innocent play *Shotgun Wedding*—and, for another, this was an Aarons-Freedley production: high twenties, Arden and Ohman in the pit, quick jokes, fleet plot, fast fun, and easy on the risqué. "Spring Is Here (in person)" runs the second number's refrain: everyone's young and cute, so what else matters? Here was the musical comedy made of interchangeable parts that had been stock-in-trade throughout the decade. A spring show, young and dizzy. Let's dance. Betty thinks she loves Stacy but eventually realizes that it's Terry whom . . . what nonsense. But then, this was the history of musical comedy in the 1920s: every now and then a dart into the unknown, but mostly one size fits all. None of our Great Men—not even Kern and Hammerstein, the outstanding pioneers of this decade—showed consistently progressive work. Still, one does have to let the public catch up with the revolutions. That takes time, even in a golden age.

One of the shows that proves how golden the age in fact was closed out of town in 1927 during a dismal tryout. A political satire, very ahead of its day, it presented the Great War as a once-in-a-generation capitalist plot in which young men risk death for the gains of plutocrats, while photo ops are scheduled, advertising space is sold, and magazines profile the famous. This show was the first, of many to follow, that interpreted the theatre's naturally liberal inclinations as a mandate for merrily savage commentary on a few of the culture's Big Lies: *Strike Up the Band.*

"Legendary" is a word that perhaps should be retired unless it refers to Paul Bunyan or the Flying Dutchman. Yet there are a few legendary musicals, mostly those destroyed when tender despite fierce claims to greatness, such as *Rainbow. Strike Up the Band,* however, made its folklore when its producer, Edgar Selwyn, brought it back to the stage two years after its Philadelphia shutdown—and this time the piece went over.* The legend has it that a wholesale gentling of the political content, along with an extensive restructuring of the score, is what saved

---

* True, *The New Moon* had the same experience, and it owns no great folklore. But *The New Moon* was an operetta of the Romberg-Friml type, not a breakthrough piece that first alienated customers and then attracted them.

Strike Up the Band. The inference that we are to draw is that 1927 was bold while 1930 was cowardly and commercial. *Nothing like it at all,* as Captain Andy says. *Strike Up the Band* was born scornful and revived scornful. This is one unique show.

"Satire is what closes Saturday night," said George S. Kaufman. Then why did he keep writing it? In his original book, the United States manipulates Switzerland into a war over the tariff on cheese and wins a glorious peace only to prepare for war with Russia over caviar as the curtain falls. All the action is physically possible but culturally so unlikely that it comes off as a fantasy. It has a realistic edge, though, in its two nonromantic leads, cheese magnate Horace J. Fletcher and Washington insider Colonel Holmes, pointedly modeled on Colonel House, a shadowy but powerful figure within President Wilson's inner circle. The two men's first scene together, in which they move from a phoney horror of war to an assigning of the profits, typifies Kaufman's Swiftian tone:

> FLETCHER: As a patriotic American, I feel that the United States must send an answer to Switzerland refusing to repeal the cheese tariff.
> HOLMES: Oh, delicate situation!
> FLETCHER: It's a matter of honor.
> HOLMES: Might mean war.
>
> . . .
>
> HOLMES: Terrible thing, war.
> FLETCHER: Terrible.
> HOLMES: Can't eat sugar . . . And saluting all the time. I was a wreck.

Luring the not unwilling Holmes with the prospect of numerous book deals, Fletcher gets war all but declared:

> HOLMES: What do you think we ought to have, a little war or a big one?
> FLETCHER: Oh well, if it's only going to be a little one I'd rather let the whole thing drop.
> HOLMES: Runs into money.
>
> . . .
>
> FLETCHER: Suppose that some patriotic citizen came along who was willing to help pay the cost of this war.
> HOLMES: Well, that'd help. Then I could see the steel people, Y.M.C.A., all them folks. They all ought to chip in. Gives them a lot of advertising.

All this is very much in the "debunking" mood of the 1920s, when it sometimes seemed as if all bohemia had risen up against the Babbitt, creating a media culture of muckrakers determined to expose America as greedy, evil, and, even worse, boring. But Kaufman kept his compass narrow, filling in the rest of the show's crew not with some schemers and fixers but with George Spelvin, a kind of fifth Marx Brother who wanders in and out of the action pulling weird stunts; a merry widow; her daughter and the daughter's boy friend; and Fletcher's daughter and *her* boy friend, a key player in the game in that it is he who tries to unmask Fletcher's motives and thus alienates his inamorata. In all, what Kaufman wrought was a typical musical comedy structure (two love couples, one "serious" and the other cute and silly, with various lead and supporting comics in a linear narrative with a beginning, middle, and end in that order) processing the least typical subject matter. Call it a newfangled business as usual.

The Gershwins wrote the score, falling in beautifully with Kaufman's scheme. They wrote, in their Aarons-Freedley manner, songs and musical scenes that were too sophisticated for an Aarons-Freedley show. We get a Gilbert and Sullivan feeling for the first time from the brothers, perhaps because Gilbert's librettos, like Kaufman's here, were so devoted to social commentary. Ira came up with two Gilbertian "How I came to be what I am" patter songs, Fletcher's "A Typical Self-Made American" and Holmes's "The Unofficial Spokesman." George laid out several exuberant finalettos that dwarf even Kern's efforts in this terrain. The ballads are admirable, from the lyrically jaunty "Meadow Serenade" and the urgent "Hoping That Someday You'd Care" to "The Man I Love"—a boy-girl duet, by the way, renovating itself as "The Girl I Love."

The unusually extensive choral activity especially enlivens Kaufman's bleak worldview. He says that the profiteers always win; the music says that entertainment always wins, because it delights as it enlightens. It's yet another case of progressives smoothing their path with song, as in "Patriotic Rally," which, in praise of the diversity of American culture, cites Henry Ford and Morris Gest in the same line, an oxymoron if there ever was one. And consider the title song, a jingoist rabble-rousing anthem for a show that exposed jingoist rabble-rousing.

Let's go back to 1927. Producer Selwyn has taken his troupe to Philadelphia and good reviews but to consternation in the ranks. Kaufman had the Fletcher, Herbert Corthell, fired. But Corthell's replacement did even less well. Comic Lew Hearn, the Holmes, was known for his vibrating high tenor that suggested a goat in rut—but Holmes should be a con man in a business suit, slimey but ordinary, Babbitt's boss.

Edna May Oliver felt uncomfortable as the giddy widow. Oliver's shtick was dour beldame and control freak. ("How I *hate* not to know things," she was to utter in her Great Role, that of Parthy Ann in *Show Boat*.) Jimmy Savo, the George Spelvin, was the only one of the comics who was perfectly cast; Savo *was* a fifth Marx Brother. But, meanwhile, Hearn and Oliver quit. (The latter had almost surely been stolen from Selwyn by Ziegfeld, who put *Show Boat* into rehearsal just about a month after *Strike Up the Band*'s Philadelphia opening.) Then Savo joined them. On top of it all, the public simply wasn't coming, despite the reviews.

An eager public might have encouraged Selwyn to replace his defectors; a dedicated cast might have persuaded him to Bring It In and see what New York thought. As it was, Selwyn had no choice but to close the show.

But only temporarily. A little more than two years later, in December 1929, Selwyn took a revised *Strike Up the Band* to Boston, once again heading for Broadway. This time, he had something lacking in the 1927 version: star comics. The duo of Bobby Clark and Paul McCullough, as Colonel Holmes and a reimagined George Spelvin, had drawing power from twenty-five years' experience, mostly in vaudeville but also in two *Music Box Revue*s and in *The Ramblers*. Straight man McCullough usually played in a top hat and raccoon coat bearing a college pennant, zany Clark in baggy southern-patriarch suit and painted-on glasses, the two developing the long-honored American trope of the small-time grifter pals, utterly without loyalty yet somehow inseparable. That suited the roles in the revised script; Clark and McCullough even went out of their way to drop their outfits and accommodate character costuming.

It was Morrie Ryskind, Kaufman's partner in the two Marx Brothers book shows, who undertook this revision of Kaufman's text, for Kaufman felt that he had done his work well the first time: what was there to revise? Ryskind's main contribution was to turn Fletcher's cheese works into a chocolate factory (why?) and to frame the war sequence as a dream. He does seem as well to have pulled a few of Kaufman's boldest punches. But the 1930 book generally retains 1927's view of war as an opportunist's revelry. Besides, as musical comedy is somewhat fantastical in the first place, there isn't much difference between a crazy evening about war with Switzerland and a crazy evening about a dream of war with Switzerland.

The Gershwins totally overhauled their score, mostly unnecessarily. "Seventeen and Twenty-One" was replaced by "I Mean To Say," "Meadow Serenade" by "Soon" (developed from a melody fleetingly heard in one of 1927's finalettos). What did the new numbers do but replace good music with good music? "How About a Boy Like Me (for a girl like you)?," for the comics and Mrs. Draper, might even be less winning than its daffy predecessor, "How About a Man?," and the waltzy new "I Want to Be a War Bride" does not console fans of 1927's losses, which take in "The Man I Love."

The musical revisions are so thorough that, except for their common use of the title song, the two overtures are entirely different. The musical revisions are also finicky. "Patriotic Rally" now turns up with the same lyrics and melody as before but with certain shifts of rhythmic emphasis. Again, *why*? But why ask? Both scores are wonderful—the second even rebaptized another Gershwin standard, "I've Got a Crush on You," rescued, we know, from *Treasure Girl*. When Selwyn brought his new, neither improved nor debilitated but, I think, simply better-cast *Strike Up the Band* into New York in January 1930, he had a hit. Audiences thronged—not to that new political fantasy, not to the Gershwins' latest, but to "the Clark and McCullough show." It had never been about cheese, or Saturday night, or Morris Gest. It had been about headliners all along.

But then, all theatre, from deep in the nineteenth century into the twentieth, was based on that notion. The crowds shopping the theatre district for a good time wanted a sure thing—the actor or actress who had fascinated before, the author who had served, the producer who had spent the money. In the 1920s, audiences were first-name-basis customers at a Fred Stone or Cohan or Astaire show, and that's why no one in Philadelphia came to *Strike Up the Band* in 1927 and why Broadway crowded it in 1930: because subject matter was of no importance and performing talent was. However, now comes the show that changes that rule. After this one, shows will need subject matter, and the personality players, being what they are from show to show, will be eased out by the character players, who change identity from script to script.

First, let's hear a little sermon on the text of *Strike Up the Band*. It folded in Philadelphia in 1927 and reigned on Broadway in 1930, but not because its message was emasculated. Not even, entirely, because it latterly had stars to attract the ticket buyers.

But because you don't try out a breakaway show in a place like Philadelphia.

9

Go, Little Boat

THE ALL AMERICAN MUSICAL COMEDY

Edna Ferber's 1926 novel *Show Boat* gets off to a theatrical flourish on the title page (actually a double-page spread, verso facing recto), in which she sets out "The Time," "The Scene," and "The Players" as if for an old-time melodrama. "From the gilded age of the 1870's, through the '90's up to the present time," she announces, going on to a detailed breakdown of her geography, first in quick rundown of the show boat itself, the *"Cotton Blossom Floating Palace Theatre"* of the Mississippi "and its tributaries," then in references to old Chicago and the contemporary New York theatre district.

The players take up an entire page: the Cotton Blossom's captain, Andy Hawks; his wife, Parthenia Ann; their daughter Magnolia, "later a famous actress on the variety* stage"; Gaylord Ravenal, "a gentleman of

---

* This word bears some scrutiny. I have used it in this book in its modern theatrical context that denotes any bill of diverse and unrelated acts: vaudeville, obviously, but also some Broadway revues that were really nothing more than a chance concatenation of performers, and, in its last incarnation, television's *The Ed Sullivan Show*. But "variety," in the English-speaking theatre world until about 1930, meant any musical entertainment that was *not* provincial, small-town, unheralded, semi-amateur. It was a social distinction. "Variety" meant Broadway or the West End or a major tour, whether of the *Follies* or *Rose-Marie*. Less than variety was, in America, vaudeville and, in England, music hall: low audiences and worthless credits,

fortune and sometime actor" who marries Magnolia; Kim Ravenal, their daughter, named for being born on the Mississippi at the junction of Kentucky, Illinois, and Missouri. (This is indeed physically possible, precisely where the Ohio River flows into the Mississippi, a few miles southeast of Cairo, Illinois.)

These five are Ferber's leads. The rest are lumped as "Julie, Elly, Steve, Schultzy, and other members of the show boat troupe"; as "Habitués of old South Clark Street in Chicago"; and as "actors and dramatic critics of the present theatrical world of New York City." (*Vanity Fair* and *The New Yorker,* Lunt and Fontanne, Woollcott and Shaw are mentioned in the novel, in a reverse of the retrospective "variety" usage: to emphasize the reality of 1926 Broadway. What Ferber had in mind was a tale to open up the ever-changing panorama of the essential American invention, show business. Or no: she was telling a love story about a sweet thing and a gambler, except both happen to be actors. Or no: she was using the Mississippi in all its romance and destructive power to remark upon American culture.

Actually, she was doing all three at once; no wonder the book was a best-seller. But how come Jerome Kern thought it would make a good musical? How could it make even a bad one, what with fifty years of narrative, the deaths of both male principals, the problem of getting the River on stage, and the huge collection of subsidiary characters? Besides, musicals weren't based on novels. A few classics underwent adaptation, such as *The Three Musketeers* and *A Connecticut Yankee,* not to mention the Duncan Sisters' *Topsy and Eva.* A few shows even were made from contemporary novels—*Show Girl* and *Chee-Chee* only a few pages ago—and Booth Tarkington's *Seventeen* was but ten years old when *Hello, Lola!* subsumed it.

But *Show Boat* was a *novelist's* novel, a great, sprawling, devious, melodramatic, shocking, unapologetic presentation, like the Mississippi itself. It's a great story, as Magnolia grows up amid the show boat folks, sees the cruelty of racism slice into backstage life, marries her heartthrob gambler, raises a daughter, goes on the stage again, and sees her daughter start to become the next Marilyn Miller while the men in her life fumble and fail and her stupendously awful mother rails and reigns. On one of its many levels, *Show Boat* is a saga of three generations of womankind.

---

though some performers did become national figures in these arenas. Ferber deliberately used the by-then near-archaic term to anchor her epic narrative in authentically passé argot.

This is a musical?

Of course, as we know, Kern's style had been broadening, and the partner he chose for *Show Boat*, Oscar Hammerstein, was the most questing, evolving, of liberettists. Perhaps, when they had worked on *Sunny* the year before, Kern had sensed in Hammerstein a despair of shows without *content*. Ferber's book certainly had that. We can also see that Kern was attracted to a property that would allow him to illustrate the changing eras of the story through music—taking a single melody through epochal transformations, say, ragging, then jazzing it; reinventing old genres such as the spiritual and the coon song; even interpolating genuine old songs into the mix, a favorite Kern device.

Oddly, the classic story of how Kern made contact with Edna Ferber to secure the rights to her novel leaves out the punchline. The anecdote finds Kern encountering Alexander Woollcott at a Broadway opening. Knowing that Woollcott is an acquaintance of Ferber's, Kern asks for an introduction. Woollcott remarks that he just *might* be able to arrange it—then turns to the woman next to him and says, "Ferber, this is Jerome Kern. Kern, here's Ferber."

Cute. But what's missing? If Kern went on to say that he wanted to make a musical out of *Show Boat*, what did Ferber reply? Let me guess: *"You want to make a WHAT out of Show Boat?"*

For this is where the twenties musical really presents its history. More than the jazz and the ethnic emergence and the intensifying expressing powers of the music was this naive belief that a musical needn't spring from an established genre. A musical might well be something that hadn't been tried before. Even: a musical *should* be.

In the event, Kern and Hammerstein's adaptation of Ferber is faithful in an overall way, incorporating, one, the five leads as Ferber created them; two, her love of theatre; three, the River; four, racism; five, the history of the Hawks-Ravenal family; and six, the concept of destiny as something that one chooses even as it marks one out for judgment—so that, say, Captain Andy creates his life by claiming the River as his territory, only to succumb to a drowning accident. The body is never recovered.

What is most interesting in the adaptation is how much of the book shouldn't rightly have been good theatre material (but ended up in the musical) and how much might have worked (but the two authors ignored). First, they tightened the time scheme a bit by starting not in Ferber's 1870s but in the late 1880s (and even this still leaves daughter Kim, portrayed as a young flapper in the show's finale, set in 1927, at the actual age of thirty-one). They reduced the size of the show boat troupe, meanwhile promoting Julie Dozier and her husband, Steve, from "general business team" to heroine and hero and demoting Elly Chipley, billed as Lenore La Verne, from "ingénue lead" to comic support. Julie also got Elly's *nom de théâtre*. Julia La Verne is the name that Julie plays under, Julie Dozier the name of her terrible secret: she's the offspring of a racially mixed couple. Elly got respelled as "Ellie" and paired off with a composite of two of Ferber's characters, Frank (the company's heavy) and Schultzy, the "juvenile lead," who become Frank Schultz, a comic villain.

This was sharp thinking. Julie *had* to be the show boat's principal player, for she is *Show Boat*'s principal player. It is her racial unmasking (by an evil-hearted suitor) and her subsequent exile that give the American musical its first tragic heroine and *Show Boat* its emotional center. True, the Magnolia-Ravenal love plot is technically the play's beating heart—but over the years it is the Julies who have graced revivals with the utmost in what the Italians call "morbidezza": what Mimì brings to *La Bohème*.

The Miscegenation Scene, as it has come to be known, marks how well the authors reinvented the American musical. They had no choice: *Show Boat* into a conventional musical won't go. This scene, which occurs about halfway through Act One, is the only episode in the novel that Hammerstein borrowed almost verbatim. It was Kern who decided to open the scene with a spiritual—that is, a taste of black folk chorale. Kern flirts with the black folk style (behind the veil of Broadway jazz, albeit) in "Can't Help Lovin' Dat Man," Julie's first song and an undetected plot number in that it's the authors' subtle tip-off that Julie is not what she seems. In this nineteenth-century America of strict racial segregation, black culture is so cut off from whiteland that Queenie grows suspicious when Julie knows a black song. And not one of those Stephen Foster creations—real black music, unheard by whites.

So, as the lights come up on the Miscegenation Scene, the black chorus is readying the auditorium for the evening's performance before a daytime rehearsal. "Mis'ry's Comin' Aroun'" is the singers' text: a general instinct that white man's trouble is seeking them out. When Julie innocently asks Queenie why everyone seems so anxious, Queenie gets a bit more specific:

> QUEENIE: When I got out a bed dis mornin', Ah knowed somethin' was goin' to happen.
> JULIE: Well, what's happened?
> QUEENIE: Nothin' . . . yet.

In fact, what she really means is that something has been wrong ever since Julie knew More Than She Should—ever since the White Over There and the Black Over Here got displaced. And when that happens in a place like Mississippi, people get hurt.

"Mis'ry's Comin' Aroun'" is an extraordinary number, more impressive than the *Deep River* choral music because it is composed right into the action—not commenting on it but feeling it. Tense and restless in its first half, it grows achingly lyrical in its second. By then, Julie, caught up as if by instinct, takes over the number in a dialect prayer for a black funeral, wherein the mourners chip in small change to finance the burial. Julie knows More Than She Should because she's More Than She Should Be. Realizing this, she turns against her choral support, shouting, "Stop that rotten song!"

Too late. Within minutes, the sheriff will board the Cotton Blossom to arrest Julie. She is saved only by her husband's long-planned defense, something so rich, so effective, and so bizarre that it rightly belongs in the old melodramas that the show boat company performs: Steve cuts Julie's finger, sucks her blood, and, when the sheriff arrives, announces that he, too, has black blood in him.

Ridiculous! But it is Ferber's use of a typical melodrama shock scene in her real-life narration that supports one of Hammerstein's pet notions: theatre does not invent but reflects life, and thus it redeems and enlightens us. We call it fantasy, but it's truthful, and this is why Magnolia and Ravenal meet to a song called "Make Believe (I love you)." They *aren't* making believe: they're in love, for in Hammerstein it only takes a moment.

Another intriguing thing about the Miscegenation Scene: while taking down Ferber's dialogue, Hammerstein introduced his own material to advance the story line in ways Ferber didn't need to consider in a 400-page novel. In the musical, the scene not only decisively reunites Magnolia and Ravenal but launches Magnolia's stage career, as the two must stand in for the departing Julie and Steve. Interestingly, Ferber had Elly throwing a racist fit upon learning that her former friend is part black. Hammerstein decided to sacrifice realism—his Ellie is extremely sympathetic—to treat the Cotton Blossom as a Safe Place for Julie, making it all the more regrettable that she is forced to leave it. With the information of the vaguely unnerved "Can't Help Lovin' Dat Man" and the keening "Mis'ry," we sense that the rest of Julie will be despair and death.

In Ferber, Julie makes one last appearance, many years later, in a

Chicago bordello, where Magnolia gets but a fleeting glimpse of her while paying off Ravenal's debt to the madam. (Ferber leaves it ambiguous whether Julie is one of the working girls or more of a clerk.) Obviously, Kern and Hammerstein were not about to lose the chance to get some music out of this, so they expanded the moment into a major episode.

Opera historians praise the wonderful narrative jolt in Puccini's *Manon Lescaut*, whose first act ends with young lovers merrily running off together and whose second act begins with the girl now a grouchy, pampered plaything in some rich man's house. What happened to love? *Show Boat* pulls off a similar coup in its second act, third scene, as the lights come up on a rehearsal for the New Year's show at Chicago's Trocadero Music Hall, with the pianist banging out Sousa for the dancing girls, the manager looking on, a few employees cleaning up . . . and Julie, who was last seen an hour ago, about fifteen years in the past.

Granted, the authors had something luminous in the Julie, Helen Morgan. To spend her conclusively in the first half of Act One simply could not have happened. But Julie does not return just because Helen Morgan needs another song. Julie returns because it was one of Hammerstein's most fervent notions that certain important relationships, even important encounters, can change our lives: that humankind is a community in which some teach, goad, and inspire the rest of us. This is not in Ferber, who exercised the realism of the cynic. Hammerstein was a Believer, and *his* Julie ends up not as a functionary in a brothel but as a blasted alcoholic mess who has one gallant act left in her. Magnolia has turned up, out of nowhere, to apply for Julie's job. Hearing the song she herself had taught the girl in perhaps the only happy time in her life, back in that Safe Place, Julie steals out of the Trocadero. And this time she does not reappear.

Ferber was sparing in her use of coincidental reencounters, Hammerstein greedy. But then, Ferber saw American life as a rushing, destructive force that yields nothing but change. An avalanche. Hammerstein saw the change as affecting only the facade of the culture: the worthwhile elements hold steady. Family. Home. Self-belief. Naturally, friends will meet again. Love rules destiny.

Hammerstein may have overtaxed the credibility meter in his final scene, when he brings Captain Andy, Parthy, Magnolia, Ravenal, Kim, Joe, Queenie, Frank, and Ellie all back together—every principal but Julie. By contrast, by this time in the novel Andy, Parthy, and Ravenal are dead and of the rest, all but Magnolia and Kim are dispersed or forgotten. Moreover, while we gape at the utterly questionable return visit to the Cotton Blossom of Frank and Ellie, how are we to react to the simultaneous materialization of Ravenal? Out of the narrative for twenty-three years, he just "bump[ed] into" Captain Andy "at Fort Adams yesterday," as a line reveals even as it dismisses one of the most striking coincidences in theatre history since Oedipus and a surly king arrived at a crossroads at the same moment.

Historian Miles Kreuger claims that Hammerstein eventually regretted having resuscitated Ferber's Ravenal. But how else to close up an epic than by bringing one small yet salient piece of it to a resolution? And Hammerstein leaves us with a tasty irony at the very instant of Magnolia and Ravenal's meeting, in the intrusion of a character simply called Old Lady on Levee. The last of *Show Boat*'s thirty-three speaking parts to be heard from, she tells them that she was in the audience for that veritable act of performance art forty-odd years before, when Magnolia and Ravenal were married:

> OLD LADY: My, my, how excited we all were! That was a real love match! Well, glad to see it turned out well and you're still happy together.

Of course, it turned out very badly. But then we recall how Magnolia, when she and Ravenal first met, invoked the seventy-five-year separation of aunt and nephew in *The Village Drunkard*, and we realize that life is no stranger, no more wonderful, than art. The theatre may magnify but does not exaggerate. As I've said, ours is a culture that has made show business its definitive contribution to Western civilization. It is not an avalanche, this American energy, but an evolution that never rests. "It's like a person," says Magnolia, in Ferber, of the River, "that you never know what they're going to do next, and that makes them interesting."

How often critics complained of twenties musicals that authors had to pad the second act out of sheer lack of story. The Aarons-Freedley format, which replaced plot interest with performer charisma, created a near-black hole of a second act; as there was no real character interaction in the first place, the script had nowhere to go in development. *Show Boat* is the twenties musical with *too much* story—real characters undergoing real life. Yet we can lament the loss of scenes in the novel that might have strengthened the authors' intentions, such as the moment when Magnolia has been lullabying Kim with the home songs, hears something in their hotel hallway, and opens her door upon a group of black employees, arrested by the sounds of the only music they know, otherwise unavailable in the north. For of course Magnolia thinks of Negro spiritual as "music" while Negroes think of spiritual as "our music." When Julie sang it, an era before, it was. But, by 1900, the white appropriation of black music is a crucial piece of cross-cultural integration. The best in American culture is starting to unite the sections, seeping out to all open eyes and ears. In Kern and Hammerstein, as in Ferber, show business is the key. It opens the mind.

Ferber, as a chronicler, sees the races as separate, because she looks for but cannot find tolerance. The musical harmonizes the races, perhaps because music is the only language both white and black can speak. The very center of this transaction is "Ol' Man River," a white man's spiritual—written by white men out of a white woman's book, to be performed by a black character. This River Number is *Show Boat's* theme song, as the River is virtually the central character in the novel. For this strange tale has no human protagonist. Who, Magnolia? So overshadowed by mother Parthy, even by father Andy? So controlled by Ravenal after their marriage?

Is Parthy the protagonist? She is without question Ferber's great invention, an enraged control freak so relentlessly mean-spirited that one wonders why such a life-denying creature lives so fully, emphatically, tirelessly. Did *Sally* or *Lady, Be Good!* or *Dearest Enemy* give us unique characters? Hear Ferber:

> In [Parthy's] stern code, that which thrilled was wicked. She belonged to the tribe of Knitting Women; of the Salem Witch Burners; or all fanatics who count nature as an enemy to be suppressed; and in whose veins the wine of life runs vinegar.

There is no love whatsoever in this woman; she is a triumph of of suspicion and denial. But musicals thrive on vital characters, and Hammerstein centered his libretto on Captain Andy, the very opposite of Parthy. Surely Ferber had it in mind to divide her epic Americana, like Caesar's Gaul, into three parts: the out-of-control River of money and opportunity and corruption; the Fundamentalist hatreds of Parthy; and Andy's loving openness. Here's the country, says Ferber, tying up her package. It is all you need to know on earth.

Hammerstein tips the show over to Andy to tell us that *his Show Boat* is not about power but about redemption. Not about who runs the company but what the plays are saying. Not about reality but about poetry. Not about the River but about "Ol' Man River." Ferber ends her story with Magnolia standing proudly on the Cotton Blossom's upper deck. "Isn't she splendid!" cries her daughter. "There's something about her that's eternal and unconquerable—like the River." Hammerstein and

Kern don't spotlight Magnolia quite so brightly at *Show Boat*'s curtain—but what do we hear? The River Song. Maybe "Ol' Man River" is the show's protagonist—the stupendous continent and the democratic explosion, implied in the limited vision of one black man, all America itself.

As Kern and Hammerstein plotted their piece and began to sketch in the numbers, they saw immediately that what they had done on any previous show would not work here. First, "Ol' Man River," which came along very early in composition, told them that they had something unique on their hands, brawny, poetic, simple, overpowering. Neither of them had written anything like it before.

Then, too, Kern was creating leitmotifs for the lead characters, not just calling cards but germs of melody to be expanded throughout the score. Kern also decided to exploit the musical scene to the fullest, pumping music through the show as even *The Student Prince* had not done.

Some things came more easily than others. The all-important meeting of Ravenal and Magnolia seems effortlessly to have produced a brilliant musical scene, fluid, romantic, dramatic. Ravenal enters, establishes his character in "Who Cares If My Boat Goes Upstream?," hears Magnolia's offstage piano playing, makes her acquaintance, surges into "Make Believe," converts her to his point of view, then fends off the intrusive Sheriff Vallon. Already, in the show's first out-and-out song, the authors are pursuing their themes, gambling and transforming, telling us ten things at once about her innocence and his slyness, or her willingness and his romanticism, bringing up the idea that all life is performance, a "make believe" that yields a truth.

Some things came hard. The love duet that at first clinched this pair's affair, "The Creole Love Song," seemed a misfire. What did Creole courtship have to do with these young Americans? All right, Ravenal (twenty-four years old in Ferber, at this point) is worldly. But where did the sheltered Magnolia get her intimate knowledge of love among the Creoles? This was Romberg-Friml thinking, generically acceptable but realistically absurd. And *Show Boat* was the realistic musical. Long before rehearsals began, the authors junked "The Creole Love Song" for something appropos: "You Are Love." Simple. Direct. Passionate. Right on the money.

As they worked, Kern and Hammerstein found many a chance to delineate the immense time scheme in the score, borrowing nineteenth-century tunes for the show boat performance of *The Parson's Bride*, ragging "Can't Help Lovin' Dat Man" a generation or so later, building

Magnolia's piano theme into a gigantic hot jazz anthem for the finale called "It's Getting Hotter in the North." Most puzzling was the question of Julie's second-act spot. She's rehearsing a song in 1904, so obviously it will be a story ballad, the key pop concert piece of the day. The authors came up with "Out There in an Orchard," suitably old-style, with a dying-away pathos perfect for Julie's emotional state. But the song was of the second rank as sheer melody.

Then Kern had a brain surge. Two great songs, historians will tell you; were dropped from show after show by their frustrated authors—the Gershwins' "The Man I Love" (which never did find a home in a hit) and Kern and Wodehouse's "Bill." It was Kern's notion that the intrinsically neutral "Bill" could, through the alchemy of Helen Morgan's plangent vocalism, become a torch song. Here was an irresistible solution, especially after Kern refashioned a key phrase in the refrain and Hammerstein rewrote some of the lyrics. The revision lost us one of Wodehouse's best couplets:

> Whenever he dances,
> His partner takes chances.

But it saved the song, and the spot.

Unfortunately, Magnolia's cabaret debut, a bit later, gave greater trouble. Another story ballad was written, "A Pack of Cards," but it lacked . . . well, everything. Again, interpolations were considered—this time, not anything by Kern, but antique pop songs, such as "Ta-Ra-Ra-Boom-Der-E," the signature hit of the English music hall star Lottie Collins. Finally, Kern suggested that they give Magnolia "After the Ball," Charles K. Harris's superhit of 1892. "Ta-Ra-Ra-Boom-Der-E" was too hectic for this poignant moment, when Magnolia struggles to win over a hostile crowd and does so only with the help of her father, who has suddenly reappeared in her life just when her husband has deserted her. It's quite a moment, and it needs a sentimental waltz, not a can-can. Besides, "Ta-Ra-Ra" was so much the vivacious Collins's personal property that it would have sent *Show Boat*'s public an incorrect signal. Magnolia isn't a source of energy; Magnolia is a source of love. Like the Overture to *Sweet Adeline*, "After the Ball" would root the audience in the generalized nostalgia the scene required, especially because by 1904 it was a beloved "old favorite"—precisely the words used in Magnolia's Trocadero introduction.

I think this was flawed thinking. Interpolations have their use, but the employment of so gigantic a hit unsettles the rest of the score. It worries us: why didn't the authors write their own "After the Ball"? It distracts us: many in the audience today don't know where this song comes from but have a *feeling* that it's not by Kern. Some think it *is* Kern's, which is worse.

Kern was perfectly capable of writing a stunning story ballad in flawless period style for this spot. Besides, most of his generation appeared at about 1920, while Kern published his first song as early as 1902. Surely he had trunk material—like "Bill"—waiting for exposure. Kern, anyway, could *create* trunk material, as in Frank and Ellie's "I Might Fall Back on You," composed in the two-step style that Kern had all but abandoned after the Princess shows.

But it appears that, at some point, Kern and Hammerstein decided to give the entire New Year's Eve scene at the Trocadero to interpolations. For Frank and Ellie, too, turn up here, to sing "Goodbye, My Lady Love" and dance to "At a Georgia Camp Meeting," while Offenbach opens the scene, and, as midnight rings out, the lights fade on "There'll Be a Hot Time in the Old Town Tonight." All old tunes. By coincidence, Bessie Smith recorded this last title for Columbia in March 1927, just about the time that Kern and Hammerstein were working out these decisions on what kind of music a musical *Show Boat* should have. The 1920s brokered a dialogue between old and new art, rough and fine art, strong and silly art. This, too, is part of what "jazz" means: striving to find meaning in the discords, keeping afloat in the River.

What kind of music *Show Boat* should have is a major point, for Kern and Hammerstein figured it out only after it was too late: after they'd already written a show so special that its score must be one of a kind. Unlike Romberg-Friml, *Show Boat* created no formula: how many more forty-year epics was the musical going to need? The authors endowed the comic characters with a musical comedy sound, as in Ellie's "Life On* the Wicked Stage" or Queenie's "Hey, Feller!" They pillowed the lovely people in operetta's lavish melody. They kept creating genre numbers in bygone style that seemed neither of musical comedy nor of operetta, like "Ol' Man River" and "Can't Help Lovin' Dat Man." They laid out musical scenes at tapestry length, involving whoever happened to be on stage at the time, whether of the comic or the lovely variety. They kept Captain Andy and Parthy out of the music almost entirely, as if seeing them as too piquant or too lordly or too ineffable to be given conventional voice.

* Ellie sings "upon," but the song was programmed and published with the title as I give it. Hammerstein wanted to associate it with a cliché phrase of the day, but Kern gave him that extra note and Hammerstein had to fill it in the lyric.

So, in the end, *Show Boat* is neither musical comedy nor operetta; nor is it a blend of the two, like *Rosalie* or *Sweet Adeline*. *Show Boat* is a musical comedy with epic dimensions, an amazing intimacy, and music of uncommon rightness, beauty, and depth. That's why so many mistake *Show Boat* for an operetta: musical comedy scores of the time were shallow. They were "Tea For Two," "My Heart Stood Still," "Let's Do It." Nice tunes, sure, but nothing next to "Ol Man River," "You Are Love," "Mis'ry's Comin' Aroun'." Even "Bill," a musical comedy ditty when it was written for *Oh, Lady! Lady!!*, has turned into something very large because of who's singing it when: Julie, at her wit's and life's end.

This is a rich entertainment. Only an operetta would have wanted to field so much story, but only a musical comedy could have had such fun in telling it. It is the biggest show, not only in content but in its eight scenes in Act One and nine in Act Two. Remember, back in 1920, when most musicals offered one set per act? By 1925, the rule was three sets per act, the two middle scenes of course just set-change throwaways. For a 1927 book musical to take in seventeen scenes was extraordinary. Hammerstein, who directed the show, gave his staging credit to Zeke Colvan, the stage manager, simply for keeping the huge production flowing.

A piece of this size needed one of the Big Three: Ziegfeld, Dillingham, or Arthur Hammerstein. What other producer could afford it? Dillingham had a strong relationship with Kern, who had composed nine shows for him, and Oscar owed a great deal to uncle Arthur. But the authors may have mistrusted producer Hammerstein's acumen in the treatment of so unusual a work, especially given his loyalty to Romberg-Friml operetta. As for Dillingham, wasn't he too commercial for this project, not to mention old-fashioned? But when was Ziegfeld ever uncommercial?

One can only speculate, but it may be that Ziegfeld really was the Great. Somewhere in that Glorifying the American Girl head of his must have been the instincts of a genuinely stupendous showman, the kind that ennobles your work in a manner unknown to all others.

At any rate, Ziegfeld jumped at it and quickly began casting: Elizabeth Hines as Magnolia, Harry Fender as Ravenal, and Paul Robeson as Joe. Robeson was a right-as-rain choice. But Hines? She was a beauty, but never more than a dependable musical-comedy heroine, a questionable singer at best. Fender was both a beauty and a singer—he'd played Captain Donegal in Mr. J. J. Shubert's 1920 revival of *Florodora* (the one who trumpets "I Want To Be a Military Man") and worked for Ziegfeld in romantic leads in *Kid Boots* and *Louie the 14th*. But of late

Fender had developed stage fright and would in fact retire to become a cop in Missouri. Ziegfeld decided to go with the more securely motivated Guy Robertson. But in the end the show took its own time to evolve, and Ziegfeld had to release his three leads and postpone rehearsals for more than six months.

The three roles ultimately went to Norma Terris, Howard Marsh, and Jules Bledsoe. Terris was not that well established, having played leads on tour and a couple of Shubert revues. But she did boast of an oddly appealing look that would allow her to age convincingly and translate, in the last scene, into Magnolia's daughter. (One wonders if Ziegfeld ever considered Jeanette MacDonald, who opened in *Yes, Yes, Yvette* two months before *Show Boat* opened and then in *Sunny Days* [1928] two months after.) Marsh, Romberg's original Student Prince, was something of a stick, but that was also true of Bledsoe, whom we last saw driving Arthur Hopkins crazy with his dead stage presence in *Deep River*. Both men sang well, however, and Joe, at least, doesn't do all that much but deliver "Ol' Man River" and its reprises.

The supporting players could not have been better cast—but are any of *Show Boat*'s nine principals supplementary? We think of Ravenal and Magnolia as the leads simply because they're the lovers and because their reunion closes up the plot, and Joe always has a place of honor because of the central position that "Ol' Man River" occupies not only in the show but in American music. Hire a mediocre Joe and the boat founders. But it's one of the show's many brilliant peculiarities that only Steve (Julie's husband and the tenth principal, in a minor way) actually leaves the show when he appears to. Everyone else turns up again— not only Julie at the Trocadero but Frank and Ellie at the Trocadero *and* in the final scene, when they drop by the Cotton Blossom to glory in their new career as managers of "Little Frankie Schultz, the boy wonder of the screen." (This last appearance is a little dubious, as it occurs in Natchez, and we get no explanation of why the Schultzes have strayed so far from Hollywood. But it does allow Hammerstein to pull another element of American show biz, the movies, into his panorama.)

Aren't Captain Andy and Parthy the show's true leads? Neither does much during the music, but Andy's is the longest speaking part and Parthy isn't far behind, at least in stage time if not in actual number of lines. Besides, isn't Andy the evening's interlocutor? He captains not only the Cotton Blossom but the entire show itself: bringing Ravenal into the backstage community, giving him the idea of marrying Magnolia, coaching Magnolia to success in her new career as a songstress, and, finally, bringing Ravenal back to the show boat at the play's end. Kern saw Andy as the basic ingredient of *Show Boat*'s score: his four-note leit-motif, with the second and third pitches in reverse order, becomes the Cotton Blossom leitmotif, and this in turn, in retrograde form, provides the first four tones of "Ol' Man River."

As Andy, Ziegfeld hired Charles Winninger, *No, No, Nanette*'s daffy Bible publisher, in the role of his life. Parthy was the inviolably sour Edna May Oliver. This was Streisand-as-Fanny Brice casting, he the re-demptive figure and she the damning one, an entire cosmos. Ferber barely suggests that this pair represents anything; she saw them as one of the many accidents that a chaotically expanding culture invents, a dysfunctional marriage that works. Hammerstein saw them as definitive. She has to be the judge who imposes the maximum penalty on every-one because *he* would let them off. Or: he has to be made of forgive-ness because she is made of hard truth. Or even: he's Mary and she's God.

Frank and Ellie, a couple in the show, were a couple in life, Sammy White and Eva Puck. Queenie was Tess Gardella, a white blackface spe-cialist who worked under the name of "Aunt Jemima." That's odd—one fake Negro in an otherwise authentically mixed-race cast, including a full-sized black chorus. I would have guessed Georgette Harvey, ideal for the role, the original Maria in both the play and opera versions of DuBose Heyward's *Porgy*. But then, the play opened only two months before *Show Boat*, and perhaps Ziegfeld didn't snap Harvey up in time.

Helen Morgan takes pride of place before these all, as the unknown whom *Show Boat* made a star. But then, the cast as a whole passed at least relatively into fame. Howard Marsh, Norma Terris, Jules Bledsoe, and Tess Gardella are mentioned today, when at all, exclusively for *Show Boat*; even Winninger and Oliver, still very available in old cinema, are primarily known as Andy and Parthy. Yet notice that none of the above, not even Morgan, was actually starred in *Show Boat*. These were gifted players, but not headliners. Besides, you think, a show as new-fangled—story-bound, really—as *Show Boat* wouldn't have room for the star stuff, right? The Entrance, timed to accommodate applause, the this spot, the that spot?

On the contrary, that stuff was a basic element in show construction. What do you hire performers for but to do what they do? Every one of the leads got his specialty moment, except this time the specialty was written into the action. For instance, Winninger was a very physical co-median. He had no automatic shtick—no Cantor heebie-jeebie fits and blackface, no Fields growl and juggling, no Bobby Clark makeup glass-es. But Winninger could devise shtick as the situation demanded. So

Hammerstein, using an episode from the novel in which a redneck gets so caught up in a Cotton Blossom melodrama that he literally shoots the villain off the stage, gave Winninger a main chance. To guarantee the audience its money's worth, Captain Andy proposes to finish off the show himself, taking all the parts. This includes a knockdown-dragout between hero and villain, capped by the sudden entrance of the heroine's "errant foster-sister Lucy," who beans the villain with a (rubber) water pitcher, killing "the dirty rascal deader'n a door nail!"

Thus, *Show Boat*'s reconstructed equivalent of the star comic got at least one little segment of the evening in which everything rested on his ability to invent fun out of his experience and expertise. It is not a self-contained set piece. It is part of the story: for it is Captain Andy's child-like belief that the enchantment of theatre, however primitive, is what holds a community together. This is what *Show Boat* itself is about, what Hammerstein's life was about: theatre is good for democrats.

Similarly, Hammerstein arranged to integrate Sammy White's dance specialty into the whole by using it to represent the typical show boat "olio"—the revue that invariably followed the play, as in old burlesque. The redneck pacified, Frank is now willing to reappear, even in his villain's moustache and cape—and, canny Hammerstein, White's dance covered the complex set-change from the Cotton Blossom auditorium to its top deck.

Tess Gardella's specialty spot also covered a technical transition. But this time Hammerstein used the scene to convey chronology, for in covering the jump from 1904* to 1927 Gardella's ample Queenie appeared in flapper attire, an instant comic visual cue to Where We Are Now. During rehearsals and the first weeks of tryouts, Gardella sang an antique interpolation, the "Bully Song," popularized by May Irwin, one of the first of the so-called "coon shouters." This occurred in an earlier scene, closer to Irwin's own time. At length, the authors decided to write their own number for Gardella's hot spot, one to cut right into the twenties ethos: "Hey, Feller!," on the aggressive courtship etiquette of the New Woman.

Looking in on all this fastidious shuffling of time, place, character, show biz history, and Americana, Ziegfeld began to worry. He was himself a fastidious playmaker, but not in the matter of villain's dances and bully songs. Ziegfeld was fastidious about the important things—how the costumes looked on the girls and how the lights hit the set. Heav-

---

* Actually 1905, as the Trocadero performance ends with the bells tolling in the New Year.

en knows what he was expecting when Kern and Hammerstein first pitched him the project, but now that he had it, what exactly did he have? No stars, except Helen Morgan, *maybe*. No girls, except during the Act Two opening on the midway of the Chicago World's Fair in 1893, so all those beautiful! *girls!* had to walk around *dressed!* from! *neck! to! toe!* Think of it—the story covered forty years, and the show itself lasted almost as long. As *Show Boat* packed up for its first stand, at the National Theatre in Washington, D.C., in mid-November 1927, Ziegfeld pondered the timing of the final dress rehearsal: three hours and fifty-five minutes, not counting pauses for technical mishaps. The producer had to wonder if he had, at long last, come up with Ziegfeld's Folly.

For this was no *Kid Boots*. *Kid Boots* was a country club. *Show Boat* was white and black, south and north, country and city, show biz from the primitive to the technical, tolerance and hatred, patience and anxiety, several bad marriages, alcoholism, and the River. It was such a rich evening that the tragic "Ol' Man River" was coming off as exalted and the affable "Bill" was playing as tragedy. Ziegfeld was putting on something that the musical had never even thought of being: vast. Bowing to fate, the producer billed it, with the mildest implication of its grandeur, as "an all American musical comedy."

But first an hour of it had to go. Unfortunately, Hammerstein's plot-obsessed script contained none of the extraneous comic scenes we've seen so much of in these pages, as when two zanies get handcuffed together in *Lady, Be Good!* or when a "naive" girl cleans out *Good News!*'s crap game. *Show Boat* counted nothing extraneous; the piece ran four hours because it had a good deal more to delineate than the average musical.

What *could* go, alas, was a hefty fraction of the music. Bits were tucked here and there. A number called "Cheer Up" (for the Hawkses at the World's Fair) was dropped, only to be replaced by the freshly written "Why Do I Love You?" Reduced to mere underscoring was Magnolia's narration of her meeting with Ravenal, "I Looked Down at Him" (a new setting of the verse to "If We Were On Our Honeymoon" from *The Doll Girl* [1913], which also provided Kern with *Show Boat*'s "fate" theme, the lowering music first heard directly after the Overture).

But three major numbers were also lost. Dropping almost all of "Mis'ry's Comin' Aroun'" saved six minutes, though it denuded the play of a crucial element in its view of race relations: that blacks see them as oppressive and whites see them as functional. Remember, through the River, Ferber, Kern, and Hammerstein identify America as a nation eternally in development, self-reinvention, progressive at its best. To isolate racism as immobile—a misery that relentlessly "comes around"—is to declare it anti-American, a bold apprehension for 1927.

"I Would Like To Play a Lover's Part," for Frank, Ellie, and the chorus, was a plot number that worked as a dance, for it in fact tells us (through the sighing of the separate male and female choristers) that Magnolia and Ravenal have become stars along the River. Here was another four minutes to pick up; deleting "It's Getting Hotter in the North" saved nine more minutes of running time.

But what was lost! "Hotter" was, musically and dramatically, a culmination of much of what the show represented. It is a dear little nineteenth-century piano ditty transformed into stamping modern power, the white-black thing seen at last to be reaching a stage of cultural interaction (as jazz makes its way north to the cities), the chronology hammered home, and the only chance for Kim to ingratiate the third generation of the Hawks-Ravenals with the public. There is a tale that Norma Terris, who of course played Kim as well as Magnolia, got Kern to drop the number because she thought it tawdry. (It must have been quite a comedown from the George M. Cohan, Lewis Gensler–Milton Schwarzwald, and J. Fred Coots scores that Terris had previously sung.) Supposedly, Terris talked Kern into letting Kim reprise "Why Do I Love You?," while working in imitations of Ethel Barrymore, Bea Lillie, and Ted Lewis.

I don't believe this story. First, nobody talked the touchy Kern into anything. He was an extremely experienced theatre man by 1927 (*Show Boat* was his thirty-first complete score), and he knew what was tawdry and what wasn't. Norma Terris is going to tell Kern to drop a song? More likely, the authors were looking to turn a very long number into a short one. A reprise of a solid tune like "Why Do I Love You?" never hurt, and, if nothing else, Terris's imitations would help root the scene in the 1920s, when virtually everyone in show biz did "impressions," not necessarily all that well.* So Kim did reprise "Why Do I Love You" with imitations. But it threw the finale off, thinning out the musical climax and losing all the thematic climaxes. Many critics commented on how lamely the show concluded.

Actually, Hammerstein might have cut certain portions of the book that set up what ultimately doesn't need explanation, such as Pete's vi-

---

* Terris's were terrible. She privately filmed a reel of them at about this time, apparently as a screen test for Hollywood work. She hastily restyles her hair for each one and gives it all she's got, but you still have no idea whom she's supposed to be doing.

cious denunciation of Julie's background to the Sheriff, or Captain Andy's picking up of his three New Year's Eve tarts. But the one was embedded in an important character scene for Ravenal, containing "Till Good Luck Comes My Way," outlining his essentially flighty, opportunistic nature, and the tart business covered a set change.

In all, *Show Boat* lost about an hour on the road, to trim the running time to the standard union contract, quite as if it were *No, No Nanette* or a *Music Box Revue*. Why this one-size-fits-all timing? If the Great American Movie, *Gone With the Wind*, can last four hours, why not the Great American musical? The cuts didn't cripple *Show Boat*, but they masked it—so thoroughly that today, seventy years after, we're still not sure exactly which music this national treasure should contain.

Let's ponder a moment. Ziegfeld is handling *Show Boat* with care, virtually curating it as he brings it from D.C. through Pittsburgh, Cleveland, and Philadelphia. The Broadway that he is heading for stands at the height of a theatre boom, with almost three hundred Broadway productions in the 1927–28 season. One reason is the increase in theatre realty. The territory south of Forty-Second Street had become undesirable by the late 1910s, after a spate of theatre construction pushed the entertainment district ever higher into the West Forties. By the 1920s, managers and entrepreneurs were filling the area with new auditoriums, twenty-six in all from 1920 through 1928, when the building stopped and the total stood at sixty-six. But more theatres meant more productions, which called for a larger and larger public—whether or not it actually existed.

Some years brought a single birth: the Times Square in 1920, the Imperial in 1923, the Martin Beck (but also the Broadway, originally a cinema) in 1924. However, 1921 saw in the Forty-Ninth Street (now demolished), the Jolson (demolished; and, from the beginning, too out-of-the-way, across the street from Central Park), the Music Box, the National (now the Nederlander), and the Ritz (now the Walter Kerr); 1925 gave us the Biltmore, Chanin's Forty-Sixth Street (now the Richard Rodgers), the Forrest (now the O'Neill), and the Guild (now the Virginia); and amazing 1927 added the Ziegfeld, the Hammerstein (where David Letterman now works), the Alvin (now the Neil Simon), the Gallo (no longer in use), the Majestic, the Royale, and Erlanger's (now the St. James).

Another reason for the rise in theatre productions was the rise in newspaper publicity for theatre events. In 1900, PR was in the hands of theatre newspapers, read by the thespian community and dedicated theatregoers. By the 1920s, columnists led by Walter Winchell created new PR venues in their gossip columns, reaching a wider audience than that already mustered for theatregoing.

There was, of course, competition from the movies and radio. But radio popularized Broadway performers and the latest show's hit songs, enlivening interest in the theatre itself, and Hollywood gave New York producers an economic boost by buying up rights to virtually any filmable title, once sound came in.

So *Show Boat*'s Broadway was booming, at least for the moment. The piece opened at the Ziegfeld on December 27, 1927, to almost unanimous acclaim as the Awesome Musical. "A work of genius," Robert Coleman called it in the *Daily Mirror*. It "shows that managers have not until now realized the tremendous possibilities of the musical comedy as an art form." *Variety*'s Abel Green, while praising the work, completely misunderstood its revolutionary nature: "Meaty and gripping, rich with plot and character, it's almost a pity that the novel wasn't dramatized 'straight,' sans the musical setting." Is he kidding? The point isn't that the subject was too busy for a musical but that musicals had been getting by on thin subject matter. *Show Boat* was a wake-up call.

Oddly, when *Show Boat* came to London's Drury Lane in 1928 (with Edith Day, Howett Worster, Marie Burke, Cedric Hardwicke, Viola Compton, Paul Robeson, Alberta Hunter, Leslie Sarony, and Dorothy Lena), the reviews were mixed. The two big guns, the *Times*'s James Agate and the *Observer*'s St. John Ervine, were astonishingly perverse. Agate called it "inane," and Ervine declared himself "appalled." The 350-performance run marked a solid success, though not comparable to New York's seventeen months.

Interestingly, Kern and Hammerstein did not simply hand *Show Boat* over to the Drury Lane management as it was: they were still tinkering. For the Trocadero New Year's show, they gave Frank and Ellie "How'd You Like To Spoon with Me?," an old Kern number from 1905, which would register with the London public more certainly than "Goodbye, My Lady Love." They wrote a new song for Robeson, "Me and My Boss," dropped before the opening and now presumed lost. They cut "Hey, Feller!" at Edith Day's insistence, because Alberta Hunter was attracting too much attention with it (thought Day). And they made an entirely new stab at an eleven o'clock number, not reinstating "It's Getting Hotter in the North" but writing a new song for Kim, "Dance Away the Night." Perhaps "Hotter" was simply too hot for England in 1928. Too jazz.

Another point: *Show Boat* was not the first classic musical in the chronological sense, but it was the first musical to be *perceived* as a classic. For, just three years after the first New York production had closed, Ziegfeld revived it at the (new) Casino Theatre with virtually the entire original cast (save for Dennis King and Paul Robeson as Ravenal and Joe), as if acceding to popular demand. It was a success, though revivals were extraordinarily rare in those days. The view was that, once a musical ceased to sell tickets, it should be permanently retired, partly because the performing talent could not be duplicated, but also because the era teemed with creative talent, so shows were believed to be infinitely replaceable. That Shubert remounting of *Florodora* and the periodic repetitions of Gilbert and Sullivan were exceptional, and the notion of a *new* show's being brought back for an open run within a generation was unheard of.

Show Boat underwent two movie adaptations from Universal at this time, in 1929 (a part-talkie derived from the novel with infiltrations from the show) and in 1936. The latter cast, headed by Charles Winninger, Irene Dunne, Allan Jones, Helen Morgan, and Paul Robeson, is justly celebrated; and the authors, in charge of the script, troubled to write three new songs and tried yet another finale. This time, Ravenal (as a theatre doorman) was reunited with Magnolia (gala in her box) while their daughter, onstage, was opening a new show. In place of "It's Getting Hotter in the North" and "Dance Away the Night" was a big dance on the same premise as "Hotter," a white-southland-meets-black-Harlem special that, like "Hotter," was designed to update a song heard earlier in the action, "Gallivantin' Around," one of the three new titles. Unfortunately, this dynamic jazz rave-up was almost entirely cut and can be viewed only in production stills.

Ziegfeld had died during the 1932 run, but in 1946 Kern and Hammerstein themselves produced a revival, again at the Ziegfeld. Now the tinkering became acute. Stage technology had so advanced that "scene-change dialogue" could be tightened or even dropped entirely. Three musical numbers vanished, and yet a fourth finale, "Nobody Else But Me" was given to Kim. There were small changes: the switch of the first word heard in the show, "Niggers," to "Colored folk," the dropping of tuba and banjo from the orchestra, to distance the sound from the jazz band noise that the 1927 original exploited. In all, this 1946 *Show Boat* altered the scope of the work, tidied up its epic contours, limited its comedy, organized its dance from fun-filled hotcha to Very Prestigious Ballet. Thus Kern (who died two months before the production opened) and Hammerstein changed their musical comedy into a Rodgers and Hammerstein musical play. This was the *Carousel* version of *Show Boat*, transformed to be the kind of musical it would have been had it been written in the mid-1940s.

But that isn't *Show Boat*. This magnificent omnium-gatherum is—or *was*—a kind of container of everything that American show biz thought important in 1927. It was story-vaudeville, the comic operetta, the *musical* comedy. It's not a tragedy, it's a backstager. And it's not Magnolia's story: it's America's. We can see by the 1946 cast how much *Show Boat* had already lost, with a baritone Ravenal (Charles Fredericks)—no, he's supposed to sing *tenor,* high, skittish, unmanly, the charmer who leaves his wife and child because he thinks the marriage was about *him.* With nobodies as Captain Andy (Ralph Dumke) and Parthy (Ethel Owen), and as Frank (Buddy Ebsen; yeah, that Buddy Ebsen) and Ellie (the scream-voiced Colette Lyons), and with a lively Queenie (Helen Dowdy) but a dull Joe (Kenneth Spencer), the all-important ensemble effect of the constantly interacting principals was lost. Jan Clayton, previously *Carousel*'s Julie, was fine, and Carol Bruce sang a great Julie, in lowered keys, again to suit the 1940s, which liked its torch singers on the husky side. *Show Boat* was losing its identity while gaining one: as the show that could be redevised to suit the era.

There was a third movie, this one from MGM in 1953, a project of the unspeakable Freed Unit. American stage revivals in the 1950s and '60s honored the 1946 version, sometimes with the addition of a number it had dropped (such as "I Might Fall Back on You") or the deletion of one it had retained (such as "In Dahomey," the black dance scene at the Chicago World's Fair), but invariably ignoring "Nobody Else But Me," which wasn't even published in the 1946 vocal score. London saw an extremely successful *Show Boat* in 1971 with further modifications, including the building of Julie into the star part for Cleo Laine by the addition of an extra scene (between her leaving the Cotton Blossom and her reappearance at the Trocadero) in which she put "Nobody Else But Me" through the jazz-cabaret treatment. Actually, this production generally was anachronistic, as if it were all taking place on, say, Rudolf Friml's birthday. But it did have a stuffed-full-of-fun presence that 1946 lacked, and it boasted a variety of Caribbean black accents that were historically close to how some southern blacks sounded in the years covered by *Show Boat*'s first act.

The 1980s ushered in the archaeological era in the musical's history. With so little that was new and worthy, reconstructed old titles became trendy, and the Houston Grand Opera, which had reintroduced *Porgy and Bess* to the world without the traditional cuts, now elected to do a similar job on *Show Boat*. Unfortunately, Houston's underpowered staging, in 1983—loaded with cuts, by the way—made the work look like just another twenties operetta.

Perhaps the most important of all *Show Boat* revivals was not staged but recorded, by EMI, in 1988, on three discs that contain the entire original score in its original Robert Russell Bennett orchestration, along with all of the cut material that could be found, the new songs written in 1936 and 1946, and early numbers that may never have even been rehearsed. Suddenly, in the atmosphere and punch of 1927, the orchestra jamming with the *snap!* of a jazz band, *Show Boat* came back from the dead of *Oklahoma!* Ravenals and lounge singer Julies, the huge music reverberating as it was meant to, *at length*. As a "crossover" album, EMI's *Show Boat* cast opera singers in the romantic roles, but then so did twenties musicals. In fact, it was the musical comedy players who were weak on these discs.

The set got a lot of attention, and the way now seemed clear for restudied *Show Boats*. Paper Mill Playhouse in New Jersey (in a staging taped for PBS) reinstated "I Still Suits Me" (from the 1936 movie) and the Trocadero New Year's chorus, never before performed anywhere. England's Opera North put *Show Boat* into repertory while reclaiming "Mis'ry's Comin' Aroun'," to spectacular effect. Finally, Hal Prince directed a new version for Toronto in 1993 that reconsidered the text in all its variants. Prince's ecumenical edition collated 1927, 1928, 1936, and 1946 to create a wholly Kern-Hammerstein *Show Boat* that nevertheless would appeal to contemporary audiences.

There was first of all the racial thing. It's already in *Show Boat*, of course. How much more racial can a musical get than "Ol' Man River"? Prince pointed up some of the dialogue for a slightly revisionist view. This is 1927:

> PETE: *(angrily, espying a gem on Queenie)* Where'd you get that, nigger?
> QUEENIE: *(merrily ignoring his brutality)* You mean this scrumptious piece of jewelry? It was give to me.

This is Prince:

> PETE: *(as before)* Where'd you get that, nigger?
> QUEENIE: *(stopped flat out by the word "nigger," hurt, speaking low, defiantly undefiant)* You mean this? It was give to me.

There were other very telling yet small touches throughout the production, in the staging as well as in the text—black instrumentalists maintaining their dignity while wearing idiotic party hats as they play for the Trocadero show while the drunken white customers behave like savages; black street dancers inventing the Charleston, which is later commandeered by whites. There were broad touches, including a powerfully jagged Brechtian gesture when "Ol' Man River" was at first backed by a black-and-white "lithograph" of a cotton field, which was angrily pulled down by the black choristers.

There was second of all the musical thing: which songs to use? Prince wisely opted for as comprehensive a program as possible; he in fact played more *Show Boat* music than any production since the Washington, D.C., tryout in 1927. The basic contents were of course on hand—the six standards and "Life On the Wicked Stage," the first-act opening (cut down, but now sporting a taste of "I Might Fall Back on You" for Frank and Ellie's dance) and finale (surprising, as it's one of those finalettos, incredibly quaint for the 1990s), "Who Cares If My Boat Goes Upstream?" (the lead-in to "Make Believe" and thus virtually uncuttable), "Queenie's Ballyhoo" (basic, yes, but, shockingly, cut to a verse and dance in 1946, without a vocal chorus), and the two Trocadero interpolations.

This much is expected. But to this Prince added "Mis'ry's Comin' Aroun'" in its first complete hearing in New York and retrieved "I Have the Room Above" from the 1936 film, to fill in what he felt was a missing piece in the development of the Magnolia-Ravenal romance. (It had been missing since the authors dropped "I Would Like To Play a Lover's Part," which traces the romance from the *audience's* point of view.) Prince even found room for "Till Good Luck Comes My Way," lost since Hammerstein dropped it in 1946. Most daringly, Prince invented two numbers, narrative dance-pantomimes cleverly spun (by David Krane) out of *Show Boat* melodies. Thus, while Prince was clocking the passage of time through newspaper headlines and changing fashions, actually *showing* us the decline of the Ravenals and a final post-"Bill" look at Julie, begging on the street, Krane and orchestrator William Brohn were serenading us with that extra helping of Kern—"Hey, Feller!," "Dance Away the Night," and even "It's Getting Hotter in the North," now a military march to mark World War One.

There were niceties for *Show Boat* buffs, too subtle to address any but the expert. For instance, while cutting out the too-dated verse to "You Are Love" Prince reinstated the song's original ending—not the crashorama climax that we've known for seventy years, but a gently loving farewell for the two singers that was dropped during tryouts because applause drowned it. Prince, or someone on his team, realized that if the orchestra launched its peroration and *then* Magnolia and Ravenal sang their final lines, the ovation would have died down and the words could be heard. Why didn't Kern think of that? There was even a nicety for buffs of Second-Age musicals, an hommage to the vamp of the *Florodora* Sextet in the middle of "Life On the Wicked Stage."

Then there was the question every *Show Boat* production must answer: what to do with the finale? Prince's solution builds on that of New York, 1927, in which Terris scammed "Why Do I Love You?" with her clammy imitations. Prince turned the reprise into a duet between Kim and Parthy, then let the ensemble loose on a hot jazz turn culminating in a long line of dancers virtually spanning the stage, the left half facing the right half. Whether choreographer Susan Stroman knows it or not, this is the very picture of a twenties dance number, though Prince got somewhat modernist at the curtain. "Look, Gay—there's Kim," says Magnolia, as a last choral bit of "Ol' Man River" ties this family saga to the notion of an America ever-changing yet constant. In most productions till now, of course, the Magnolia would have just changed out of her Kim costume to become Magnolia again, and Kim, on the Cotton Blossom's upper deck, would be a double turned upstage. But Prince's view of theatre doesn't allow for this shifty mother-daughter double role with last-minute cheat effect. That's so . . . twenties. He hired a Kim from scratch. So when Ravenal looked at Kim, it was not some dimly glimpsed chorine, but *his daughter, Kim,* perched atop a roadster down front, with Magnolia by his side and Parthy and Andy at stage left. Now the modernist touch—a freeze-frame on that giant stage, the Hawkses cooing, Kim boiling in the guiltless revelry of the young, Magnolia watching as Ravenal gazes in wonder upon this lovely thing that is all that is left of his marriage, his life.

Prince made one error in showing Kim's birth in a scene borrowed from the 1936 film. It makes a better second-act opening than the old-hat World's Fair music, but it specifically dates Kim's birth to 1889, which makes that dear little flapper of the finale thirty-eight years old.

Prince also pulled a gaffe in his handling of "Bill." Like all moderns, Prince doesn't understand these autonomous numbers that the twenties musical doted on. Who's Bill? he wonders. He doesn't understand that the singers of Julie's day—and of the 1920s—didn't need to know a Bill to sing a "Bill." It's not a character: it's a song. Nor does Prince get Hammerstein's *coup de théâtre* in tossing Julie back into the story without explanation or fanfare. Do we need a year-by-year rundown on her life since the Cotton Blossom to comprehend that Steve is gone and Julie's a wreck? Maybe he died in a fight defending her honor. Maybe he abandoned her. Maybe she left him, sacrificing herself to free him from her clouded destiny. It's enough to know that Julie is a tragic figure and that events have brought her to this place at this time because Hammerstein isn't yet finished with the Magnolia-Julie relationship. But Prince isn't satisfied. He wants motivation, maps, diary entries, breathless confidences from bystanders, backstory. Where is Steve? Prince cries. And, above all, *Who's Bill?*

So, in lines that cannot be found in any extent *Show Boat* script, Prince's Julie virtually "dedicated" her singing of "Bill" to the guy who left her (Steve? Bill? Herbert Stothart?), as if she were on *MTV Unplugged*. In 1904, singers did not dedicate performances to anyone. *Authors* dedicated songs on rare occasion; singers only sang them. This failure to trust the material sheds light on a flaw in nineties dramaturgy: the musical has become so "realistic" that it has lost its vital instincts. The twenties musical says that Helen Morgan's way with a song is so touching that she can convey where Julie is at this point in her life with virtually any sentimental number, especially one written to sound cheery. (It's called "irony.") The nineties musical says, Who's Bill?

Prince's literalistic survey, however, failed to catch the one mistake that *Show Boat* has contained since 1927. As we know, "Can't Help Lovin' Dat Man" is meant to be a black song, unknown to whites. But, come the first-act finale, what does *everyone* onstage, black and white, break into as Magnolia and Ravenal set off for their wedding? "Can't Help Lovin' Dat Man"!*

These are cavils, for Prince scored a well-deserved triumph for taking *Show Boat* into the age of the dark concept show. Ziegfeld was right in terming it the "all American musical comedy," for it defines each new era in American theatre by the very changes that are wrought upon it. Even the variations in that first sung line record a miniature history of American race relations, as 1927's "Niggers" demands attention from a public unused to socially aware musicals, 1936's "Darkies" euphemizes (for the day), and 1946's "Colored folks" is blandly neutral. Fifties LPs favored "Here we all work [on the Mississippi]," which suggests a grammar-school citizenship class before the volatile 1960s changed the rules. The line is dead, but then so were the 1950s. The 1966 Lincoln Center production shows how tense the whole question had become by cutting the section entirely.

---

* Perhaps we will never have a truly realistic *Show Boat* till some bold director has his Queenie first startled, then suspicious that the white folk ken this ghetto exclusive. Queenie could produce paper and pencil, take down the culprits' names, and pass the note to Sheriff Vallon—who just happens to be onstage at this time. There's a lot of race fraud on the levee.

Show Boat grows in large and small ways along with American culture. Its platonic conception never alters, but each new format that is
traced on it—what other twenties title could turn into so many different *kinds* of musical?—tells us something about America, and the American musical, and how we regard the ones from the era when the American musical was most truly created.

For one thing, we don't quite get them. If we ever had an honest revival of one, we'd laugh at the constant infusion of work-for-hire talent,
like the exhibition dancers who entertain during a set change or the
lengthening of a party scene while a vaudevillian does his twelve minutes. We'd gape at the Albertina Rasch girls in disbelief, resent the stock
jokes ("Marriage is an institution . . ."), marvel at the sensory-overload
song cues.

But then, how could there be an honest revival of an art dependent
upon performers whose like are gone? Old-time Captain Andys found a
little comic apocalypse in the four-minute solo in which he singlehandedly completes *The Parson's Bride*. Charles Winninger registered his
patent in the 1936 film, but we've seen it brought off recently on PBS
by Eddie Bracken. Prince's New York Andy, John McMartin, presented
a very understandable and rational character, not Winninger's encompassing jester but more Ferber's Andy, a man making the best of a hard
road with a mean wife and a lovable daughter. McMartin's four minutes
were a disaster, for, as an organic actor, he was given nothing to play.
In 1927, Hammerstein let Winninger loose to devise his horseplay; by
the 1990s, the very language of the horseplay is Etruscan. McMartin
cannot speak it.

On the other hand, Prince's modern inquisition of the 1927 script
found a real character in Parthy, utterly brought to life by that ruthless
pixie Elaine Stritch, one of the few Parthys since Edna May Oliver to
refuse the audience the slightest humanist concession. As early as 1936,
Helen Westley was putting a "dear" spin on Parthy, giving a bend to a
character of steel. Even the Wicked Witch of the West, Margaret Hamilton, at Lincoln Center in 1966, was feeding the audience knowing
looks: this isn't me. That isn't Parthy. Stritch was Parthy, even to the
point of singing a rhapsodic "Why Do I Love You?" to the newborn Kim,
emotionally seeing off her departing daughter . . . and walking right past
the intruding Ravenal without as much as a glance.

In the 1920s, they were talents. In the 1990s, they're actors. Charles
Winninger wasn't an actor. Helen Morgan wasn't an actor. Howard
Marsh, Tess Gardella, and Sammy White weren't actors. Alone of
Prince's cast, Joel Blum (Frank) summoned up the self-starting merri-

ment of the old-time performer, with his crazy steps, dippy faces, and hat tricks. But Blum's Ellie, Dorothy Stanley, is a modernist, playing character. Prince almost certainly cut Frank and Ellie's last reappearance, in the finale, as too coincidental, but it would have been difficult for Blum and Stanley to play it in any case, with Stanley knowing that the whole thing is poppycock that gives her nothing real to portray and Blum not getting any room to step and face and trick his way around it. We haven't lost the twenties musical, but we have lost its style. All we can do today is rehabilitate it, by rewriting the book (as with *No, No Nanette*), rewriting the book and tarting up the score with "and then they wrote" interpolations of irrelevant hits (as with *Good News!* and *The 5 O'Clock Girl*), or reshaping the entire structure for the modern, sometimes charmless singing actor, which can leave a piece gasping for warmth.

Nonetheless, by what is possible at this point in the musical's evolution, Prince's *Show Boat* is a fine and even true one that the age can grow old on, with its extra scoopful of *Show Boat* music, its respect for the original's sense of investigating a panorama, and, most important, its refusal to assault the authors' intentions with trendy sociopolitical propitiations. The production's power is all the more arresting in that this tireless director of musicals had never before wanted to stage a revival. And this: in two major ways, Prince's version mirrored the achievement of the original. For, in 1927, *Show Boat* marked the culmination of two energies that we have seen in development throughout this book, this era. One was devoted to artistic development and the other to a social agenda. How could Kern and Hammerstein have even contemplated adapting Ferber's novel without wanting to advance the integration of story, character, music, and dance and also without wanting to promote the musical as a form of inherently progressive socialistic sympathies?

Comparably, Prince instituted what one hopes will prove to be an era of rethinking old shows, not by doodling them up with fake scores and gauche new librettos but by returning to the shows themselves, to what they meant when new. Prince's political viewpoint, too, preserves that of the original, even elaborates on it, though the usual professional victims picketed the Toronto opening, screaming for an *Oprah* date and a book deal.

We take *Show Boat* for granted now, so it must really be the all-American musical comedy. Yet it was only just possible in 1927—was, in fact, a freak of timing. Five years earlier, it would have been impossible: because Kern's style had not broadened sufficiently, because Hammerstein was still learning, because multiset shows were technically impossible except in the revue (wherein stagehands could take ten minutes while a star earned his fee alone before a curtain), and because racially integrated casts were unthinkable. Imagine "Ol' Man River" sung by a white man in blackface! All this demonstrates how quickly the twenties musical was sculpted, how simultaneously all the elements of the Third-Age musical came together.

Yet how small the start of big things. Hammerstein himself tells this story, so we know it's true: way back at the beginning of it all, just after Kern had met Ferber and bought the rights from her, he called Oscar and said, "How would you like to do a show for Ziegfeld? It's got a million-dollar title—*Show Boat.*"

Hammerstein recognized it. "Isn't that Edna Ferber's new book?" he asked.

"Yes. I haven't finished it yet, but get a copy and read it right away. This is a story in a million. It's a *big* show, too, grand and touching and really special."

"Is Ziegfeld enthusiastic?" asked Hammerstein.

Kern laughed. "He doesn't know anything about it yet."

10

My Future Just Passed

WHAT HAPPENED AFTER

Reader: as *Show Boat* is the exponential twenties musical, our curtain has fallen, and this is no more than exit music. We should, however, consider, first of all, this show's immediate influences: it had none. It liberated Kern and Hammerstein, no question; but there were too many twenties matrices for any single one to conceive preponderantly. Formula remained popular.

We notice small signs of a maturing process after *Show Boat*, such as the sudden disappearance of the New Dance Sensation, a growing interest in integrating choreography into plot lines, and songwriters' increased expertise in trading in genre songs for the character numbers that *Show Boat* is stuffed with. But wasn't all this in progress throughout the decade anyway? Isn't *Show Boat* as much a son of this revolution as its father? In the main, *Show Boat*'s effect was longterm: as the work uniquely inimitable yet eternally inspiring.

Now we have to consider 1929 as a cutoff point in several important ways. The most obvious is economic. Though *Show Boat*'s 1927–28 season was the biggest in Broadway history, everyone on The Street was aware that the second half of that season was a virtual bankruptcy court because of overextension. As I've said, there were too many theatres to fill with too much inferior product. There were too many producers, too many writers, too many actors—and everyone was working. The 1928–29 season saw a substantial slowdown. Then came the Crash in the fall of 1929, a cataclysm on Broadway as everywhere else in the nation. From then on, Broadway began to shrink, losing theatres to film or the wrecker's ball, losing talent to Hollywood, losing audiences to television, and losing its lucrative control of American pop music when rock took over.

The year 1929 marked the end of an epoch also as the first year of the *movie* musical. Of course, this is a completely different form from the stage musical—but then why was it so dependent on Broadway properties and Broadway names? Some of its major talent—Bing Crosby and Judy Garland, for instance—was generated entirely on the West Coast. But Hollywood made a kind of interacting alternative in the evolution of the American musical. One could tell the history of the stage musical without the slightest reference to Hollywood, if one wished to. To tell the history of the Hollywood musical without bringing in the stage would be impossible.

The most striking, yet heretofore unremarked aspect of 1929 is how utterly the Third Age freed itself from almost all the trend makers of the Second Age. A very few people—Kern and Berlin, Victor Moore, Sam H. Harris, Mr. J. J. Shubert—had an impact both before 1920 and after 1930. Yet the list of those who formed the very infrastructure of the Second Age who then died or significantly lost power in the musical during the 1920s is amazing.

It starts with the Big Three, Ziegfeld, Dillingham, and Arthur Hammerstein. Each lost his theatre. (Dillingham's was the Globe, now the Lunt-Fontanne, a money-spinner because of its gigantic orchestra and the unusual number of top-ticket shows its hosted.) Ziegfeld never had a hit after *Whoopee* in 1928, Dillingham demoted himself to absconding with his actors' wages out of penniless despair, and Hammerstein was so ruined by the Crash that his entire output was put up for auction. Bizarrely, no one showed up but Lee Shubert (Mr. J. J.'s brother), who bid unchallenged for the rights to all of Arthur's shows—*The Firefly, Wildflower, Rose-Marie,* and *Sweet Adeline,* among others. They went for $700 and netted the Shuberts millions.

Other major producers passed on, such as fierce Abe Erlanger and dodgy Henry W. Savage, who brought *The Merry Widow* to New York and changed the course of operetta. The two most influential voices of the Second Age, Victor Herbert and George M. Cohan, gave it up, the one dead and the other written out, though he did pull off a superb last *appearance* in a musical, playing Franklin Roosevelt in *I'd Rather Be Right* in 1937. Julian Mitchell and Edward Royce, the only director-choreographers of importance in the Second Age, passed from the scene, as did both Joe Weber and Lew Fields.

Such sterling composers of the Second Age as Ivan Caryll, A. Baldwin Sloane, Raymond Hubbell, and Jean Schwartz vanished, as did Rudolf Friml, after two thirties flops. Anne Caldwell's last credit was in 1928. The most distinguished librettist of the bygone day, Harry B. Smith, presents perhaps a most typical report, for by even the early 1920s he was being offered only the most outdated projects and seldom worked with a top composer. Once he had been a darling of Herbert and Kern; latterly he partnered Hugo Reisenfeld, Karl Hajos, and Jean Gilbert. True, Smith worked with Romberg at this time and translated two major Kálmán shows, but his reign and power were long over. Like Caldwell, he died in 1936.

Performers? Such mainstays as Fred Stone, Eddie Foy, Sam Bernard, Nora Bayes, Marie Cahill, Christie MacDonald, Joseph Cawthorn, Julia Sanderson, and Walter Catlett all bowed out in the 1920s. Even the Casino Theatre, Broadway's first house built specifically for the presentation of musicals (the list of habitués takes in *The Passing Show, Florodora, The Maid of the Mountains, Oh, Boy!* on its transfer from the Princess, *Sally, Irene and Mary, Wildflower, I'll Say She Is!, The Vagabond King,* and *The Desert Song*) was demolished in 1930.

Clearly, the American musical underwent a house-cleaning in the 1920s. It was partly inadvertent, an accident of the timing of births and deaths, but also inevitable, for as new trends developed, many old-timers were virtually driven out of power. This is why the lineup of Kern and Berlin (a bit before the 1920s), Vincent Youmans, the Gershwins, Oscar Hammerstein, Rodgers and Hart, De Sylva, Brown, and Henderson, Cole Porter, and (a tip over into the 1930s) E. Y. Harburg and Harold Arlen seems so unified. These are the people who presided over the American musical after its formative years and after its early evolutions but during its age of mastery, when it became without question the greatest of all the world's forms of popular lyric theatre. These are the names of those who swept away the old stuff—*A Chinese Honeymoon, Naughty Marietta,* even *Irene.*

Jazz swept them away. City music. Know-how. Sex and guts. Yet there was still room for charm, as when Nanette and Tom sang the first choruses of "Tea For Two" and stood gazing at each other at center stage as the boys and girls strolled in from the wings in time to the music, step by step, the boys stage right and the girls stage left, two great lines pairing off boy-girl to match Nanette and Tom there at the center, all smiles and welcome and a keen yet easy delight, till the eye was filled with tea-for-two couples and ear was lulled, so sweet, such elegance, so *smooth,* pure entertainment.

Index

237